# PRAISE
## ——LOVE AND RAGE——

"Lama Rod Owens's voice is a distinct coming together of streams of identity that pour forth an ocean of wisdom that is relevant to anyone that has ever experienced anger. He speaks with a rawness and candor that is both disarming and invitational, creating space for the whole of who you are to enter fully into—regardless of race, religion, sexual identity, body type or ability. Drawing equally on the endless suffering of peoples and bodies marginalized and oppressed, and the timeless wisdom that lies beyond identity and circumstance, he asks that we fiercely honor and hold the complexity of it all to heal ourselves to become the ancestors in training we are meant to be. His language draws from Buddhism, experience from Blackness, and he beckons toward a wide path of Love that has room for everyone."

—REV. ANGEL KYODO WILLIAMS, sensei,
founder of Radical Dharma Movement
Project, and coauthor of *Radical Dharma*

"This work is personal, political, and practical. Lama Rod Owens is wildly generous in letting us see him wrestle his way through his own pain, rage, and arousal. He weaves us from his own story to ours, from his Blackness, gayness, his prophetic nature, to our collective need to feel, harness, and express anger. And then every other page offers practices, practical guidance on how to be in right relationship to anger, to understand the power and wholeness of rage. What a gift!"

—ADRIENNE MAREE BROWN, author of
*Emergent Strategy*

"*Love and Rage* is a deep dive into how we are shaped by our perceptions of anger in a culture marked by dividedness and contempt. Through the lens of mindfulness and compassion-based practices, Lama Rod Owens shows us how the power of rage can be transformed into a force of healing in our fractured world."

—TARA BRACH, author of *Radical Compassion*

"As a book, *Love and Rage* is uniquely situated. Informed by the depth of practice, liberating insight, sincere love, and humor to which Lama Rod Owens is well known as a Buddhist teacher, this work is a true multifaceted gem. Offering practical techniques for working with anger and the profound work of touching the earth, this book helps meet our need for getting free in ways unlike any other. *Love and Rage* is as old as the human relationship to anger, while also being rooted in the hot fire of the present time in such a way that it is more than a book; it is an Ark that helps the reader journey to the promise land; liberation into authentic embodiment. Lama Rod Owens proves again that he is a vital teacher with a vast impact who is shaping the future and helping us all make the journey ahead of us."

—JUSTIN VON BUJDOSS, Buddhist teacher and chaplain

"With a nakedly honest voice, Lama Rod Owens takes us beyond the spiritual harm of unconsciously repressing, exiling, and indulging anger, opening a courageous path to its vigorous transformation. Here anger is not the enemy to be assailed, but an energy that when held with loving attention becomes a powerful and indispensable discerner. In a time and a nation where unconscious trauma continues to threaten the well-being of so many precious lives, we desperately need to be guided past shallow harmonies to the honest conversations that deliver the possibility of authentic love. I am grateful that this is exactly what we have here in *Love and Rage*."

—KOSEN GREGORY SNYDER, Dharma Teacher, Brooklyn Zen Center, and Senior Director and Assistant Professor of Buddhist Studies, Union Theological Seminary

"Audre Lorde, Black lesbian feminist poet-philosopher, once said: 'There are no new ideas. There are only new ways of making them felt.' In *Love and Rage*, radical dharma teacher Rod Owens brings fresh texture to another of Lorde's classic insights: how to mobilize the energy of anger without being poisoned by the toxicity of rage. Relevant, wise, and generous, *Love and Rage* shines a much-needed queer Black freedom light onto one of the greatest challenges of our time: living honestly with fury, while deepening compassion. With the grace of a good teacher and the warmth of an old friend, keenly attuned to the stark realities of personal and historical trauma, Owens helps readers dig down gently past anger's sharp brambles to find the loamy soil of heartbreak underneath. A must-read for those of us ready to stop either bypassing or glorifying rage, and start embracing its powerful lessons on the path to liberation."

—KATIE LONCKE, Director, Buddhist Peace Fellowship

"Lama Rod stands on the shoulders of Dr. King, Malcolm X, Essex Hemphill and others to continue the important work that still needs to be done. He offers us his alchemy to work with anger that has been epigenetically passed down to us from historical trauma. His Radical Sermons teaches us how to metabolize Love and Rage. A Bible of kindness for anyone who wants to face their rage with dignity and pride. This book is timely, and inspirationally gritty."

—VALERIE (VIMALASARA) MASON-JOHN, author of *Detox Your Heart*

"Lama Rod Owens is an absolutely essential new voice of leadership and wisdom on so many of the most important issues today: race, politics, religion, sexuality, masculinity, and, of course, love and rage. Reader beware: in this book Owens will probably obliterate your most entrenched assumptions about spirituality, mindfulness, and Buddhism. He will then proceed to offer something so much better, truer, more life-sustaining to take their place."

—GREG M. EPSTEIN, Humanist Chaplain at Harvard and MIT

"*Love and Rage* gives us a deep dive and courageous view of what it means to be radically alive and present to everything that makes us impossibly human. From staying awake to the rawness of personal experience, to our communal disappointments and fears, and our historical and ancestral traumas, Lama Rod holds nothing back. This timely and relevant book shares brilliant quotes, teaches crucial techniques and meditation practices that allow us to celebrate joy as well as disrupt systems of anger, and helps us see that anger and rage make us human and not spiritual punching bags. This book wakes us up and reminds us what it means to live fully."

—JOANNA HARDY, Dharma teacher and author

"The latest from [Lama Rod] Owens is an insightful personal narrative steeped in Buddhist wisdom on how he disentangled from rage, specifically, rage created from being a marginalized body living in the United States today. . . . His reflections allow readers to understand how engaging with emotion can begin to reveal one's lack of embodiment and help locate emotions, such as anger, that often accumulate from years of oppression."

—*LIBRARY JOURNAL*

"[Owens's] appealing tone and easy-to-follow instructions on meditation, breath work, processing trauma, and visualization make Buddhist principles open to any reader."

—*PUBLISHERS WEEKLY*

# LOVE
### AND
# RAGE

# LOVE
## AND
# RAGE

## THE PATH OF LIBERATION
## THROUGH ANGER

## LAMA ROD OWENS

North Atlantic Books
Berkeley, California

Published by
North Atlantic Books
Berkeley, California

Cover art © gettyimages.com/CSA-Archive, gettyimages.com/undefined undefined
Cover design by Jess Morphew
Book design by Happenstance Type-O-Rama

Printed in the United States of America

*Love and Rage: The Path of Liberation through Anger* is sponsored and published by the Society for the Study of Native Arts and Sciences (dba North Atlantic Books), an educational nonprofit based in Berkeley, California, that collaborates with partners to develop cross-cultural perspectives, nurture holistic views of art, science, the humanities, and healing, and seed personal and global transformation by publishing work on the relationship of body, spirit, and nature.

North Atlantic Books' publications are available through most bookstores. For further information, visit our website at www.northatlanticbooks.com or call 800-733-3000.

Library of Congress Cataloging-in-Publication Data
Names: Owens, Lama Rod, 1979- author.
Title: Love and rage : the path of liberation through anger / Lama Rod Owens.
Description: Berkeley : North Atlantic Books, 2020. | Summary: "Reconsidering the power of anger as a positive and necessary tool for achieving spiritual liberation and social change"—Provided by publisher.
Identifiers: LCCN 2020003934 (print) | LCCN 2020003935 (ebook) | ISBN 9781623174095 (trade paperback) | ISBN 9781623174101 (ebook)
Subjects: LCSH: Love. | Anger. | Self-realization. | Social change.
Classification: LCC BF575.L8 O94 2020 (print) | LCC BF575.L8 (ebook) | DDC 152.4/1—dc23
LC record available at https://lccn.loc.gov/2020003934
LC ebook record available at https://lccn.loc.gov/2020003935

2 3 4 5 6 7 8 9 KPC 25 24 23 22 21 20

This book includes recycled material and material from well-managed forests. North Atlantic Books is committed to the protection of our environment. We print on recycled paper whenever possible and partner with printers who strive to use environmentally responsible practices.

*This book is dedicated to
my friend Ruddy Ligonde and
all the beautiful ones who left
this realm of the living too early.*

# CONTENTS

# PREFACE

ON NOVEMBER 9, 2016, the day after what may forever be known as "the elections," I woke up to a reality that felt as if it was going to crush me. In my despair and anger, I posted this as part of a longer sharing on social media:

> *I let myself cry and admit that I am not trusting many people right now. I can say that if you think we are friends and you supported Trump, not only will a Trump administration not work out for you or anyone, we now have a serious issue in our relationship. You should know that. You should know I'm not in the mood for your shit right now. I can also say that the most disadvantaged bodies in this country must once again reinvent survival strategies and must also at the same time work to liberate all bodies. I must continue living amongst people who let their selfish concerns outweigh the health and freedom of people like me.*

Ten months later on September 26, 2017, in a crowded room on the campus of Columbia University Law School in Manhattan, my colleague and friend Rev. angel and I had been asked to explore how to challenge racism and whiteness through the practice of mindfulness. As we always do together, we used our lens of Radical Dharma and had a dynamic and insightful dialogue. After the dialogue, we invited the crowd to ask questions. A young Black man was the first to raise his hand. "As a Black man, I have no choice but to be mindful, and it brings me to a place of anger. I need a little of the happiness, or I am just going to be really angry all the time."

I responded first, sharing how we must allow the anger to be in our experience. I continued on and spoke about letting ourselves be angry as the first step to healing the hurt that is beneath the anger. I talked about my anger and how learning from my anger about all the hurt inside me that the anger was covering. And that if we don't wrestle with anger, we never get to the heartbreak. And if we don't get to the heartbreak, we don't get to the healing.

Rev. angel spoke next about how dangerous it is for a Black man to inhabit the space of anger. She continued speaking about how moving into the space of anger helps us to understand why we are angry, and for many Black folks our anger points to racial injustice. She also suggested our anger points to the grief beneath the anger.

After the event, we walked out onto the streets of a warm Manhattan evening. There was something else I needed to say to that young man. There was something else I needed to figure out for myself. Before I knew it, I was uttering these words: "I think I need to write a book about anger."

# —ACKNOWLEDGMENTS—

WHEN I BEGAN WRITING this book, I had no idea how much it would change me. It seems that when you write with a purpose to help people get free, you yourself must be willing to experience that process of freedom first. And what I know now, and have known for a while I suppose, is that getting free is not easy, fun, or sexy. It is messy, frustrating, confusing, and dull. And yet it can also be invigorating, dynamic, inspiring, and joyful.

However, there would be no teaching, struggling, liberation, let alone a book without the kindness of all my teachers and lineages. I offer these gratitudes knowing that no lineage or teacher is perfect and that despite these imperfections, I have been the recipient of profound transformative wisdom that has saved my life. I first offer the deepest gratitude to my *lamas* in the Kagyu School of Tibetan Buddhism, including my root teacher Lama Norlha Rinpoche, who authorized me as a teacher, as well as Lama Tsering Wangdu Rinpoche, the first Tibetan lama I felt a heart connection with. I offer gratitude to Lama Willa Miller for her friendship and guidance since the beginning of my path. I also offer gratitude to Lama John Makransky for his kindness and early teachings on love. I also remember Lama Palden, who helped me to understand the female Buddha Tara in such a simple and direct way.

I am also deeply grateful for the Kashi lineage founded by Ma Jaya Sati Bhagavati, who in her death has become a close guiding teacher for me. I am forever grateful for the love of Ma's spiritual daughter and my swami, Swami Jaya Devi Bhagavati, for always reassuring me that she is holding me and for her influence in helping me to become so much more myself. To these two lineages, Kagyu and Kashi, I bow.

As always, this book would not be possible if not for the example of my mother, Rev. Wendy Owens, who taught me how not only to be a minister, but also to have a ministry that invites people to be their most authentic selves. I also am grateful for my father, Dr. Hershel Holiday, for introducing me in my early teens to Black radical thought, which became my first real *dharma*.

Writing this book was a struggle, and I had no choice but to call on my personal deities, guides, protectors, and ancestors to support and hold me through this process. I offer them the deepest gratitude and my continued devotion. I especially express my gratitude to Ganesha and Chadrupa for their protection, as well as the compassion of Mother Tara, whose energy saturates this text.

I offer appreciation to my mentors, elders, and spiritual guides. First, I thank Kathe McKenna, who has been a staunch and loving example of how to be both a committed change maker as well as a devoted spiritual practitioner.

I also remember all the elders whose love and examples have held me in this process as well as inspired me to understand that I am an elder in training. These elders include Colevia Carter, Karen Ziegler, Darla Martin, Jan Willis, Alice Walker, Ericka Huggins, Susan Morgan, Bill Morgan, Noliwe Alexander, Metta McGarvey, Mark Jordan, Daigan Gaither, and Cheryl Giles.

I do not know if this book could have ever been finished at all without the guidance of my friend and spiritual guide Leah Tioxon of the Seed to Star Collective. Her magic, insight, and maturity as well as her joy and honesty created the conditions for me to translate what felt like ephemeral and vague impressions into ideas and words.

I am also indebted to Anna Gallagher for her realness and spiritual intuition that skillfully aided in moving these teachings through my body.

I have so many personal friends whose friendship has made this journey easier. My gratitude first goes to my closest and oldest friend, Jamie Fergerson, who has held me since we were teenagers and whose generosity in sharing her home and resources has been deeply moving.

I also thank Top Upcoming Legendary Child, Sister Sadada Jackson, for her years of ride or die friendship and for her intense loving honesty. Her insights into how to embody this book for the rest of the children are deeply appreciated.

I also thank Lama Justin von Bujdoss for being my brother on this path and for being a lifeline that has kept me in relationship to our lineage.

I thank Lisa Jessogne for her many years of spiritual friendship, as well as Josh Bogart for all his loving support.

I am also appreciative for the dialogues included in this book with my friends and colleagues Ravi Mishra, Kate Johnson, Sarah Beasley, and Leslee Goodman.

Also a special thanks to the Liberation Through Anger group for helping to clarify these teachings for Black, queer, trans, indigenous, and people of color activists.

I am deeply grateful for my team who not only have supported this book, but have made it possible for my teachings to be sustainable in the world. I am especially grateful for Daniel Sutton-Johanson for really making the growth I have experienced in the past several years possible. I also want to thank Abby Allen for her incredible branding support, as well as Ericka Phillips and Seth Freedman for representing me. I am honored to have their support and to be in friendship with them.

xviii    *Love and Rage*

I am grateful for Radical Dharma and all the impact it has had on people's lives. I offer gratitude to my coauthor Dr. Jasmine Syedullah for her comradeship and her deep kindness and fierce insight into liberation struggle that have so deeply influenced me. I am always indebted to Rev. angel Kyodo williams for her mentorship and helping me believe that I could write a book. So much would not be possible if she had not taken me under her wing. The relationships I have cultivated with these fierce comrades and co-conspirators have shown me how revolutionary Black love can be when we want people to be free instead of wanting to dominate them.

I am grateful for Tim McKee and Shayna Keyles and the folks at North Atlantic Books for taking on this project and for extending such patience as I completed the manuscript. I am deeply grateful for the effort Tim put into shaping this manuscript.

I am so appreciative of all the Buddhist and meditation retreat centers around the world for their support. I am very grateful for the Thomasville Buddhist Center, who supported me in retreat as I prepared a significant portion of this manuscript.

Lastly, thank you to everyone for your support of these teachings.

# INTRODUCTION
## What Is This?

But anger expressed and translated into action in the service of our vision and our future is a liberating and strengthening act of clarification, for it is in the painful process of this translation that we identify who are our allies with whom we have grave differences, and who are our genuine enemies. Anger is loaded with information and energy.

—AUDRE LORDE

Anger is better. There is a sense of being in anger. A reality and presence. An awareness of worth. It is a lovely surging.

—TONI MORRISON

Between stimulus and response there is a space. In that space is our power to choose our response. In our response lies our growth and our freedom.

—VIKTOR E. FRANKL

*The very first thing a writer has to face is that he cannot
be told what to write. You know, nobody asked me to be a
writer; I chose it. Well, since I'm a man I have to assume I
chose it; perhaps in fact, I didn't choose it. But in any case,
the one thing you have to do is try to tell the truth. And
what everyone overlooks is that in order to do it—when the
book comes out it may hurt you—but in order for me to do
it, it had to hurt me first. I can only tell you about yourself
as much as I can face about myself. And this has happened
to everybody who's tried to live. You go through life for a
long time thinking, No one has ever suffered the way I've
suffered, my God, my God. And then you realize— You read
something or you hear something, and you realize that your
suffering does not isolate you; your suffering is your bridge.
Many people have suffered before you, many people are
suffering around you and always will, and all you can do
is bring, hopefully, a little light into that suffering. Enough
light so that the person who is suffering can begin to com-
prehend his suffering and begin to live with it and begin to
change it, change the situation. We don't change anything;
all we can do is invest people with the morale to change it
for themselves.*

—JAMES BALDWIN

TO BEGIN WITH, this is not a mindfulness book on how to
bypass anger and focus on happiness. Nor is this a book about
using any other spiritual path to transform the nature of anger
into something more profound or transcendent. This book is
about facing our anger and welcoming it as a teacher and friend
so it can help us to benefit ourselves and others.

Herein I synthesize the many traditions of beliefs that I have
trained in to create a system of practice that guides you into
being in a new relationship with your anger. I pull together
Buddhist philosophy and a wide range of meditative traditions,
including mindfulness, *tantra*, *pranayama* (breath practice),

ancestor practices, energy practices, and classical yoga. All of these practices have helped me work with my basic discomfort associated with anger.

This is a book that comes out of where I am: Black, queer, cisgender, and male-identified, fat, mixed-class, Buddhist teacher and minister, yoga teacher, and shit-talking Southerner, among other identities. Though I am these identities, I am much more as well. However, these identities have come to shape how this book is being expressed. The privilege and disprivilege I have experienced as well as the oppressions that have shaped me have had a direct relationship with my own anger as well as my hurt beneath my anger. The practices and insights I offer emerged from ancient lineages and are reflected through my relative identities like sunlight through a prism. As the prism breaks the sunlight into the colors of the rainbow, so too do my identity locations break these spiritual teachings into strands of wisdom.

This book is also a continued expression of the Radical Dharma tradition grounded in the seminal text *Radical Dharma: Talking Race, Love, and Liberation* that I coauthored with my homegirls, sisters, and co-conspirators, Rev. angel Kyodo williams and Dr. Jasmine Syedullah. That book centers on a dialogue about the reality of race in American Buddhist communities. Many other people outside of Buddhism or even religious or spiritual spaces have found benefit in it. Radical Dharma is simply an expression of who I am; it means I see spiritual liberation and social liberation as being bound to each other.

Though there is an eclectic community of practices and ideas in this book, they are all accessible. When people come to hear me teach publicly, I lay out a buffet of different practices and approaches and invite all in attendance to fix a plate full of whatever I am offering for the purpose of reducing suffering and violence. The next few pages will help you orient yourself on how to use the book and will introduce you to many of its key concepts and practices.

## – A PRIMER TO THE RADICAL DHARMA FIVE –

One of the guiding narratives of this book is the five principles of a Radical Dharma practice, which weaves together both social and spiritual liberation:

- Contemplative Approach refers to being in relationship with the material of our minds. To get free, we must free ourselves from our compulsory relationship with thoughts and emotions, especially anger.

- Embodied Approach means that we are practicing not just with our minds, but with all the ways that we show up in our bodies. And when I say body, I am not speaking of just the physical body, but the body of our emotions, the body of our energy, the body of thoughts, and our community body.

- Liberatory Practice is the work of understanding what it means to be free and to exercise a self-agency in making choices to experience more spaciousness, wisdom, and compassion. I actually define "freedom" as the space I am able to cultivate around the material that I have felt trapped by in the past. In getting space around this material, I am earning freedom to make different choices to deepen what is virtuous and to let go of what is not virtuous.

- Collective Practice is the recognition that I am connected to countless beings and an awareness of how I impact these beings. I am interested in receiving care and sharing care. So when I practice, I want to embrace the collective, not just me as an individual. However, the care I offer myself is the same care that I can offer to my community.

- Prophetic Praxis is about establishing a practice that tells the truth of who and what we are as well as the situation and context we are living through. Prophetic Praxis is also about believing that we can get free through the appropriate strategies and effort.

When we practice all of these principles together, we will have no other choice but to experience a liberation that is both socially and spiritually based. As you continue through the book, these principles will be the heart of this dialogue between love and rage. Although I may not formally refer to these principles often in the book, they are beacons throughout.

## —— CONTEMPLATIVE-BASED PRACTICE ——

This book is grounded in contemplative practices that are meditative in nature. Meditation is the practice of developing a deeper awareness of our minds and the world around us. Meditation is at the heart of my personal path of transformation and was the key practice that helped me to manage my early struggles with anger as well as depression.

Though the theory and philosophy of mind and meditation in Buddhist traditions are quite thorough and detailed, I represent a brief introduction to the mind informed by my training in Tantric Buddhism. To begin with, it is understood that everything in the world, including all of reality as well as ourselves and others, is an expression of mind. Whoever I think I am, I am an expression of my mind, and whoever you think you are, you are also an expression of your mind. While you and I may have individual minds, our minds ultimately are expressions of the one unified nature of one mind or ultimate reality.

I understand the mind, like ultimate reality, to be spacious and limitless. This spaciousness is often paired with a description of emptiness as well, but this emptiness is not void or nihilistic in nature. Instead, this emptiness is imbued with an energetic potential that gives birth to phenomenal reality that we experience as the world and our lives. Yet floating around in this spaciousness of mind is what I call material, expressions of energies that we identify as thoughts and emotions. Thoughts arise from the energetic potential in the mind, whereas emotions are thoughts that label and respond to sensations in the mind felt by the body. There is also the experience of an ego, or this sense that we are autonomous selves we call I and me. The ego or this sense of I is simply a thought. To understand the nature of my mind is to understand the nature of all reality, which opens the door for my mind to merge back into the ultimate reality. In Buddhist philosophy, enlightenment happens when I recognize the nature of my thoughts and sustain that recognition until it is permanent, leading also to recognizing the illusionary nature of my ego. Nirvana is the intentional re-emerging back into the ultimate mind or ultimate reality.

In meditation, we are honing various degrees of our ability to pay attention to and understand the nature of the mind. These degrees of paying attention are concentration, mindfulness, and awareness. Concentration practice is the ability to focus tightly on one object of meditation that we call an anchor. Mindfulness is a relaxing of the concentration whereby we are able to focus on an anchor while having space to have a sense of other things that may be going on. Awareness is not just paying attention to the anchor but broadly having a sense of everything that is in our field of awareness. Each training relies on the other two trainings.

## MINDFULNESS

For this book, I define "mindfulness" as training the mind to return to the present moment over and over again with a sense of nonjudgmental curiosity and kindness guided by an intention to reduce harm for ourselves and others.

I have also developed a justice-based philosophy of mindfulness that guides my relationship to mindfulness practice, study, and teaching called Adaptive Intersectional Mindfulness. Adaptive Intersectional Mindfulness is the promoting, teaching, and practicing of a mindfulness that helps us to tell the truth of who we are, how we are, and what has made us and continues to shape us. It is decentering of materialistic happiness and redefining it as acceptance of what is. This acceptance is not condoning or celebrating what is. It is telling the truth that it is. It remembers the body as being intricate in needing to be noticed and cared for. Most importantly, Adaptive Intersectional Mindfulness offers us insight into adopting what is conducive to the diminishment of harm for self and others.

The characteristics of Adaptive Intersectional Mindfulness are:

1. Intentional focus supported by curiosity and friendliness.

2. The development of an individual practice that supports the practice of the collective.

3. Understanding that everything in our experience is ours to experience.

4. Divesting from experiences that create harm for ourselves and others.

5. Reinvesting in helping ourselves to be well and then helping others to be well.

6. Self-care as self-preservation.

7. Adapting to the needs of the practitioner.

--------------------- TANTRA ---------------------

I am trained as a Tibetan Buddhist lama. *Lama* means "teacher" in the Tibetan language. I earned the title as well as my teaching authorization by completing more than three years of (mostly) silent group meditation cloistered away from the world. It was a time that helped me to transform my relationship to myself and heightened my capacity to be as open and honest as I can in the face of a lot of violence while at the same time experiencing a sense of mental spaciousness from which I connect to the experiences of gratitude and happiness.

Tibetan Buddhism is an expression of a spiritual tradition called Tantra, which was developed in Southeast Asia. *Tantra* means "weave" or "system" and suggests a weaving together of various practices to produce a certain result. Tantra connects us to the liberating nature of our own minds using a variety of methods. The early traditions were esoteric or secretive, but over time the teachings and practices spread through teachers to communities throughout the world. The principal expressions of Tantra are Hindu and Buddhist. It is important to understand that much of how we have come to understand these traditions has been influenced by white Western colonialist scholarship. I identify as a Tantric Buddhist teacher and minister as a way to more authentically embody my intersectionality as a Black queer man in a tradition where I am underrepresented. Yet beyond that, the concept of tantra offers me the freedom to weave together practices that help me to express my authenticity within this body that I have been born into while doing the work to experience mental and spiritual freedom.

Buddhist tantra is a complex system of practices developed to help practitioners awaken to their innate Buddhahood. We also call Buddhist tantra Vajrayana Buddhism. Vajrayana is a collection of skillful practices, including, but not limited to, mantras, visualizations, meditation, breath practice or pranayama, ritual, and philosophy that help practitioners perform activities to unlock the reality of one's awakened nature.

## YOGA

I have been practicing yoga for almost as long as I have been practicing Buddhism and meditation. I started practicing yoga for the physical benefits that it offered. However, I was drawn to something else that I couldn't articulate in those early days. Over the past fifteen years or so, I have gone in and out of periods of practicing formally and informally. In 2019, I decided to train to become a classical yoga teacher. I made this decision to help create a stronger foundation to maintain a serious practice. However, a more important intention was to engage in training to deepen my own embodiment. Another way to put this is: I wanted a strategy that invited me back into my body. Without my body, I cannot experience liberation.

Yoga is about union or returning to the reality that we are never separate, outside of the thought of separation that most of us believe. Yoga is a whole lifestyle that is centered around the reduction of violence and embracing that which is conducive for our liberation. *Asanas,* or the physical exercises of yoga, are important in this lifestyle, but asanas alone will not get us free. In this book, I embrace the path of yoga, including the liberation philosophy of yoga. I also call into the practices of pranayama and a few asanas to provide other strategies to work with our anger. Breath practice helps energy to move while being the glue that binds our awareness to our body and its movements.

The approach of this book may be new to you regardless of your spiritual practice. I suggest taking your time with each section. I think of the book as being a really hearty meal. It's hard to eat a hearty meal quickly. This book is the same. Take your time. Be patient. My only goal is to present something that you can use to experience a little more liberation from your anger or perhaps any other strong emotion. If you allow it, this book can change your life.

## USING THE TERMS "ANGER" AND "RAGE" IN THIS BOOK

I am defining "anger" as the mental and physical tension we experience between being emotionally hurt and determining a strategy of self-care to tend to the hurt. From this tension, aversion and rigidity arise, resulting in the expression of aggression, whose energetic force distracts us from self-care into self-protection, often resulting in violence. Anger and rage are expressions of the same experience of being hurt, and the tension from needing to care for ourselves while also trying to figure out how to be safe. Although we may assert that rage is more intense than anger, I would rather point out that rage is an experience of anger wherein we lose a sense of self and an awareness of anything outside of the anger. In other words, when we lose ourselves in the anger, then we have lapsed into rage. I will often use "anger" and "rage" interchangeably, but all the practices in this exploration address the root of both experiences.

# 1

# A SERMON ON
# LOVE AND ANGER

*It is easy for a spiritual teacher to say, "Give up anger." There is reason for anger if we look at the plight of the world's children—and I don't just mean the babies, I mean all of Earth's children who are caught in war, hunger, disease, injustice. Sometimes it looks as if there's no justice anywhere in the world.*

—MA JAYA SATI BHAGAVATI

*I'm for truth, no matter who tells it. I'm for justice, no matter who it's for or against.*

—MALCOLM X

SINCE THE 2016 PRESIDENTIAL ELECTION, shit has been hard for some of us. For the rest of us, shit has been hard for a while. Yet since the election, people have been asking me publicly and privately what they should be doing about the intense anger they are experiencing. Other folks have been asking me about the extreme fear that won't go away. Still others have been concerned with the experience of overwhelming despair.

As people approached me with these concerns, I checked out my own experience. I was pissed off. I was afraid. I was definitely experiencing my share of despair. However, I was also experiencing a lot of spaciousness, contentment, and confidence. I was thriving. I am thriving. Not only was I thriving, I was having a good time in life despite the apparent apocalypse that was happening around us. I would sum up my experience in four words: friends, dates, Netflix, and cocktails.

I had to get really critical about what was happening for me. On one hand, shit was scary. I did feel a little unstable. On the other hand, I was having the time of my life. How could I explain that things are really falling apart, but I'm having a lot of fun in life? How does that happen? I'm having even more fun now than what I was experiencing back then. I had to explore my relationship to love and loving and that somehow love was holding my experience of anger and despair.

In my practice, anger arises out of tension. There is a tension between being hurt and wanting to take care of myself but not knowing how to do that. This tension leans into energy that I get sucked up in, and I label it anger, and that anger feels as if it needs to be exerted and directed somewhere. There's something that I have to blame, and if I blame it and if I can eradicate it, then somehow maybe I will not feel angry anymore. Strangely enough, even when I "did" that, I still felt angry. I had to learn to turn my attention back to the hurt, to the woundedness beneath the anger. Taking care of the woundedness was the path out of this suffering.

When people would come to me and say, "Oh, I'm so pissed. I'm so angry," I would help them turn their attention to the woundedness beneath the anger by saying, "Where are you hurting? Where is the aching? Where is your woundedness? What is your anger trying to protect?" Sometimes it's okay to think that our anger is trying to protect us. However, it is more truthful to think that it's actually protecting something else that's a little deeper than that. It's protecting our hurt. It's protecting our broken hearts. The work to turn our attention back to the woundedness is this really intense, profound path of transformation, which doesn't feel as good as just responding to the anger, because the energy of anger makes us feel powerful. Some of us, particularly if we're coming from positions and communities where we feel marginalized or erased, use that anger to feel powerful, to feel valid.

I come from activism. I've been doing the work since I was a teenager. First I engaged in teenage pregnancy education and substance abuse education. Then I found out about the Black Panthers and became a Black radical, which was really scary. Not scary for *me*—scary for everyone else around me. In my teenage years, I was waking up to anger, but I was also really connecting to the hurt as a young person.

I grew up north of Atlanta in Rome, Georgia. That part of north Georgia was a site of the Trail of Tears, where members of the Cherokee Nation were gathered and forced to walk hundreds of miles to the northwest to resettle on reservations. I am descended from stolen people who were resettled and enslaved on stolen land. I, my ancestors, and indigenous Americans, as well as the land, are all still in trauma from this violence.

Growing up around these sites of violence and within the systems of violence made it hard to experience healing. I needed to channel the anger related to my deep hurt. Activism and community service became the way that I tried to channel my rage, beginning with teenage pregnancy, then hunger and homelessness, HIV/AIDS awareness, sexual assault advocacy and education, and soon after, LGBTQ+ organizing. I figured if I could just stay active, I could keep this energy moving, and do something productive with it.

Deep down I knew that I was hurt, but I just didn't know what to do with that. I wanted to feel powerful, and I knew that my anger made me feel powerful. I ended up breaking up with God. I grew up in church, but ultimately I was not interested in the message anymore. The branding was a little off. It wasn't God exactly, but the people who believed in God. I felt as if people were using religion to perpetuate harm for themselves and for others. I gave up and said to myself, "I want to continue to dedicate my energy to liberation, to education, to service, to advocacy." I didn't want to just sit around and talk about how good and great God is, which God is, but I didn't get that back then. I wanted to actually do the work that Jesus asked us to do.

That led me to an intentional community inspired by the Catholic Worker Movement, which began during the Great Depression in New York City, in which radical Catholics got together and started doing activism, feeding people, serving people, getting arrested, all kinds of actions to disrupt systems of violence. Dorothy Day was one of the leaders of that movement. I was so deeply influenced by her life. She was angry. In pictures she's very staunch, with strong jaws and forehead. She was deeply loving, but also there was rage there. I resonated with how love and anger lived in her activism.

I was very fortunate to find myself struggling with severe depression. Of course, back then, it wasn't a blessing. It was a pain in the ass. I say it's a blessing now because for me, in my life, it's always been great moments of struggle and great moments of suffering that have lit the fire under me to change. I started asking, "Okay, but what else? What am I missing?" That led me into interactions with people around me where I would ask them about their lives, how they understood happiness, and how they were practicing to get free. That led me to a spiritual teacher who was willing to help me. For the first time in my life, someone was speaking a language that I could understand. She began teaching me how to make choices to save my life.

What I had to do was actually start meditating and watching my mind and changing my whole life around. Of course, all that meditating and change I was experiencing was only reorienting myself back to the hurt. I had to learn how to start grieving and mourning in a way that I had never learned how to do. It's not as if I was instantly liberated from my anger, but that was the beginning of the work for me. That was all based on love, not only the little love I had for myself, but the love I had for other people wanting me to be different than I was, because I knew that I was a source of suffering for people around me because of anger. Not only was I angry, I was really disconnected from the anger as well. People would come to me and say, "Oh, Rod, you're really angry." I would be like, "Fuck you. You're angry!"

It took a lot of work for me to connect to the experience of anger. Everyone has been conditioned to relate to their anger in very different ways. As a Black man, I was conditioned to believe my anger was dangerous—if I channeled anger and expressed anger, then I would be punished. I would be killed. I would be put in jail. I would be silenced. I would be erased. To protect myself from my dangerous anger, I learned to bury it and distance myself from it. When I buried it, it became passive aggression. It also fed into my experience of depression, because the muffled anger made the depression seem even heavier and immobile. Some of us have been conditioned to believe that we're good and so we don't get angry, or that it's not ladylike to be angry. I would get that too, because I'm kind of like a lady in my mind. Some of us have been taught that it is our right to be angry and thus our anger is celebrated.

So much of my work with this healer in meditation was actually about learning to be embodied, learning to bring awareness back to all the bodies that manifest for me. Not just the physical body, which is a key manifestation of our bodies, but my mental body, my spiritual body, my energetic body.

I needed to come back to start learning how to move the energy of anger through my system. Instead of saying I was mad or pissed off, I had to learn to start saying how I've been hurt, while identifying the energy of anger around my hurt. I started learning how to take care of myself.

And what I needed to do to take care of myself was not going off and whooping people's ass or cussing people out or being passive aggressive. Matter of fact, passive aggression is my working edge. And it is just as dangerous as other forms of anger because we're not tuning into how we're actually feeling. Passive aggression happens when we are afraid and/or disconnected from our anger. When we are touching into the hurt, the hurt begins to inform us. When we actually begin to mourn and grieve, that mourning helps us to experience a spaciousness within our experience. The hurt isn't the central thing anymore; it's something that's happening within the spaciousness of other things that can arise. I grieve every day. When I give the mourning lots of space, the anger has lots of space. The anger is like, "Thank you, finally, for taking care of the hurt." The energy of anger is still there. If I am grieving, then I can actually channel the energy of anger, not into trying to protect myself, not into trying to hurt other people, but rechannel it into benefiting others.

Sometimes thinking that we can be skillful with responding to anger is like believing that we can hit a target with a ball after we get twisted and turned around and really dizzy, then trying to hit the target. That's how anger is. We may actually hit the target sometimes, but mostly not.

The problem is, if we're responding to anger, we think that we will always hit the target. We think we can be angry and have agency over how we respond to it. We tell ourselves we are not going to get violent. If there's no space there, if we are not taking care of our hurt, we will actually lapse into violence, because the anger will have agency over us. If you want to be angry, that's wonderful; but if you're actually concerned with nonviolence, you also have an ethical responsibility to have a relationship with your hurt. I can be hurt and angry at the same time, and I can love both my anger and my hurt.

We have to understand that at some point we have to develop an attitude of needing to love everything, especially what is unlovable. Everything has to be loved if you're interested in getting free. I'm talking about free from duality. I'm talking about freedom from binary thinking. I'm talking about freedom from always being triggered. I'm talking about freedom from the ways in which I'm deeply attached to ego, freedom from always performing for other people, freedom from always living outside of my body. That kind of freedom, coming back into wholeness, coming back into privileging what I need. I am not saying that my needs are better than those of other people, but rather that my needs deserve to be in consideration as I am considering other people's needs. If we don't have that spaciousness, if we're not taking care of the hurt, then we're going to be very limited in the choices that we make.

I want to be very clear about how I believe that anger is important. At no point have I said to get rid of anger, because you shouldn't. Just like I will never say get rid of ego, because you shouldn't. When I say that everything should be loved, what I'm also saying is that everything has a place. If it's outside of our experience, then it begins to become really dangerous for us. It becomes subconscious and then that becomes a demon or a monster. People come up to us and say, "Don't you see that demon that's following you around?" I'll just put it in another language: "Don't you know that you're super misogynistic?" "Don't you get that you're racist?" And you're like, "What? What are you talking about?"

That's the shadow. We've learned how to pack everything away, because we're really invested in being good people. You can

say, "I am a good person. I am not a misogynist. I am not trans-
phobic. I'm a good person." Sometimes being a good person or my
attachment to being a good person actually gets in the way of me
looking at all the rough spots, at all the shadows that I'm working with. I don't even go there anymore. I don't care about being
good. I care about actually being in relationship to the shadow,
to the hurt, to the woundedness, to the rage, and to the ways in
which I'm really addicted and attached to power.

Look at how the narratives keep us from actually doing the
really important work of liberation within our own experience.
It's not supposed to feel good. It's supposed to be hard. It's supposed to be really uncomfortable. If it were easy and fun, everyone would be doing it.

People come to me and say, "Oh, this practice that you gave
me, it hasn't helped me to feel good." I get that, because when I
started my practice, it didn't feel good either. I felt as if I was suffering more. I wasn't. I was just finally paying attention to how
I've always felt. It's really not fun, but it definitely gets better.
It gets better because I learned how to get really curious about
my experience. I learned how to be re-embodied and to actually
understand that all these really difficult experiences I was having
were composite—there were all these different pieces of things
smashed together.

That began to transform my relationships to everything,
especially my anger and hurt. There's no liberation without actually leaning forward and looking at the things that we habitually
run away from, in order to see things as they really are, not as we
have imagined them. This is the path of liberation through anger.

# 2

# WOUNDEDNESS AND RAGE

*And the thing about white colonialist fear and rage is that I have nothing to do with it but my body still becomes a receptacle for this unmetabolized woundedness. At the end of the day I find myself hauling not just my trauma but also the trauma of whiteness.*

—LAMA ROD

*I'm dying twice as fast
as any other American
between eighteen and thirty-five.
This disturbs me,
but I try not to show it in public.*

—ESSEX HEMPHILL

MY ANGER IS OLD, personal, and dependable. It is older than me yet younger than the youngest child I know. It is so old that most of us no longer believe that it was ever born to begin with. It is the primordial deity that we come to worship, thinking that somehow it will be the revolutionary leader who will set us free. And yet it is also our jealous master.

Anger is actually trying to tell us something. Anger is confessing that it's not the main event. There's tension arising from my unwillingness to be with this deep sense of being hurt. When I begin to look at that, one of the hardest things that I could ever admit to myself was that I was just hurt, that I wasn't just pissed off. I wasn't pissed off because of racism or homophobia or something else. I was actually deeply, deeply hurt. I was deeply in despair because of the situation. This realization just made me feel weak.

And never in my life had I ever been told and ever been supported in touching deeply into this woundedness. I call it heartbrokenness. To sink beneath the anger or to move through the anger was to recognize the anger for what it was: an indicator that my heart was broken. When I allowed myself to experience my heartbrokenness, my activism began to change. I wasn't out there in the streets any longer trying to do stuff because I was angry. I was out because I was just really hurt and I wanted someone to recognize that. I wanted someone to recognize that for the first time my struggle wasn't to get people free or to disrupt systems. My primary struggle was to embody and communicate that I was not okay, that I was struggling to be happy, and that I wasn't, above all, being distracted by the anger. I suppose, in other words, my activism was to first give myself permission to be free to feel deeply into my experience so I could enter into change work more myself and in deeper attunement to other people's struggle.

Strangely enough, when I got into activism I didn't notice anger. I was doing really intense activism living in an intentional community and building a life that was about service and disruption. In my world, that's what one did in your twenties. My elder mentors invited me into becoming curious about my anger. They gently asked me to become aware. I attempted to start a meditation practice. Most folks in my community either were

Buddhist or at least had a contemplative practice of meditation or mindfulness. Most of them were members of the same *sangha*, or meditation and spiritual congregation, which sat weekly with that community. Sometimes we would have meditation sessions in the house.

I had attempted meditation well before being encouraged to, and I realized how much I hated it. I thought it was another thing white people could do magically without any problem, because they weren't Black! My attempts to practice meditation, particularly mindfulness, were a disaster. I could sit for all of a minute before I became irritated and pissed and ran out of my room. I remember everything so clearly now. I remember the acute mental suffering that was deep sadness surrounded by flaming rage. It was horrible and overwhelming. It was impossible. How did people do this shit for hours?

I realized that this energy of anger as well as hurt was deeply rooted not just in my mind and spirit, but in every part of my body. It informed every way I showed up in the world, from activism to sex! Yet at the same time, it was also very difficult to see because of my stellar performance of being the nice Black boy. It was beautifully and frustratingly hidden. And because of such internalized and hidden anger and rage, I felt as if my experiences of mental illness, especially severe depression, worsened. My anger and rage were turned inward, where they started to eat away at my efforts to remain well, and it was hard for me to feel joyful or even basically present. It was definitely impacting my physical and chemical biology.

I gave meditation another shot after I began to work with a healer who explained that meditation would be the foundation of self-care that would help me to address not just my anger, but also the debilitating experience of depression that I was also connecting to. So I took practice seriously and took risks in learning how to sit with all the discomfort that I previously ran away from.

And somehow I knew that I was taking a huge risk. This was the risk of beginning to work with my own mind, which meant that I wouldn't be able to hide from the secrets my mind had to reveal. I began to pull the veil back. When you pull that veil back, you can't just put it back if you don't like what you see, because you've seen it and there's no unseeing it (though we may try!). We can't undo the things that we witness, unfortunately, even though we try to forget.

And I definitely tried to forget. Each time I saw the anger, I attempted to deny it. I was still attempting to tell myself that I wasn't angry. There was a lot that I was angry about, and I began to realize as I continued my meditation practice that I was doing the work of activism, organizing, and attempting to create change because I was pissed off at the world. I was deeply pissed off at being born into this body, deeply pissed off at the system of racism, the system of homophobia. I was very pissed at my trauma and woundedness. I was pissed at all these acts of violence that were perpetually laid upon my body and mind. None of this was fair. I was pissed that I had to deal with this and other people didn't. I think I was ultimately pissed at the utter unfairness of all this shit! Yet I still believed that I could somehow use my anger to shatter this system, and once that happened I wouldn't be angry anymore.

In activist communities, our relationship to anger is immature, ill informed, and overly romanticized. We manipulate anger as a false source of energy and inspiration. Many of us have no idea how to really use anger to see the changes we need to see in our communities. Our relationship to anger is a reactive and compulsory one. We feel the anger and respond. When I am asked to illustrate this point, I talk about finding yourself in a burning room and reacting to the danger by jumping out of a window to escape. You didn't have time to think about how far up you were or what you would land on. You just reacted to the fire and split.

This is how I see our compulsory relationship with anger: jumping out of a burning room with no space to think of where you might land. And maybe the room is on the ground floor and you jump out onto land. Maybe the room is several stories up and you jump out; maybe you land and don't get too badly hurt. Or maybe you jump out and, like in a movie, luckily land on a stack of hay or in water. Or maybe you jump out with no way to break your fall and end up hurting yourself. When we are just reacting to anger, we have no idea if this reactivity will be harmful or beneficial to ourselves or others.

It is this energy that distracts. We think it is crucial to our work on activism, but it is not. Our being pissed is an indicator that there is something off. However, it is love that directs and motivates me, because it is the love for myself and others that helps to maintain the humanity of everyone involved in my work to challenge injustice. When I am rooted in love, anger reveals itself as trying to point us to our hurt; and when I am taking care of my hurt and loving at the same time, the energy of anger becomes an energy that helps me to cut through distractions and focus on the work that needs to be done.

The great activism needed today entails bridging our personal grieving with the grieving of our communities. Our anger arises over our pain and is only pointing back to our pain. To hold space for our pain is a way that we begin to take care of our pain. Taking care of our pain softens our hurt as we do the work of empathizing with ourselves. Empathizing with ourselves makes it easier to empathize with others around us. This empathy is at the root of the love and compassion that will begin to disrupt the systems that create harm.

If we refuse to acknowledge our hurt, we will never understand how to relate to our anger in such a way that we are not reacting to it. If we are always just reacting to our anger, we will never be fully empowered in our agency to channel the energy of anger into clarity and directness while reducing harm. I want to see a culture of activism where we can celebrate our anger and rage while realizing that they are not the issue. Our anger and rage are not the reason why we and the world around are struggling. We and the world struggle because we have misused our anger by reacting to it instead of partnering with the energy of anger to address the roots of why we hurt.

I have had to learn to love my anger, to treat it as I would treat anyone or anything that I consider precious and beautiful. My anger is my precious and beautiful thing, and it was because of this new relationship that my anger was no longer something that controlled me.

I thought I needed anger. I needed anger not to be weak. I needed anger to bless me with the ability to push through situations, to push through violence. I needed anger to keep me connected to the suffering of communities, the suffering of individuals. I needed anger to keep me connected to my own suffering. I needed to suffer, and suffering was how I understood being in solidarity with other marginalized folks and communities. There's something about our identity as activists that is so closely related to the anger that we experience. What would it look like if we formed our activist communities around joy, not the suffering or the anger, as a basis for our change work?

## BLACKNESS AND ANGER

*It's often hard to communicate how beautiful and fearless Blackness makes me while at the same time making me unbelievably vulnerable. I am vulnerable to the wild whimsy of white colonialist fear and rage.*

—LAMA ROD

When I am with other Black folks in gatherings, I always sense the energy of anger beneath the surface. I remember heated family talks about O. J. Simpson, Bill Cosby, the 2015 Charleston massacre, and Trump. Also I remember gatherings with Black friends, venting about issues ranging from racism and other injustices to our favorite Black celebrities doing stupid shit that challenged how we related to them. I believe that is intentional and functional. First, it provides a way for us to express our anger in the safe space of family and friends. Second, it establishes a sense of safety in the community, because each member gets a sense of how others feel about and are thinking about issues. Third, all this contributes to an experience expressing belonging to the community. One of the things that I learned growing up and had countless dialogues about is that so much of what it meant to be Black and to belong to the Black community was to be angry. The message I seemed to get was if you were not angry, then you did not belong.

Blackness and anger are not the same thing. This has taken me years to understand. Blackness for me is an identity location that not only articulates my race and my ancestral African roots, but also is a political identity that speaks of how those like me have survived systematic violence, marginalization, and cultural erasure in a social context that was created to use my body for production and now sees my body as expendable. I believe the Movement for Black Lives emerged to highlight this violence while at the same time seeking to restore value and care to the lives of Black folks. Yet this political Blackness also embraces the lives of all people who survive systems of racial violence. My identity as being Black means that I am always on the side of those of us who are targeted by systematic violence—including but not limited to racism, queerphobia, transphobia, misogyny, ableism, and ageism—translating into a personal slogan of mine, which is that if you are marginalized, you are Black.

However, my Blackness is not anti–white people; it is anti-oppression, including anti–white supremacy. My expression of Blackness is a recognition that we are all indoctrinated into systems of dominance and oppression, yet it is up to people to do their work of undoing their role in maintaining dominance. Moreover, my expression of Blackness is a demand that this work be done. In my experience, when white folks hear me or others speak of white supremacy, there is a tendency to hear this critique as a personal attack rather than an invitation to understand how whiteness in America is and remains an expression of dominance if there is not effort to interrogate this expression. To be white is to be racist. That's how America was established. I am deeply hurt by this system, and that hurt means that I experience being pissed at the system of white supremacy as well as how white folks continue to buy into this system.

When I first started practicing meditation, I had to start confronting difficult mental states like anger. Even early on in my practice, I knew that my anger was important and that it was connected to the pain that I was experiencing having been raised Black in this country. Yet when I started getting space around my anger, I found myself experiencing so much spaciousness in my mind around the anger that I was getting concerned whether I was becoming less Black!

I experience a lot of settledness from this spaciousness. Some may view my settledness as apathy. However, my experience in the moment is one of having space around what I feel and thus having the agency to make decisions about how to react to what I am feeling. When I am pissed, I can feel the energy of being pissed, but I am not trapped in a compulsory relationship with that energy. This settledness is an expression of wisdom in relation to all my emotions.

I am Black and many other things. But to be Black-identified does not mean that I am also anger-identified. To be Black has come with significant woundedness and trauma from having to survive a white supremacist culture and having to hold the transhistorical trauma of my ancestors who also survived the same trauma and passed it on unknowingly to me. Yet because of my meditation practice, I have an experience of Blackness that is based upon resiliency, community, deep joy in the face of violence, and a profound gratitude for my culture that continues to transform marginalization into celebration. My trauma and anger are still a part of this celebration, but they are not what Blackness means. They are only some of the struggles of being in this system.

## ——— THE WISDOM POWER OF ANGER ———

I've come to realize that when I don't have agency over my anger, it actually has agency over me. Or in other words, I am a slave to my anger. Wisdom means clarity, and that clarity has the power of getting to the point. When this clarity is coupled with compassion, then we can accomplish profound benefits for many people, including ourselves. Anger is full of wisdom, and with the appro priate practice, anger can actually transform into wisdom, and that wisdom is deeply liberating. But as with anything else, we have to practice. There is no liberation without practice.

The self-agency that I speak of is an ethical expression of power that helps me to meet my needs and express myself in the world in a way that reduces violence against myself and others. Having self-agency doesn't always mean that I get everything that I want or need, but rather is the clarity that I have to know what I need in order to be happy and reduce suffering. Further, agency is my personal power to articulate my boundaries.

Many of us have a complicated relationship with power. This is probably because of how many of us have been abused by the expression of power in interpersonal relationships as well as have been victimized by systematic power and other forms of abusive hierarchical power. Power is often judged to be a negative. However, power is neither positive nor negative. Power is power. Power is always happening. We are always making decisions, influencing others, or adhering to the prescription of systems and institutions. What determines our expression of power is our relationship to it.

In my practice, self-agency as well as agency over my anger mean that I am in power *with* my anger, whereby I have confidence that my anger will not overwhelm me, which will make it easier for me to take care of the hurt beneath the anger. I am not running away from it nor am I forcing it to do anything besides be itself.

## FEAR OF POWER

The issues we have with anger are rooted in our ambivalence toward power and our struggle to embody our power or agency effectively. Many of us fear our agency and can't take responsibility for its manifestation in the world, particularly in interpersonal relationships. One of the ways I struggle with this is being afraid to assert myself in my relationships. My personality is such that I feel very comfortable going with the flow and basically being super chill about everything. Some of this comes from my fear of being seen, which would expose my insecurities as well as potentially make me a victim in spaces where I have learned how to survive by trying to be invisible. On top of all of that, the work that I have been doing for more than two decades to understand my social positioning as a cisgender man in patriarchy has made me hyper-aware of my relative social power, even as it is disrupted by my more disprivileged identities.

I have also noticed how I tend to be afraid of asserting my agency because it will disrupt my identification with the person I have become comfortable in being, even if this person is not who I need to be. It is hard to let go of our ways of being in the world, because we simply do not know who we will become after we let go of our old selves. The expression of our agency moves us into a dynamic articulation of how to be our most authentic selves.

When our expression of our personal power is hampered, then that energy is often expressed as anger. Thinking about my issues with anger, my need in the moment when I am experiencing anger is to be taken care of, and when I don't know how to do that in the moment, I get swept up in reacting to anger. It takes work and time to understand that I have agency over my anger and I can make decisions to take care of myself in the moment and not lapse into a narrative of how I am powerless to hold space for my anger, to take care of my hurt, and to have the space to make different decisions to reduce violence.

## —————— PASSIVE AGGRESSION ——————

My superhero ability is passive aggressiveness. It's not as sexy as flying through the air or walking through walls, but it has kept me alive and helped me to manage the difficulties of living in a socially oppressive culture. From an early age, I learned that my anger was dangerous for others and especially for myself. As a little Black boy, I learned that it was not okay for me to be angry, let alone express it. There were consequences to my anger. As I grew older, I learned that my anger was extremely policed, because Black anger and rage were like a mirror reflecting back to white folks their participation in a white supremacist system that came at the expense of Black and brown folks. My experience is that most white folks were afraid of my anger, because it reminded them of the violence of their whiteness. The unbearable suspicion that their whiteness has had and continues to have a brutal impact on Black and brown folks creates a tension from which their own rage emerges, which is often directed back at Black and brown folks.

I found that my white male friends could express anger as much as they wanted with few if any consequences. However, when I expressed anger, I was labeled dangerous and angry, which establishes a narrative for white folks that our anger was not due to an oppression that they participated in but instead was part of our nature. Intuitively understanding that from an early age, I believe that passive aggressiveness was what my anger devolved into, and as it devolved I lost direct contact with it. Those of us who have not been allowed to be openly angry have often reverted to passive aggressiveness to express our upset without being punished.

Passive aggression is a disembodied expression of anger that occurs when we have decided that an outward reactivity to anger is in some way not beneficial. We call it passive because most often the energy of the anger itself has been channeled into other ways of expression that are not easily identified as anger reactivity. Despite anger being channeled into other expressions, it is still anger that is active; and when this energy is active, it is aggressive. Though it may not seem like aggression is happening, because someone isn't getting cussed out or getting their ass whooped, there is harm still being done. Passive aggressiveness can be just as dangerous as direct anger, because passive aggression is a form of deception and manipulation that can cause much more harm than an ass whooping.

Passive aggression is rooted in a fear of our anger. If I don't respond to my anger, then I am a good person, and furthermore we feel that bypassing anger is the best way to cut down on the violence stemming from our response to anger. However, this means that I am still not relating effectively with my anger. If I am afraid of my anger and not dealing with the energy of anger, then that energy is left sitting in our experience and will start to become a source of frustration. It will become a kind of trauma as this energy keeps cycling in our experience with no way for it to be expressed or metabolized.

The shifting of anger into passive aggressiveness is also a process of disembodiment. To disconnect from the reality of how my anger is expressing imbalance from hurt, I have to numb my physical sensitivities. This numbing makes it easier to rechannel my anger into something more indirect and passive. And because I am numb, I can't rely on the data from my body to figure out what I need, and therefore I get trapped in a confusing ambiguity from which it is hard to express clarity. Though I do believe that people can be intentionally passive aggressive to manipulate people and situations, I also believe that this expression does come from real unmet needs.

Moreover, balanced self-agency is completely dependent on my own embodiment. When I am not embodied, I have no real-time sensitivity to how my body is speaking to what is happening around me as well as inside of me. The reality of trauma is thus called into consideration, because trauma does disrupt the equilibrium of the body, making it difficult to understand what the body needs, because its sensations are not necessarily in line with what is happening around us in our environment at the time. On top of that, trauma may make it difficult for us to be in our bodies because of pain. Therefore, it can be hard to trust myself, and it is hard for me to know what I really need.

At this point, I have been working with passive aggression for years. I am now able to identify when I am experiencing anger, yet sometimes I still struggle to connect with that anger to exercise self-agency. As it is said, knowing is half the battle. In any case, I do express passive aggression in a variety of ways. A common expression is finding myself in interactions with others feeling an aversion to what's happening or just feeling angry but not knowing how to connect to that anger. Therefore, it is expressed as passive aggressiveness that looks like me smiling and nodding approval in the interaction while mentally cussing (or cursing) out the other person. During the exchange, I am also making a vow to do whatever the hell I want! To be honest, I very much enjoy this practice; but at the same time, I do recognize how immature the whole thing is. I know that I am struggling to have agency in the situation. My passive aggression in this case is a form of manipulation that I have justified in the past by saying that I will never get what I want by being direct and confrontational. However, it is not about what I want, but what I need. The practice is to stay with what I am feeling in my body and mind while trying to articulate what I need, first to myself and then to the person I am in interaction with.

**3**

# A CONVERSATION
# ON LOVE AND RAGE

WITH BUDDHIST TEACHER Kate Johnson from the series
*U Mad?* hosted by the Buddhist Peace Fellowship

**Kate Johnson:** *I am just really excited to talk to you about this
topic of love and rage and accessing the wisdom that's available
in the* dharma *for working with our own rage, for working
with rage that we experience coming from outside sometimes
directed at us, and certainly in this turbulent political time it
feels like a prescient topic. To start, I know you hold a dual role
in your community as a dharma teacher and as well as an activist, and someone who spends a lot of time in politically active
communities, and so I'm wondering for you—how do you hold
the role of anger? And is it different for you in moving in these
two communities? Is there something you bring from one to
inform the other? How does that work for you?*

**Lama Rod Owens:** *I would say anger was really the first material I had to work with, that began my practice. Actually,
there were senior practitioners that I was around who were*

*coming to me initially, before I really had a practice. They were coming to me saying, "Rod, I think you have a problem with anger." I couldn't see it; it was so normalized for me. People would come and sit me down, and they would be like, This is what I'm seeing. I would be like, Fuck you, and I couldn't see that reaction as an expression of anger.*

**KJ:** *That reaction to being told you were angry.*

**LRO:** *Yeah, it was so ingrained, like anger was so much a part of my life, and I was heavily in activism so it was really fueling something for me. But as I moved out of my early twenties, I began to see what people were talking about, and for me, clinical severe depression was really the first time that I began to understand the impact of anger in my experience.*

**KJ:** *What was the relationship between the anger and the depression?*

**LRO:** *What I began to see was that anger was deeply turned around, like I wasn't acting angry. I had redirected it, and deeply internalized it. That began this process that led into depression for me, and I think that I was so hesitant to externalize anger because externalizing anger as a Black man was dangerous.*

**KJ:** *Yeah, when you said that about teachers coming to you and saying, "I see your anger," it's such a sensitive place because.... My experience as a Black woman is that often I'll be expressing some other kind of emotion like excitement or sadness or fear, and people will say, Oh, you're angry, you're angry; and that can be so hurtful. So it's been hard to work with my own anger just because I am so busy trying to convince other people that I'm not angry when I'm not angry, that when I am actually angry it's like, oh no, this is exactly what other people are scared of.*

**LRO:** *Exactly. I think as Black-bodied people we are moving in the world in a hypersensitive way, and we know the consequences of being angry outwardly, and we know how we can be policed, and that policing actually puts our life in danger. So I was really working with that kind of etiquette of not performing anger, because I needed to stay alive. And then in my interactions with people, it's really easy in my situation to get this label of being a nice Black man, and that completely erases my validity as someone who experiences anger because of injustice and who is actually deeply responding to something that is putting me at risk. And when I do express anger, I get toned policed.*

**KJ:** *Yes, uuggghh.*

**LRO:** *People will say, "I don't like your tone." Well, my tone is not the point.*

**KJ:** *Right, right. Well, I won't talk to you until you calm down, you know?*

**LRO:** *And again, that triggers that anger for me. Where I'm like, I don't care what you're thinking, I'm still gonna be communicating with you. So it doesn't matter if you're shutting down or walking away; I will be walking with you.*

**KJ:** *Right [laughing]. I will be by your side, communicating.*

**LRO:** *Right. And that's what happens for me and my practice. I actually had to let go of being affected by those strategies. So if someone says, "Well, I don't like your tone. I think you're angry. I can't listen to it," I say, "Oh well then. That's where you're at." That's not gonna affect me, because I'm actually trying to hold space for my experience. I know that in the past I have privileged the ways other people have censored* *me, and that's actually been a cause of the ways in which I've suffered.*

*In my dharma training and in retreat, what I began to see was that my anger was valid, and that it was trying to teach me. In dharma communities where we're taught that we just need to suppress our anger and that anger is wrong, that there's no place for anger in our dharma spaces. And that's just another strategy that these spaces are using to control bodies, to police bodies. You know? Because our anger, especially if we're in dharma spaces, our anger is actually helping us to look at things that feel really off. I'm just not angry for the hell of it.*

**KJ:** *Right, or 'cause it's fun or 'cause I have a problem.*

**LRO:** *Yeah, it's not cool to be angry, you know? It's not like what the kids are doing these days, you know? But anger is actually pointing to a really real kind of woundedness, of hurt.*

**KJ:** *I think it would be beautiful if in our dharma spaces or in our activist spaces or just with our friends we could have that kind of agreement not to problematize the anger but to have a commitment to look at what the anger is pointing to. To be able to mine that experience for the information that's available.*

**LRO:** *It's okay to be angry. It's okay to have this experience of being pissed off right now. And I'm not gonna hide out from it, I'm not gonna push it away; I'm gonna hold it and take care of it. Even if it's not legitimate—maybe it's coming from the ego fixation, which anger is—but I'm still going to allow space for it to be there.*

**KJ:** *Making space to have that experience of anger: is that how you do it? You just say, "It's okay that I'm angry right now"?*

**LRO:** *Yeah. It's okay, because I'm trying to allow there to be space for me to notice it. Because if I don't see it, if I don't notice it, then I start reacting to it subconsciously, and that's where harming begins for myself and for others, and in relationship too. Now having said that, yes, I am angry and I'm actually communicating out of this anger. This is where mindfulness and awareness come into play. So I have practiced in a way that I can actually communicate while being angry. It's a slippery slope.*

**KJ:** *Well, it's a skill, because often when I'm angry, I'll feel it kinda rising up from my belly like up to my throat, and there's so much force there that I don't necessarily know what's gonna come out. And it depends on if I'm in a safe space, and it's okay not to know; but as you mentioned, we can be in different spaces of high risk involved with expressing anger depending on how we present in the world.*

**LRO:** *I think it was Suzuki Roshi who wrote in* Zen Mind, Beginner's Mind—*to "give your sheep a lot of pasture"—and I've been working with that for years, for years, early on. And that's the way that I approach my anger when I am having to interact with others in tough spaces. I give that anger a whole lot of room; I give it a lot of room to roam and to be there. But I still need to do what I need to do in the situation. I can only do this because of having to make anger my primary project in my practice.*

**KJ:** *That's a beautiful image. It just takes the pressure off so much to just think about the anger having this open pasture to do what it needs to do, and have its own evolution, whatever that's gonna be. I'm wondering if you have any advice for those of us who are finding ourselves targets of anger and of hatred right now and actually experiencing or are under constant threat of experiencing violence by other citizens or, you know, people or* *by the state. That's something that I find to be so frustrating too, is the accusation, or the fear of my anger, at the same time as there are greater powers that are full of hatred that are directing themselves toward my communities. I hear what you're saying about the cost of anger when it doesn't have space, when it turns inward, or when it gets fixed, and also I struggle sometimes with appropriate response when I'm the object.*

**LRO:** *Yeah, and this is where dharma becomes really important for me, specifically in terms of what is the ethical relationship to my anger. And when I think about ethics, I think specifically in this case of what is okay for me to do in the moment. Knowing that each moment is very different. So when I am experiencing being the object of anger, when anger is being directed towards me and has actually increased since the election, not for me but for all my friends, all my queer friends, friends of color, who actually don't have any way of performing or fitting in, who are honestly just simply visible, are really receiving a lot of hate. Even on the day of the Women's March in 2017 we had people yelling at us.*

**KJ:** *At the Women's March you had people yelling at you?*

**LRO:** *Yes. I had left the march and gone to another part of town with some friends, and people were yelling out of their cars at us.*

**KJ:** *I'm so sorry.*

**LRO:** *Thank you. I think many of us have been experiencing so much violence for so long, and then you get to this place where you're just like, How do I actually strategize against this? For me, one of the things that dharma has helped me to understand is that I am not the reason for someone's anger. I did not put anger in someone's mind. That helped me to* *take responsibility for my anger. I had to understand that is part of my experience; however, there are people who trigger the experience for me, but they don't create the experience. I create the experience. I am the creator of my anger. So that's disrupted the ways in which I blamed others; and when I disrupted that blame, I actually created the causes and conditions in which I empowered myself to work with my anger. Before it was like, Well, I can't do anything with my anger because this person pissed me off, so it's actually up to them to come and apologize and to reconcile.*

*So I'm giving all of my power away and all of my agency away to another person, and I am left powerless. If I'm left powerless, it's hard for me to believe that I can actually do anything about this, about the anger, about the rage, so I had to actually take that power back.*

**KJ:** *And that radical responsibility was really a pathway to that power?*

**LRO:** *Yeah, and that kind of perspective helped me to start moving in the world in a healthier way. So when someone is exhibiting anger-based violence towards me that I had no hand in triggering, I can think that it has nothing to do with me. It has everything, however, to do with that person's mind and their ignorance. Further, I reflect on how this person has no idea who I am. They see me, and they perceive me to be a certain thing, and their own ignorance is attaching a lot of meaning and narrative to who they think I am.*

**KJ:** *Right. They probably believe that their anger is related to who you are or who they think you are, right?*

**LRO:** *Yes, and there is the reality of anti-Blackness, which is also an expression of anger. Anti-Blackness positions Black*

*people as the problem with Black bodies deeply scapegoated
in this particular context in the States. So we always have to
hold that as well. That's when loving-kindness practices, or
metta practices, have actually been extremely useful for me,
because those practices have helped me to cultivate a sense of
self, of belonging. A self-compassio n that has actually begun
to disrupt these deeply internalized feelings of being unloved,
unheard, unseen, of being devalued, which is why I love the
Movement for Black Lives so much. I love that there is space
for us to start understanding how to practice loving ourselves
and loving our communities. At least for me, that's my inter-
pretation of the movement.*

*I love the movement 'cause I'm able to talk about Black
love. I think we're all able to step in and say, Okay, this is
the piece I'm gonna do. I may not be at the marches, I may
not be trying to do civil disobedience and all this stuff, but I
can start creating spaces where I can cultivate love of Black
bodies, and I love seeing that happen. I love that everyone
has a place to get involved.*

KJ: *Yeah, it's really brilliant.*

LRO: *But yeah, so going back to being the recipient of anger:
it's recognizing that this isn't personal, and secondly, I have
these practices of loving-kindness that actually help to hold
me in these moments, to hold the fear, to hold the trauma,
the woundedness that comes up, and also allows me to create
boundaries, where I'm not setting myself up all the time to be
in situations where I'm just accepting this.*

KJ: *Yeah, 'cause we're not like machines or something.*

LRO: *It's that agency again. It's like well, you know what? If
you're yelling at me, then I have the agency and the right to
walk away. I actually don't have to sit there. I actually can*

*ignore you as well. I can put up these boundaries that create spaces for me to take care of myself in the moment.*

*And so this next thing is really controversial, but this is kinda where I am because I come out of radical anarchism. I'm not a 100 percent believer in nonviolence.*

**KJ:** [gasp] [laughing]

**LRO:** *I know, they're gonna take away my teaching card now!*

**KJ:** *Oh my gosh, but don't you love peace though??*

**LRO:** *I love all kinds of peace. I love, I love peace! But peace can be used to bypass the work. Here's the basic struggle: Sometimes I have to realize that I am not capable of allowing my body to be used as a vehicle to absorb physical violence. I have these images in my head of footage from the civil rights movement where Black bodies are being bitten by dogs, sprayed with fire hoses, and people are being physically assaulted by bystanders and cops. Those images are very strong in my mind, especially the ones of people balled up and allowing themselves to receive physical violence as a strategy of nonviolent resistance advocated by Dr. King.*

**KJ:** *Right, and one that was strategically involving media, not just the taking of it, but the display of it in a public space to call out the kind of basic decency of the mainstream American sitting at home listening to this on television.*

**LRO:** *And I can't say that I consent right now to that positionality of Black bodies and lives. So if my life is in danger, if I'm being threatened with violence, more than likely I will react to protect myself and to protect others around me from physical violence. And I wonder if I can do that out of a place of love? I think it's possible. I think that we can actually come from a place of saying, Yes, I* *need to be happy and safe and I want you to be happy and safe, but you are out of control, and now I actually have to use physicality to limit the damage that you're doing to my body. And that's where I come from, and I think that that's why we're seeing such a rise in self-defense classes, for instance.*

KJ: *Yes. It's amazing. There's something about being ready to defend oneself or to defend someone who is vulnerable to attacks. My mind kinda stopped when you said, "Can I do that with love?" because I think, I can imagine that in that moment it would be more like, you know, survival instinct, which maybe that's a form of love too, a form of self-love, just the will to protect myself and protect others in order to survive, and I know that ultimately if someone causes harm to me or anyone, that that's not good for them, that's not good for their self-esteem, that's not good for their karma, it's not good for them either, you know? But yeah, in that moment, I don't know, I want to be ready, but I also hope that I don't have to find out. I would love to live in a world where that wasn't an imminent threat—violence against my body or bodies of the people I'm walking with.*

LRO: *Yeah, and that's the thing about* samsara. *Samsara isn't black and white; it's extremely complex and nuanced. I think that when we're in dharma communities, they are telling you, "Oh well anger: there's never a place for that; and violence, there's never a place for violence." That's not actually taking into account the very real and different realities that different bodies are living. There's a point of anger being triggered for me when I think, "How dare people tell me how to survive when they have no idea what it means on a relative level to inhabit this particular body." And I'm okay with saying that, being very clear about that; that's what I'm known for.*

*And this is another thing that I think about, so I think about the Black Panthers. I was into the Black Panthers when I was sixteen. Those were my heroes. And because, I don't know what drew me to them, but it was something about a kind of confidence. They also dressed hot!*

**KJ:** *[laughing] Those berets and those leather jackets!*

**LRO:** *All of that was so intentional. That's the thing that you have to understand about those movements from the '50s and '60s. What you saw in the media was very intentional. It was performance. They wore leather and black and berets and dressed for a reason, because they were trying to shift the perception of Black folks; they wanted us to deeply embody this confidence, and that included what we wore.*

*And then you saw Black folks, especially women, walking around with guns. That was something that was really galvanizing for me, because I didn't see violence: I saw love with those guns. In my early research as a teenager, I understood that the guns were about protection and self-defense; they weren't used to commit violence. They wanted to communicate their right to carry guns just like white people had the right as well. And I grew up in the South, where everyone has a gun. So that wasn't weird for me to see people carrying around guns, 'cause people had gun racks on their trucks, so you saw that, and people hunted, and everyone had a gun in the house, and I fired a gun by that age.*

*And I know that's complicated for people. I know that's like a really tricky thing for folks, but again it's like, I have to acknowledge the complexity of samsara. What I saw about the Panthers was not about anger; there was anger there, but it was actually about love. And then when you start meeting some of the original leaders from back in the day, it's nothing but love. It's nothing but love, and that's what I was feeling in those early things that I was noticing as a teenager.*

KJ: *I wanna thank you for opening up that space and offering that invitation to maybe folks who haven't even . . . considered that possibility of . . . the multiple meanings of the holding of a gun. Can we see the love here? And also to just be able to hold that space as a dharma teacher to kind of come out and say, You know what? I'm not sure I'm 100 percent with the framework of nonviolence. That there might be some times when it's necessary to protect ourselves, to protect the ones that we love, to block greater harms from happening; and that . . . it might be possible to do this from a place of love and in a way that doesn't revoke our dharma cards.*

LRO: *And we have only to look at the past lives of the Buddha, the* Jātaka *Tales. There are stories about him committing violence, taking the lives of others because he was able to discern, "Oh, if I don't do this, then the impact that this person may have will be far greater." Compassion arises when he says, "I will take on the karma of taking this person's life in order to save the lives of all these countless other people." But again, that's a slippery slope, because we can easily trick ourselves into saying that our violence is justified because I believe that this person is gonna do x, y, and z.*

KJ: *Absolutely! That's what I was thinking. How do you know then?*

LRO: *Yeah.*

KJ: *I'm asking you! [laughing]*

LRO: *[laughing] I thought that was rhetorical, so I was like, Yeah.*

KJ: *How do we know?*

LRO: *You have to be very clear, and I think there has to be a community process around that clarity. So it's not individual, but you have to be in dialogue with others who possess some clarity.*

KJ: *Right, and like, talk it over with folks.*

LRO: *That's why we have affinity groups, so that you have a community to process with, and you're able to say, "Should we do this or not?" and "Is this the right thing to do?" But it's problematic when we have people who are going out alone and saying, Okay, I got this; I don't need anyone to help me discern this.*

KJ: *If it's just on our own, it's real easy to get weird with your thinking.*

LRO: *I think that one of the things that we as practitioners really struggle with is the complexity of everything. We want everything to be really neat, and I have never related to dharma as being really nice and neat and black and white—that was never my experience. What it did was reveal complexity for me, and it gave me an awareness, and helped me to train in an awareness, and it gave me these tools to figure out what to do and how to do it.*

*Ultimately my basic ethic is: do no harm. No harm to myself, no harm to others. But then the complexity comes into play and these questions: How do you neutralize the harm that someone is doing? How do you meet violence that actually needs violence to neutralize it? These are the questions I get really excited about because I think they deepen my practice and help me to really think critically about the role of anger.*

**KJ:** *I think what you're pointing to is just a much more subtle and mature kind of process of being in the questions, and that suggestion of being in the question in community. It may not be that I ever come up with the final answer, but I can see how that's a solid path to spiritual growth. Ultimately, I think that's what I'm more interested in than the right or the wrong or the good or the bad.*

**LRO:** *That's the beauty of* koan *practice. Before I started practicing, I was like, oh, this is really stupid. I hate riddles!*

**KJ:** *You've begun working with a koan practice?*

**LRO:** *Well, not necessarily. But I appreciate them more, because it's process. After you practice and study dharma, you can figure out a koan in a couple seconds. And that's not the point. The point is actually to allow these koans to change you. Koans are actually meant to be experienced, which is exactly what we've been talking about. I think the most important teachings my teachers have given me is encouragement to figure out my own life. The most important answers that I've gotten are: No, you figure it out. Use your practice to figure this question out. It throws the ball back in my court, and it reminds me of my own agency and my own wisdom. It forces you to work. And that's what anger's been like: my work with anger has only come because I've been forced to work with it. I've been put in containers where I've had nothing to do but to look at my own anger.*

**KJ:** *Literally, right?*

**LRO:** *Yep, literally. To look at it and say, Okay, I can't run, so maybe I should start befriending it and learning from it. It's always telling me, "Rod, you're hurt right now and you just don't have the courage to look at that, so I'm protecting you. I'm going to protect you as long as you choose not to look at* *what my function is." That's what anger is always telling me: No, look deeper, look deeper, don't get distracted.*

**KJ:** *I love that. We talked earlier about what anger is pointing to, but also what anger is protecting. Framed that way, it seems like something you don't want to get rid of so easily.*

**LRO:** *Yeah, it's important. And yeah, it feels powerful. Sometimes I say that anger and rage are some of our superhuman abilities—what makes us able to be enraged and then fly out the door in my cape.... It just gets old. I hear people say, Anger is important; we need it to be effective. I believe anger is like a controlled fire. We do controlled fires in forests to create room and space for new growth and to fertilize the soil. But that fire can get out of control if there aren't any skilled people there controlling that fire. For us, if we have no wisdom, then our anger gets out of control, and it starts burning up everything. I see so many people burning up everything.*

*That gets to your question about how do we actually create community with people who are enraged; their rage is really unchecked. For me, it's that I really need to hold space for my anger, not add fuel to their fire. If I'm going to be in community with someone, then I feel that I'm holding space for their anger and for them to be angry. I'm not going to fuel their fire, throw logs on it, say, Yeah, you're justified; I would never say that. I would say, Yes, this is your experience right now, and you should own it and be with it, and yes, that anger is pointing to something. But I'm not going to say, You're justified in being angry just for the hell of it.*

*And once we gain some wisdom, we start asking ourselves what's that anger about, what's that anger pointing to? We can start to channel that anger a little bit. For me, I can hold space for it, and I can actually use it to allow me to have a little more courage in standing up for myself. Beneath that anger is often the hurt of being unseen. So I remind myself I am experiencing this anger because I'm hurt in this situation, so I need to remember that this anger is reminding me to set boundaries, or to say something right now, or I'll return to being hurt over and over again. But I still have a lot of work to do, though I've come a long way.*

*I can't say I'm less angry, but I can say anger is something I see as important for me in my practice, not an inconvenience I'm trying to wish away. That creates a lot of space when we stop wanting ourselves to be or feel different, and just be with it. And then anger stops controlling me, dictating how I am in the world; it just becomes a narrative that's a part of my experience, and I can choose not to believe in the narrative.*

KJ: *What is a practice that helps us to build the skills to be with anger?*

LRO: *Yeah. I think that with practices like* tonglen *for anger, it's really beneficial, a really good introductory practice to develop an experience of what anger feels like.*

KJ: *That's a great suggestion. Although every time I've taught* tonglen *or someone suggests it to me, there's always this groan.... I like that sense of this giving you a sense of what it feels like. For those of us who have ambivalent relationships with anger or even fear it—to be able to touch it in a safe way.*

LRO: *You can touch it piece by piece. So many of us don't even know what anger feels like. My process of liberation from anger was about actually developing the capacity to feel anger in my body. Then when I feel it, it's always in my gut. Of course it rises—I can get it easily in my throat.*

*The experiences of being with anger and transforming how we respond to it really become quicker the more we practice. So yeah, you could actually be in the moment and get triggered, and that practice instantly turns on. You're like, Okay, I see anger, I feel it, but I don't actually have to respond to it right now. That gives space for wisdom to emerge, so you can say to yourself, Okay, what actually do I need to do right now? Okay, someone is cussing me out; okay, I can cuss them out or I can sit here and hold space for them and actually try to listen to where their anger is coming from, because their anger is also coming from deep hurt. I can tune into that and say that this person is hurt, and they're doing their best to sit with that hurt.*

**KJ:** *Thank you so much for this talk today, Lama Rod.*

**LRO:** *Thank you so much.*

**KJ:** *The phrase that came to my mind was: I wish you everything.*

**LRO:** *And I take everything! I think about* Paris Is Burning—*that scene, OPULENCE, you own everything, everything is yours. That's how you have to move through the world. Obviously, everything isn't yours, but how do you move through the world with a sense of confidence, claiming your territory?*

**KJ:** *Yeah, and how radical is that, to restore a sense of agency for those of us for whom that's been taken away. I think there's a way—I've seen people do it with elegance and humility, to say, This world and this life is mine.*

**LRO:** *This is mine. I own everything. Opulence. Be creative with your anger; don't waste it. Create.*

# 4

# THE PRACTICES

*Where would I find enough leather*
*To cover the entire surface of the earth?*
*But with leather soles beneath my feet,*
*It's as if the whole world has been covered.*

—SHANTIDEVA

*I really don't think life is about the I-could-have-beens. Life*
*is only about the I-tried-to-do. I don't mind the failure but I*
*can't imagine that I'd forgive myself if I didn't try.*

—NIKKI GIOVANNI

*Don't feel entitled to anything you didn't sweat and*
*struggle for.*

—MARIAN WRIGHT EDELMAN

IT IS TOUGH to be in situations where there is a lot of anger, especially coming from others. As someone who is very sensitive to other people's emotional energy, this has been challenging. Early on, my primary strategy to manage this sensitivity was to try to avoid situations and people that might be hard. As you might imagine, this was almost impossible to do. Several years ago, a spiritual adviser helped me to understand how I was absorbing a lot of toxic psychic energy within spaces. Toxic psychic energy is energy that is unmetabolized, meaning that we are not holding space for the emotions we are experiencing, and we find ourselves reacting to the emotions in ways that are unskillful or harmful. Other times, we can be expressing really tense emotional energy in a space without even knowing it. Either way, the unheld energy is put out into the space where others sense it and either respond to it in negative ways or respond by trying to absorb the energy on behalf of others. This illustrates a point that I have often made: if we don't do our work, then we become work for other people.

I often notice this absorbing when I am near someone having an argument with someone else in person or over the phone. I notice how that energy begins to seep into my body. I notice the tightness in my chest and throat. There is a general tension all over my body. Next, I begin to feel an intense fatigue, and this is probably due to the emotional labor I am beginning to do to metabolize this energy. Often I begin to feel embarrassed for myself and the other person or people. I have learned a few key practices that have helped me manage these situations. To paraphrase the great Indian Buddhist master Shantideva, it is better and easier to put on shoes than to try to carpet the world.

There's a high level of anger and animosity out in the world today. Yet despite this, my primary activity is actually just being myself. I can be in spaces that are really aggressive, violent, and full of anxiety, and I don't have to engage in it. I can use my awareness practice to erect barriers within which I can just be myself—happy and at ease. This is how I get so much attention in the world. People see me maintaining my presence in a toxic room and ask, "How do you do that? How can you go sit and talk about racism with all-white audiences?" And I say it's because I don't take on their work. I'm just showing up and expressing how I see things. I'm not trying to convince anyone else. I give the work back to them. That way, I don't get drained and depleted. I'm just pointing out truths; it's up to them to decide what to do. Afterward, I'm going to go do something to have fun, and I'm not going to think about it.

I also don't carry certain experiences in my body, mind, and spirit like some people do. I know how to let things go. I also understand that it takes a lot of work to change, so I don't expect people to transform just because I walked into a room and shared my truth with them. It has taken an incredible amount of effort on my part to get where I am, and how many people have devoted full-time effort to it? I'm committed to providing the same teachings that helped me to help everyone else, but I know that they will have to do the work. I'm doing my work; I'm maintaining my practice and talking about my experiences. I know I'm going to be among people who might be hostile, even though I am not arguing or pushing back. My primary activity is actually just being honest.

## THE BASICS OF PRACTICE

Over the course of my years of practice, I have had the privilege of being taught by incredibly realized and enlightened beings, including Tibetan lamas, swamis, accomplished yogis, Reiki masters, mindfulness teachers, shamans, mediums, psychics, astrologers, and other spiritual advisers. Each of these beings has taught me valuable things about how to practice. For this book, I have developed a condensed template that can help you bring form and balance to the practices I will be introducing. Think of this template as a container that will hold the vibrant energy that you will generate while moving through these practices, helping you use this energy to transform.

When we practice, we are often engaging the three main parts of our embodiment that lie at the heart of our transformation: mind, speech, and body. My Tibetan teachers would say that exercising these three expressions of ourselves can be how great virtue is produced as well as great violence. This virtue or violence production depends on how we choose to use these expressions.

Mind is engaged through meditation and visualization, and this practice highlights how our minds are malleable and can be shaped to express more virtuous qualities through the development of clarity or wisdom. This wisdom helps us to know what to adopt or what to let go of in the pursuit of what is conducive to benefiting ourselves and others.

Speech can be engaged through mantras and speaking kindly. As the mind gets clearer and wiser, so does our speech. The more coarse and violent our speech, the rougher the mind tends to be, and that roughness of speech and body indicates that there is a lot of suffering in a person's experience.

Body is engaged through movement and breath practice. Again, the mind deeply influences how we use our bodies. An unvirtuous mind will influence us to act in unvirtuous and violent ways. Practices like pranayama help move energy through the body, making it easier for the body to respond to doing virtuous things. Movement practices like yoga help our body express itself, and we can learn how to be in our body and know how to use it to do what is beneficial.

To engage these expressions creates an interlocking dynamic. Transformation is much more rapid and lasting when we are engaging these three parts of ourselves.

## Three Parts of a Practice: Beginning, Middle, and End

When I'm working with a new group of practitioners, I ask a trick question: what are the three parts of a formal practice called? The answer is simply the beginning, middle, and end. I know, it's very complicated!

I am not a fan of prescribing amounts of time for practice. We are all different and need different amounts of time. I only advise people to practice for as long as they can to feel nourished and restored.

### Beginning Practice Sequence

#### CLEARING SPACE

When we begin a practice, it's important to clear both the physical space as well as your mental space. This clearing communicates a kind of seriousness about the practice. When you are clearing space, it is important to do several things:

1. Pick a space that has as few distractions as possible. Choosing a practice space that is quiet is also helpful. One thing that I like to do is use sage or palo santo to purify the space. You may also sprinkle salted or regular water around the space to clear energy.

2. I clear the space of things that may be distracting for me. For instance, I put my phone aside on silent so it doesn't distract me.

#### SETTING INTENTIONS AND BARRIERS

When this space is cleared, tell yourself that this is your practice space, and make an aspiration that all obstacles are removed so that you may have the space you need to practice. Once you say this to yourself, say it aloud as well. If you have a sense of how long you want to practice, even if it is five minutes, tell this to yourself first, then repeat aloud that for five minutes you will use every minute to stay as engaged as possible.

## GENERATING GRATITUDE

Generating gratitude is key here. Gratitude helps us to understand how rare and precious this opportunity to practice is. It helps us to understand that this space to practice is dependent on many other factors coming together. In my practice, I reflect on all my teachers who have taught me to do these practices out of the kindness of their hearts and how these teachings have changed my life. I feel the energy of that gratitude in my heart center, and I allow it to fill my body up and radiate out of my body into the space around me, and in doing so bless the space I'm in, making it sacred.

## TENDING TO AND INVITING THE BODY

All of our bodies have very different narratives. So many of us have experienced severe physical trauma or emotional trauma that has been deposited in the body. So our bodies can be quite uncomfortable and thus dangerous for us to be open to. As we go into practice through body-based awareness, it is important to be very sensitive to where we are and what our basic experience is. When working with our bodies and trauma, we should practice giving ourselves lots of space to make choices that are okay for us. Tending to and inviting our bodies into practice means that we begin the work of bringing our attention to the reality of the body and discerning how to make space for our physical bodies in our practice. The following is a practice I do for this. Note: If you can't enter into the body in the ways that I'm describing, please don't do so. Please turn your attention to a sensation that is restorative and manageable for you in this moment. If you are new to this kind of practice, please take it easy and go slow.

——————————— PRACTICE EXAMPLE ———————————

Though meditation is the root practice of this text, there are many ways to practice meditation. Meditation isn't necessarily sitting cross-legged on a cushion. You can sit on the floor or on a chair, lie down, stand, or walk.

Begin by asking your body what it needs right now. Take a few moments to listen. Allow it to respond. And adjust. Again, always give yourself lots of space to choose how you are relating to your body. The work and process of embodiment can be quite liberating, but it also can be quite painful. I encourage you to be kind and gracious to your body.

Allow your body to come into a position that feels okay for you to practice in for the period of time you set. The goal of this process is to minimize as much distracting pain as possible. For some of us, including myself sometimes, painful sensations are often distracting. The practice here is offering these sensations of pain space while continuing to minimize and manage the pain through adjusting.

Remember that your body is unique and carries a different narrative of pain and trauma than other bodies. As you enter your body, be careful. If you cannot sit with certain experiences, please take a break. Go only where you feel ready.

Now bring your attention to the weight of your body, feeling yourself held by the seat if you are seated, or if you are lying down feeling the ground under your body, or if you are standing feeling the ground under your feet.

## *Instructions on Sitting Formally*

Meditation traditions do come out of very prescribed ways of arranging our bodies in a formal meditation practice, or called informally a "sit" using a cushion or chair. As a meditation teacher, I am often asked what is the best way to sit formally. Recognizing that we all have different bodies and capabilities, the sitting posture guidelines below are body-sensitive guidelines that may be helpful for you. They are based both on my practice and on the traditions I have been trained in. They are meant to be as restorative to our bodies as possible. We shouldn't be struggling to have our bodies meet the demands of the posture. A body-sensitive posture includes:

1. Sitting on a cushion, sitting in a chair, standing, or lying down

2. Arranging your hands in a way that feels okay for you

3. Having your back straight but not too rigid

4. Keeping the shoulders relaxed and the chest open

5. Holding the head at whatever level is comfortable

6. Keeping the lower jaw slightly open

7. Keeping the eyes closed or open

Always remember that you can practice in any position you want and that feels okay for you.

## *Grounding Practices with Earth Touching and Breath Practices*

Later in the chapter I will introduce earth touching and breath practices. These practices are meant to help ground us and settle energy.

## Middle or Main Practice

The main practice is the focus of the practice sequence. However, any practice in the beginning practice sequence can be a main practice. In this book, the main practice is where most of the transformative experience will happen. Sometimes the main practice will be working with the breath or touching the earth or more complex practices.

## Ending Practice Sequence

The ending or completion of practice is how we begin closing up the practice. There may have been a lot of energy unlocked, and it's important to channel and ground that energy so there will not be adverse effects and also so that the energy can be channeled into deepening our wisdom. What follows is the ending practice sequence.

### RETURNING TO EARTH TOUCHING AND BREATH PRACTICE

It is important to come down out of a state that you may find yourself in after a meditation. Earth touching and breath practice can be effective for this. This is the first thing that should be done to start ending practice.

### GENERATING GRATITUDE

Once I am grounded, I like to generate this sense of gratitude for having had an opportunity to practice. I offer gratitude to the forces that protected me and kept my space clear, to my teachers and guides who taught me how to practice, to the earth for holding me during practice, and finally to myself for doing the practice.

### SHAKING IT OFF

Shaking it off means moving the body, shaking out any stuck energy, and waking up the body. Movement can include stretching, rubbing your body, doing an asana or yoga pose, walking around, etc. It is anything that helps us settle and be ready to move out of the session.

## RESTING

Before I leave my session, I like to take a few seconds to a minute to integrate or rest in silence as a way to settle even more and to help remind me to take the energy of my practice out of the space and into my living.

## ———— CORE MEDITATION PRACTICES ————

Anger was the first material that I consciously began using contemplative practice to work with. And when I say *material*, I mean my raw and basic emotional state in the moment. This material can be noticed or unnoticed, felt or unfelt. However, the material is only workable when it is first noticed and then felt.

Anger and rage were the first real things that I had to bring to the path. A spiritual path is where we are working to transform what is difficult or burdensome into wisdom or clarity, which invites us into the experience of freedom. Any path of transformation requires two kinds of offering. The first offering is material to work with to transform, and the second offering is the method or practice to transform this material to wisdom. This is called the path. The fuel that drives this work is our aspiration to transcend into something more meaningful, less violent, and more loving.

The following practices are methods that we can use to get free, to transform our anger and our woundedness into clarity.

## *SNOELL*

It is so important to have a practice strategy when beginning to work with difficult emotions. Over the years of developing my meditation practice, I have been interested in a process that speaks directly to how I show up in the world as a person who faces a fair amount of social oppression that informs how pissed off I can get. The following practice strategy is a tool that helps us to identify how we are feeling and helps us to figure out how to relate to that feeling.

Besides being a very weird acronym, SNOELL is a mindfulness-based noticing strategy that helps us to hold space for material in our minds. I have developed it to explore emotions in particular. It is really beneficial when we use this strategy with the Seven Homecomings, described later in this chapter.

Basically, SNOELL stands for:

1. See it

2. Name it

3. Own it

4. Experience it

5. Let it go

6. Let it float

## See It

When we are attempting to work with emotions or any material in our minds, we need to have a process to see them. Once we are able to see the material, then we can label it. The process of identifying emotions begins with noticing the sensations in the body. These sensations are the root of our emotions. When we begin to notice sensations, we can see how we label these sensations as emotions. When we say, "I am anxious," what we are actually identifying is perhaps a tightness or heaviness somewhere in our bodies. For others, tightness in our upper body and shortness of breath may be the sensations of anger. Learning to see the sensation rise and then notice how we label it is so important.

## Name It

After we are able to notice the sensation, two things can happen. First, we can watch how we label that sensation, and second, we can intentionally label the sensation. The labeling of the sensation is the beginning of a whole round of narratives we begin to create to think about that sensation. The actual labeling of a sensation is in many ways when the reality of pleasure and pain begins for us. A sensation is just a sensation. It is neither good nor bad. It is something that we sense. It is the language of the body. The classification of good or bad happens when we interpret the body through thoughts. This is called labeling. Now we may well interpret a sensation of the body as being unpleasant. We could then say that the body is perhaps telling us something is wrong. For instance, we may be sensing a kind of heavy pressure in our chests. We may label that pressure as painful. Chances are our bodies are telling us that something may be seriously wrong and we need to address it.

## Own It

Owning the labeling of a sensation can be a little tricky. When we see something and label it, we have to own it. Owning it means that I accept that this emotion or material is happening in my experience in this moment. This perspective comes from my experience of oppression and from working with activists. So much of what maintains social oppression is how oppressed people are kept from having agency over their own experience. Anger has been an experience that we have been conditioned to be disconnected from. Anger and rage are important expressions that can, when channeled skillfully, challenge systems of violence. When we have been taught to fear our emotions, then there can be no skillful harnessing of this energy. I have noticed that being born a Black American, my fear of emotions comes with a lack of agency over my body. This fear is actually a historical trauma rooted in chattel slavery and passed from generation to generation. Without agency of the body, we have no agency over emotions and thus we lose a vital tool not just for the disruption of oppressive systems, but we lose a strategy that can support our mental health. So when we own the labeling, then we are more likely to notice our body and its role in the production of the material we are owning. Sometimes to practice this, I tell myself: "I am experiencing this. This is mine. It is happening in my experience and in my body."

## Experience It

When I am finally able to own something, I can move into experiencing the material. Experiencing is a nonreactive activity. I am watching how an emotion feels in my body and mind. My nonreactivity offers the material space to be with me where I don't feel contracted or crowded. My first experience of this came during my long retreat. I had gotten triggered into anger over something, and the triggering happened so quickly that I had no time to react to the anger by getting lost in the thoughts around the anger, which for me often included blaming whomever or whatever triggered me. Not having time to react, I felt the energy of anger for the first time moving through my body as a sensation. It felt like lightning buzzing up through my body. Toward the end of that traveling, I noticed my mind naming the sensation as anger. I was blown away. During the experience, it felt as if time was slowing down. The whole experience probably lasted three seconds, and when I snapped out of it, I felt a freedom around anger that I had never felt before. The anger had not gone anywhere but was still hovering in my experience. I was so intrigued, because I had never known what anger felt like until that moment. From that experience, I learned how to be with the development of material in my experience, and I learned the difference between experiencing and reacting and that reacting makes it very difficult to experience my emotions.

## Let It Go

Letting things go is a profound practice. Many of us have a tendency to hold onto things that we don't need. The practice of letting go isn't about bypassing or covering up. This practice of letting go means I am determining which things are conducive to my health and happiness and which things aren't. On the level of mental experiences like thoughts and emotions, we can see it, name it, own it, and then let it go. We let it go by detaching ourselves from the mental material or relaxing our fixation on it. We are often having one of three experiences in our meditation practice: we are really attached to something (or we find some pleasure in it), are trying to get away from it (we find it unpleasurable), or really don't care about it (it is neutral). This very basic level of thought creates the orientation that extends to everything else in our lives. We are unconsciously grabbing onto things, running away from things, or just letting things be there because we can't figure out what something has to do with us or because we don't care about it. Even with things that we are neutral about, we are still in relationship to them because we have yet to make a conscious decision to let it go. To let something go, we bring attention to the thing we are in relationship to and notice the energy around how we are maintaining the relationship.

## Let It Float

Letting something float is a continuation of letting material go. In my practice, when I let something go, letting it float is my work of watching the material I have let go of and relaxing my reactivity to the material over and over again. In a way, it is an expression of resiliency to let things just float through my experience and to notice how I am attempting to react to them. For me, this practice is the spaciousness that allows me to move through the world with the space to choose how I wish to respond instead of getting lost in compulsory reactions. This spaciousness is also the same space that helps me to experience happiness. I understand happiness as being a part of spaciousness; so as my spaciousness holds all the material in my mind, so does the happiness. Letting things float helps me to understand that I can be happy while experiencing other things like anger or sadness. My happiness is not exclusionary but rather inclusionary. This helps me move through the world being able to experience happiness while confronting the reality of the struggle of being alive. This happiness and spaciousness make this work doable.

─────────── A NOTE ON SNOELL AND TRAUMA ───────────

Just as when we are working with the body, we must be sensitive to how trauma shows up in our minds. Any thought or emotion can trigger the experience of a traumatic event. So if you are a person with a history of any kind of trauma, be careful moving through the practice and always allow yourself the space to choose how to explore using SNOELL or any meditation practice. Here are some suggestions if you experience being triggered:

1. Immediately cease the practice

2. Bring your attention to the ground under you

3. Rest your attention on an anchor that feels neutral

4. Think about something that feels positive

5. Engage in some simple movements like light stretching or walking

──────────── PRACTICE BREAK ────────────

Let's take a pause to practice with SNOELL. It can be practiced on your own or in a group.

1. Start by moving through the beginning practice sequence.

2. Now bring your attention to your mind. The best way to begin noticing your mind is by first noticing your thoughts and emotions. Allow yourself to see and notice what's happening in your mind. This is the first step of SNOELL: seeing.

3. Now focus on noticing your emotions. You can begin this by asking yourself how you feel. You may be feeling several emotions at once. You can go through each of these emotions and name them. Pick one emotion that feels pleasant for you like happiness, joy, gratitude, contentment, etc. Name this emotion in your mind by saying, "This is _____." This emotion will be your anchor material for this practice. This is the second step of SNOELL: naming.

4. Once you have named your anchor, just keep your attention on it for a few moments. Afterward, tell yourself, "This emotion is happening now in my experience. This is my emotion." This is the third step of SNOELL: owning.

5. Relax with this emotion and say to yourself, "I am experiencing this _____." Notice how this emotion feels in your body and mind. Even notice some of the other thoughts that come up about this emotion. This is the fourth step of SNOELL: experiencing.

6. Now that you have owned and experienced this material, you can let it go. While noticing the emotion, try to relax and again tell yourself, "I am experiencing this emotion." Try to let go of the emotion. Letting go of the emotion feels like staring up at clouds passing through the sky. You can't touch them, but they are there. Imagine that this emotion is a cloud passing through the sky of your mind, and that you are gazing up at it not being able to do anything but watch it pass. This is the fifth step of SNOELL: letting go.

7. Now just sit and let the emotion pass through your mind. Notice all the ways you attempt to touch it or grab onto it. Whenever you notice that, just return to relaxing and watching. This is the final step of SNOELL: letting it float.

8. Move through the ending practice sequence.

## The Seven Homecomings

*Yea, though I walk through the valley of the shadow of death,*
*I will fear no evil: For thou art with me;*
*Thy rod and thy staff, they comfort me.*
*Thou preparest a table before me in the presence of mine*
*    enemies;*
*Thou annointest my head with oil; My cup runneth over.*

—PSALM 23

*You need to call from the inside the thing you want to liberate.*

—SISTER SADADA JACKSON

When I started my meditation practice in the Buddhist tradition, I was introduced to the practice of taking refuge, which means that I acknowledge that if I want to suffer less, experience happiness, and ultimately be free, I need support beyond what I can consciously offer myself. In Buddhist traditions, we take refuge in what are called the Three Jewels, which are the Buddha, the dharma, and the sangha. Traditionally at the beginning of our formal practice or even the beginning of our day, we reflect on these sources of refuge to inspire us and remind us that there are resources we can rely on to meet the challenges of life.

When we reflect on the Buddha, we are reflecting on an example of a being who modeled a particular path of enlightenment based on the premise that we can train the mind to let go of delusion and to embrace clarity. When we reflect on the dharma, we reflect on the teachings of the Buddha as well as the truth, or the law of how things really are as they relate to letting go of delusion and embracing clarity. When we reflect on the sangha, or spiritual community, we are reflecting on the community of fellow practitioners who are working together supporting one another to let go of delusion and to embrace clarity. These are the traditional three supports we rely on in our practice to obtain liberation.

I think of the Three Jewels as legs of a stool. It's hard to sit on a one- or two-legged stool. You need at least three legs to support you. It is the same not just in our dharma practice, but also in our lives. We need support to carry us through the bullshit. But more than that, we need to be reminded of our better selves, because those around us are often all too good at reflecting our ugliness back to us. If this is all we are seeing, it becomes hard to get a sense of who we really are. Without support, we get lost in the delusion and lose our relationship with clarity.

I practice taking refuge each day. Over the years as I have worked to talk about my spiritual practice with others of different faiths and beliefs, I noticed that my relationship with these traditional sources of refuge began to expand. I began experimenting with framing the Buddha as a doctor offering the medicine of the dharma to the community of practitioners in rehab and recovery from the violence of being lost in delusion. I was getting creative with my refuge practice.

This expansion was triggered by one question: What else do I rely on to reduce delusion and increase clarity? I was also connecting to the challenge of being in the world right now. Over the past few years, being out here in these streets has been no joke! Developing a relationship to our tough emotions is hard. All of this is even harder when we are dedicated to helping others ease the burden of living in the world. When you are doing this incredibly important and also draining work, you need support.

These reflections were transformative. I understood that the Three Jewels are wonderful and profound, and they have guided me into this present state of emotional well-being; but as I interacted with communities outside of Buddhist spaces, I found myself reflecting on other sources of refuge. I wanted to bring my whole life into this practice in a way that embraced my cultural, racial, sexual, and radical identities.

In my personal practice, I gradually began reflecting on other important sources of refuge that I was relying on, like my ancestors, the earth, silence, and, just as importantly, myself. When I combined these with the three traditional sources of refuge, I began calling them the Seven Homecomings. The Seven Homecomings are now reflections and evocations of the guide, the wisdom text, the community, the ancestors, the earth, silence, and ourselves. I see the Seven Homecomings as an expression of love that forms a container to hold the intensity of my anger and rage. It holds my despair under the anger and rage as well. When I spoke about the intersection of love and rage, I found myself returning back to this practice as a primary example of how love holds the violence and sadness of anger.

In my practice of the Seven Homecomings, I evoke each of the sources of refuge, which I call a homecoming. When all my homecomings are gathered together around me in the formal practice, I call it my homecoming circle or my circle of care. However, before getting to the formal practice, let's explore each of the homecomings.

## The Guide

In traditional refuge, the Buddha represents the teacher, guide, and guru. We need a guide who shows us how to travel the path. The guide doesn't have to be super realized or enlightened. Yet they need to possess some advanced wisdom or at least more than we have. Even if the guide is only a little ways ahead of us, it's still enough for the guide to show us how to best navigate what they have passed through and what is coming up for you. The guide can be anyone we seek advice and guidance from or any being who for us is a master of our chosen path. Depending on our traditions, we call this person shaman, healer, medicine woman/man, minister, guru, rabbi, priest, priestess, imam, elder, healer, counselor, chaplain, swami, sensei, or even lama. Ultimately, the guide is any being who teaches us how to be wiser and kinder.

I reflect on my own relationship with my teachers and guides. I have been fortunate to have what I call authentic teachers who have been very concerned with my well-being and success and have done extraordinary things to support me. The earliest memory of guides was my grandmother Betty, who taught me the ways in which love can be expressed. I think about my mother, Wendy, and her guidance helping me to navigate life as a Black male while at the same time supporting my dreams and the things that made me happy. My dad has also been my teacher who has offered me a vision of what I could accomplish in my life. This vision has guided and sustained me into this very moment.

My teachers have also included schoolteachers and professors. For instance, I think about my middle school in-school suspension teacher Mr. Monroe. I was assigned to the weeklong alternative class after being involved in a fight (which I won!). I went into the class feeling extremely ashamed; but instead of treating me or any of the mostly young Black boys there with unkindness and making us feel more guilty, Mr. Monroe expressed kindness by getting to know us and learning about what gave us joy. I have had amazing academic teachers all the way through graduate school whom I have loved and still love, but I hold Mr. Monroe as the first teacher who really embraced me and didn't use my anger and its violence as the basis to judge me as a person. I believe that one of the primary roles of a teacher or guide is to reflect our basic wisdom and joy back to us so we can see for ourselves that these beautiful qualities are a part of us. Seeing them for ourselves helps us to believe in them maybe for the first time in our lives.

I also reflect on my spiritual teachers whom I credit for not just shifting my life, but saving it. I have studied with not only Buddhist teachers, but other spiritual teachers in different traditions, spiritual guides, and spiritual mentors. Each of these teachers and guides had a different role in my life. However, I am remembering my root or primary Buddhist teacher Lama Norlha Rinpoche. I started practicing meditation when I was twenty-four and began practicing Buddhism proper when I was twenty-five. Early in my practice, I knew that I wanted to enter into a multiyear retreat and to become a teacher. One of my early teachers encouraged me to visit her teacher, Lama Norlha Rinpoche.

I do not have mystical experiences in my practice, so when I encounter people or situations that are extraordinary I usually only experience a sense of opening. It is an experience of deep relaxing and contracting in my mind as well as a deepened tenderness in my heart. It is the experience of trusting and vulnerability when we feel safe enough to let our guard down. Many of us experience this with people we love and feel safe with. When I met Rinpoche, I had this experience, and I trusted it, because this openness was what I was looking for in my practice. Any teacher I have had this opening with automatically becomes my teacher regardless of who they are or what their spiritual path is. I trusted Rinpoche with my practice from that point on as he began to train me to become a teacher. I know that I had a very different experience with him than other people had. My teacher was not perfect. No teacher is. There were situations where he was unskillful and harmful for others. That was not the case for me. He changed my life for the best while hurting others. I can love him now even after his passing and still recognize his violence toward others. Learning to hold this complexity has been one of the most important teachings from Rinpoche.

Teaching happens in so many ways, and I allow myself to always be open to learning. I see any being that helps me to be kinder and wiser as my teacher. However, the guide doesn't have to be human. The guide can be God, the Buddha, Jesus, a deity, a saint, an angel, a spirit, or any other entity. Some people see nature as their guide source or their pets as guides. The guide can even be a celebrity or artist whose work has helped us to be less deluded. I have often helped people to embrace Beyoncé or Michelle Obama as one of their guides. Even though they have passed, James Baldwin, Audre Lorde, and Essex Hemphill are some of my guides along with Sweet Honey in the Rock and other artists and groups whose work helps me to be kinder and wiser.

When I am practicing this first homecoming, I reflect on all the ways the guide shows up for me, and I invite all the manifestations of the guide into the space around me and cultivate the feeling of being held gently, warmly, and lovingly by them. This is my sense of coming home. Like the rest of the homecomings, I can imagine receiving kindness from them while also offering things that I struggle with to them to help hold. I also pray to them for things that I need to be well and free from suffering. I always encourage people to get creative in how they use these practices for their benefit.

## The Wisdom Text

The second homecoming is the wisdom text. In traditional refuge practice, it would be taking refuge in the dharma. *Dharma* means "truth" or "law." I usually define it as the true essence of phenomenal reality. Dharma is the expression of wisdom or clarity, openness, and honesty. It is seeing things as they really are. Dharma helps us to suffer less. Often dharma is described as the teachings of the historical Buddha. In this context, I like to translate *dharma* as "gospel," which in theology is the Greek word for "good news." Therefore, the dharma as taught by the Buddha is the good news that the nature of all phenomena is free from delusion, which means it is free from suffering.

The dharma is anything that is the manifestation of wisdom itself. In the contemplation of the second homecoming, we are attempting to evoke all the texts and teachings that have us develop and deepen our wisdom. These are our wisdom texts. These texts can be actual texts like scriptures or teachings. They can be the words of our teachers. They can be movies, any work of art, or a TV show. They could be a social media meme, a quote, or favorite books. Our wisdom texts are anything that communicates wisdom and truth to us and teaches us to be kind. All this is dharma.

What helps us to think about our wisdom texts is asking ourselves: What helps me to see things as they really are? What materials am I relying on to help me develop clarity? What am I always watching or reading that helps me to feel better? For me, my wisdom texts are Buddhist scriptures, along with the scriptures of other spiritual paths and traditions: James Baldwin's *The Fire Next Time*, Alice Walker's *The Color Purple*, Essex Hemphill's *Ceremonies*, bell hooks's *We Real Cool*, and Audre Lorde's *Sister Outsider* are wisdom texts. Alvin Ailey's dance piece *Cry*, Tony Kushner's *Angels in America*, the movie *Moonlight*, Marlon Riggs's documentary *Tongues Untied*, and the '90s British dramatic movie *Secrets and Lies*, as well as many of the songs of Sweet Honey in the Rock, are also wisdom texts. All these books, plays, and shows have helped me to deepen my wisdom and have shown me how to be less violent in the world by revealing hidden parts of myself and helping me to feel less alone.

When I am practicing this homecoming, I am reflecting on all these texts and evoking the energy of these texts to join me in the space along with my guides. It is this energy that serves the function of inspiring me and reminding me of my own wisdom as something that I can come home to and be held by.

## The Community

The last refuge of the traditional Three Jewels is that of the sangha or spiritual community. It is the congregation of fellow practitioners dedicated to helping each other and supporting the jewels of the Buddha and dharma. Essentially, sangha means community. It can also mean gathering and coming together with a purpose. When I am speaking about sangha, I am reminding people that when we gather together as a community of spiritual practitioners, we take on a special purpose. We are no longer an ordinary community. We are more than just blood family or an activist affinity group. We are people consenting together to help each other obtain spiritual realization. No one has to like anyone. I have been in spiritual communities where there have been people I wouldn't call a friend. However, what makes sangha important is that I can recognize that I don't like someone, maybe put up some boundaries that protect our relationship from becoming violent, while focusing on my love for that person. Again, when I love, I am accepting someone and wanting them to be happy. We don't have to like someone to love them. I think this is so much of what makes the spiritual community important.

I believe that the conflict we experience in community is a sacred conflict. I am not speaking of the conflict that comes through the abuse of power, but the conflict that comes with trying to get along with others and navigating various personalities. A healthy community will have its share of people rubbing against each other trying to get comfortable. It is through this rubbing that we learn to bring our practice into interactions and to challenge ourselves to hold others with kindness but with a directness that expresses our needs, boundaries, and values. Relationships in the spiritual community should be a negotiation to get our core needs met, not a compromise where we feel as if it is not possible to have our core needs met. It is this work that helps me to understand the spiritual community as being sacred and extraordinary. Relating to the sangha inspires me to respect it and take it seriously.

When I am reflecting on this homecoming, I am reflecting on the places, groups, and communities where I feel loved. There are spiritual communities where I love going because the love is strong. There are restaurants and retail stores I return to over and over again because there is such a strong ethic of love in the space. My family is a community where I experience love as well, and the encouragement to return the love. When I practice this homecoming, I invite the members of all of the communities I am a part of where I experience love, and I imagine that they join my guides and wisdom texts around me.

## The Ancestors

Now we move out of the traditional sources of refuge into supports that come directly from my personal practice. The fourth homecoming is the ancestors. Ancestor practice is newer practice for me. I have been inspired and moved by friends in other spiritual traditions who center ancestor practice. One of the impacts of having a Tantric Buddhist practice has been a deepening relationship with the unseen world of formless beings such as spirits, deities, and other kinds of beings. I have always believed in this world that I could not see but could feel at times, but I had no way to express that belief. Tantric Buddhism helped to restore my belief in and connection to a personally felt truth that I was surrounded by countless beings with wide ranges of intentions and purposes.

I was not raised having been taught any connection with my ancestors. These beliefs have been largely erased from communities of African and slave descent by white supremacy and white supremacist expressions of Christianity. I was taught in church that when we die we go to heaven or hell. This teaching always felt oversimplified. My introduction to Buddhism helped reveal a more nuanced and complex view of the unseen world where heaven and hell were states of mind any being could find themselves in and where there were countless other states beings occupied and migrated through. This excited me, and I felt for the first time after receiving these teachings that I was being told the truth.

Over the past few years, the reality of ancestors has become more and more important. I believe that ancestors are beings that have passed from this physical world into a world that parallels this one and have taken on the work of supporting us. This support is expressed through protection and guidance. There are many cultures in the world that have centered the remembering and worship of ancestors in communal, family, and personal lives. I believe that ancestor practice helps us to develop a sense of connectedness and belonging to our communities and families while at the same time teaching us to open to a gratitude for what others have done before us to ensure our well-being. Ancestor practice also helps us to understand that we are ancestors in training, and this reflection helps me to think about what I am doing to ensure the well-being of others coming after me.

Ancestors can be beings that are a part of our familial line who have come before us, or they can be beings that choose to care for us because we share similar lives or passions as they do. For instance, I know that there are members of my family who are still watching out for me just as there are beings who were queer or Black in their life who have chosen to support me because I reflect an important part of them in this realm. Through my experience developing a relationship with my ancestors, I understand that passing from a physical body back into a state of consciousness or energy does not completely disrupt our relationship to a sense of ego, so these beings can still be very attached to their former identities and personalities. In my experience, the ancestors are not necessarily enlightened or realized, but their metaphysical state offers them a much more expansive view of forces happening around us, which makes their guidance valuable.

However, our relationship with the ancestors is not just them helping us; we are also helping them. Sometimes our ancestors need us to continue the work that was important for them, or are needing to transition into other states and rely on our support to help.

Unfortunately, not all beings have our well-being in mind. There are unseen beings that want to hurt us, including some of our ancestors. Again, ancestors are not enlightened; they too still struggle with ego, which dictates needs and wants. Some ancestors are still hurt and wounded from their embodied lives, and there can still be great anger and blaming. When beings lost in this hurt and anger begin to touch our lives and the world through their suffering, causing violence, we call them demons. Being harmed by demons is much more common than some of us are willing to admit to. However, as there are beings that are trying to hurt us, there are also many more beings that are trying to protect us. I see my relationship with my ancestors not just as them guiding me, but as my work of doing emotional labor for them to relieve some of them of their discomfort and pain that could not be reconciled or healed in their embodied lives. My ancestor practice is not easy in light of this aspect of the work. However, I am grateful for the opportunity to offer support for those who have come before me who are directly responsible for the benefits I enjoy.

When I am working with groups, it is always important for me to explain that we have to be intentional about how we call our ancestors into our awareness. I advise people to call only the ancestors who are invested in their well-being to be present, while asking those who are not to stay away. I ask these ancestors and other beings supporting me to protect me from the beings that want to hurt me. It is so important to do this. Our calling of beings and energy is quite powerful, and we have to be intentional about what we call to be with us and how we need to relate to what we have called. Any being who is not about the reduction of suffering and violence is not welcomed around me. (This actually goes for humans as well!) Communicating these strong intentions lies at the heart of how we can protect ourselves when calling into the unseen world.

When I teach about ancestors, I also find it important to think about our lineage. In my practice, lineage is a little different from ancestry. I define "lineage" as those beings who have come before us or who are still here in this life that share similar passions and interests with us. These beings help make it possible to engage in the things that are important for me. My primary lineage is my spiritual lineage, and this lineage is all of my teachers across the various spiritual paths I practice and teach, including the teachers of my teachers, their teachers, and so forth. My spiritual lineage is a conduit of teachings that focus on the transformation of the deluded mind into wisdom and compassion, and it is through the support of the lineage that I can transmit these teachings to others. Another important lineage for me is my lineage of great activists and change makers, including all those who have come before me and those who are with me now in the work. There are many more lineages that I am a part of, and I encourage people to think about their passions and to ask themselves who made it possible to embrace their passion.

When I practice the homecoming of ancestry, I invite my ancestors into the space to be with me and to take their place with my guides, wisdom texts, and communities. I do the same with my lineages. I ask that they support me and guide me. I come to know my ancestry and lineage and can remember that I am not alone. I also understand through this calling that I am in the process of becoming an ancestor while at the same time understanding that I am a lineage holder.

## The Earth

The fifth homecoming is the earth. Earth practice has become a much more vital part of my practice now as I am discerning what my role is in disrupting climate change. This is a real issue that is complex to navigate, especially when we are having to work as a global community to address the damage we are doing to the planet. This seems daunting to me. Having spent time looking into this feeling of being overwhelmed and powerless, I eventually started asking myself what my relationship to the earth is, at this moment. One of the first insights that came was getting curious about my body.

I believe that our bodies are extensions of all of the elements, including earth. It is interesting to study the burial ceremonies of communities in the world. Most of them involve returning our bodies back to an element in some way, including variations of cremation, sea/water burials, sky burials like ones observed in Tibet, and especially earth burials. In Christian funeral burial rites, a common phrase is "earth to earth, ashes to ashes." The rite is meant to evoke the Genesis story of how God formed the first human, Adam, from soil, emphasizing that we are primarily composed of earth. Though modern science reveals that our bodies are indeed composed of more than half water, what this story, earth burial rites, and my understanding of earth reveal is that earth is vital for forming a container to hold our bodies and the other elements.

When we are in our bodies, we can connect directly to the earth itself. When we are disembodied, then we are not able to be aware of and experience the energy of earth. Our disembodiment is due to a variety of reasons, which include trauma and which translate into a distrust of our bodies. Our body becomes unsafe, and we don't want to have any awareness of it. Because so many of us are disconnected from our bodies, we have very little sensitivity to the earth, which means we cannot really sense the damage we are doing to the earth. Yet, for those people who are embodied, experiencing the trauma of the earth is very uncomfortable.

Slowly beginning to understand all of this, I started developing a reverence for the earth through a practice of revering my body. I began engaging in the struggle of returning to my body and working with the traumas that make it difficult to be in my body and feel okay about it. This takes time, especially if you have experienced significant social oppression. Social oppression often becomes deposited not just as emotional trauma but as physical trauma as well. I noticed in my practice that internalized oppression continued as long as I remained disembodied. The work of embodiment was the work of reclaiming my body, healing and managing my trauma, and embracing agency over my own body. This agency was disrupted for my slave ancestors beginning with the Middle Passage and compounded through our introduction to systematic racism. This systematic oppression has made it possible for trauma as loss of physical agency to be transmitted through my ancestry as transhistorical trauma. A central part of my personal activism is the work of embodiment to release my ancestors from this trauma and to reduce the trauma I pass to the next generation.

My current practice of the earth as the fifth homecoming is evoking the energy of the earth and inviting that energy into my body to remind my body that it is a reflection of the earth. This evoking of the earth is also the act of allowing myself to be held by the earth. When this holding happens, then I feel as if I am being loved by the earth. I think that this is the most profound aspect of this homecoming for me: the realization and experience that the earth is always loving me. And when I am loved by the earth, it becomes my teacher, my foundation, and my lover. This experience fosters a deep sense of safety, and I am able to move a little further and open my mind to not just my personal experience of the earth, but also the experience of others who have been in dynamic and intimate relationships with the various aspects of earth, and I am able to be grateful for their relationship as well.

In the practice of this homecoming, we invite the sacred earth, the sacred foundation, and the energy of stabilization into the space with the other homecomings. We allow ourselves to rest in the love of the earth holding us.

### Silence

The sixth homecoming is silence. Silence offers me the space to be with myself without a lot of external distraction. Silence is also a mirror that reflects the work that I need to do back to me. I start each day in silence and maintain it for as long as I can. If I am traveling and teaching, I adjust my schedule to wake up early enough to get a few hours of silence. This time is important for me. It is within this silence that I do my spiritual practices. I also use this space to reflect, write, and set my intentions for the day. Silence is a natural homecoming for me because I feel completely at home in it. I would say that my natural habitat is silence.

When I reflect on silence, I think about Audre Lorde and her essay "The Transformation of Silence into Language and Action." When she speaks of the necessity of moving out of silence into language despite the risks that it presents, I think about how silence has taught me to be in relationship to language. My years of silence have taught me the power of language and how to be held accountable by the way I use language and allow it to emerge from my own vulnerability. When my language emerges from a place of openness and truth, it will be truthful and therefore necessary. The transformation of silence into language is the migration from captivity into freedom or even the migration from invisibility into visibility. However, freedom and visibility come with the burden of confronting all those who don't want you to be free and seen.

I was raised as an only child and tended to spend a lot of time alone. I think that this contributed to being shy sometimes in social situations where I found it easy to sit alone or to remain quiet. I developed a healthier relationship to silence after I started my meditation practice—I no longer used silence to avoid anything or to make myself comfortable. I really began to understand that silence was a strategy that allowed space to hold everything that was happening in the moment. I do not equate silence with space, but silence can offer us the support to notice the space in and around us.

I understand that silence can be hard for some folks. Though this has not been my experience in life, I know that some people associate silence with danger. People have shared stories with me about the neighborhoods they grew up in where silence, especially an instant of sudden silence, indicated something violent was about to happen. Silence then prompts a PTSD response to the potential of something bad happening. I do remember times in high school when we would all be in the cafeteria, and all of a sudden people went silent, followed quickly by the sounds of fighting. That instant of silence alerted everyone, and it was a habitual reaction to jerk your head up and quickly scan the space to see where the shit was about to go down.

In my training to become a teacher, I spent more than three years in a small group retreat, much of it alone and in silence, with intermediate periods throughout each day engaged in group practice and meals with my handful of fellow co-retreatants. The beginning of that experience was the first time I remember being terrified by silence. The terror emerged from the reality that the silence would be for years. I found myself paralyzed by the promise that silence would be brutally honest with me, and I felt I wasn't ready for that honesty. When silence is intentionally used to understand ourselves, then it will reveal many secrets to us. I see silence in this respect as being compassionate, because it does tell me the truth and it calls me to do the work of holding space for that truth, which is the work of spiritual transformation.

Sometimes silence isn't that silent. There is the silence many of us identify as the quiet around us that is the absence of noise. Yet it is not so much the absence of noise we are responding to but the nondistractedness we can maintain in the midst of noise. I can often find silence in the most chaotic situations because the chaos itself doesn't distract me. There is still an awareness of things, as well as an experiencing of things, but not a thinking about things happening. The same is true for my mind. Silence doesn't mean that things go away. It means that I am not lost in the material of my mind. So silence is not just the absence of noise or other distracting things; it is the state of being aware of phenomena and not getting lost in any of it.

Then again, silence isn't silent, because silence is still communicating something. Silence is itself a medium to reveal other experiences, whether thoughts, feelings, or even other kinds of energy. Silence can be loud like this. There can be so much happening even without any noise. Another reason why so many people struggle with silence is because even when blanketed in it, we are still not safe against the things we are trying to avoid.

On silent meditation retreats, I encourage retreatants to lean into the silence. I teach that silence is there to offer us the space to take care of ourselves. In silence we can have the support to look within ourselves into the places that need listening to, holding, and healing.

In my practice of silence as a homecoming, I invite the silence to be in the space along with stillness. I reflect on silence as a guide as well as a vehicle that supports my transformation. I ask the silence to hold me, and I ask all the other energies I have invited into the space to hold me. Sitting in this silence, I am at home; and just as with my other homecomings, I am being loved.

## Ourselves

The seventh homecoming is perhaps the most important one, and it is coming home to ourselves. The one thing that I desired the most at the beginning of my path was to love myself. Coming home to myself is essentially cultivating a deep acceptance for myself and allowing all the aspects of myself to be present regardless of how painful it is. It is the work of allowing that grants me the space to begin to transform my relationship to what is uncomfortable. This is the expression of love for myself.

Coming home to myself is doing the work of developing confidence in myself. I know that this confidence has been something that has been missing for me most of my life. Systematic oppression has resulted in a state of disembodiment; and when I am disembodied, I struggle to experience confidence in myself. When I say confidence, I mean developing a basic trust in my ability to be okay, to be loving, compassionate, and overall trusting that I am resilient. When I am disembodied, it is almost impossible for me to trust myself; I can't trust my body because I am not in relationship with it. The psychic trauma of oppression posits itself in the body, making it difficult to be in relationship to that discomfort. This is one of the ways systematic oppression maintains itself in our experience: by making it dangerous for us to sense our bodies.

Then again, having confidence in myself has also meant trusting my woundedness, including the trauma that stems from systematic oppression. This trust means that I am allowing my discomfort to be in my experience, and I am choosing to learn from it and to see it as a guide. Sometimes I even call my discomfort into the space as one of my guides in the first homecoming. Developing an acceptance of and an appreciation for my pain has been deeply radical. To not be afraid of the pain and to be able to hold space for it are expressions of love and compassion for ourselves as well as the first step in the process of embodiment.

Another aspect of myself that I practice having confidence in is my joy. Joy is much more than just being happy; it is experiencing the energy of what I often call bliss. This bliss is an experience of all my distractions falling away and of being left with this profound feeling of freedom. It is the realization of extreme clarity and openness. Many of us experience this during sexual orgasms or highs from substance use. The most authentic experiences of bliss are those that are the expression of deep virtue or goodness, which connects us to an expression of our most nonviolent and loving selves. This bliss, like happiness, is about connection and balance; but it is more about the experience of unity, that there is no separation anymore. Some of us will get a glimpse and taste of this; but this is all we need to be transformed, because that one quick experience will reveal to us what is possible beyond our suffering. It will reveal potential, and that potential can fuel our motivation to do the work of suffering less and getting free. I am practicing confidence in my innate capacity to experience bliss, which I ultimately believe is an expression of my true nature.

One way that I come home to myself is by trusting my practice to hold me in times when I may be caught off-guard by crisis. I often tell longtime practitioners who are dealing with serious issues to step out into your practice and let your practice catch you. Often the most powerful practice I experience is when I cannot practice intentionally. Sometimes shit just happens, and all of a sudden you are showing up and holding space for yourself and others, as well as the situation itself.

When I am practicing coming home to myself, I am inviting myself into the space along with everything that is a part of me, both the negative and the positive. I am leaning into my basic experience in the moment of this calling. When I am struggling to do this, then I call on my other homecomings to support me. In doing all of this, I am coming home to myself.

### Practicing the Seven Homecomings

The Seven Homecomings can be practiced formally or informally, individually or with a group. Often I evoke my homecomings as I move through the world. Sometimes I need certain kinds of support and find myself evoking some homecomings over others. Sometimes I need to experience connection to my ancestors more than to my guides, or I need to feel the earth more than my wisdom texts. Other times I need all the homecomings. However, the following practice is the basic formal practice in which we are evoking our homecoming circle. Sometimes in my teaching, I call it my circle of care as well. In any case, this practice will be the root practice for larger practices I will introduce throughout the book.

---

### THE PRACTICE

The meditation is a contemplation practice. It can be practiced on your own or in a group. The best way to begin the practice is by reading through the guiding instructions once, and informally evoking each homecoming. Do this a few times. Let the language and the process of the practice change to meet your needs. When this happens, it's easier to remember and internalize the practice in a way that makes sense for you. The guiding instructions are just a template. Allowing yourself to be creative with the practice is important for you to sustain the practice.

1. Start by moving through the beginning practice sequence.

2. Begin contemplating the first homecoming of the guide. Reflect on any being who has been a guide, a teacher, a mentor, an adviser, or an elder for you. Reflect on the beings in your life whom you've gone to for guidance and support. Reflect on the beings who express love and compassion for you. Imagine that you're inviting all of those beings into the space with you. Invite them to gather around you in a circle and say welcome. Relax. Inhale. Exhale and come home to being held by your guides.

3. *Short pause*

4. The second homecoming is your wisdom texts. Begin reflecting on any text that has helped you to deepen your wisdom. These texts can include any writing, books, teachings, sacred scriptures, quotes, social media memes, or any form of artistic expression like music, dance, visual art, etc. Any texts that have helped you to experience clarity, openness, love, and compassion are your sacred texts. Invite the essence of these texts into this space. You can imagine that these texts are actually present, or you can have a sense that their essence is encircling you with your guides. Say welcome to your texts. Relax. Inhale. Exhale and come home to being held by your wisdom texts.

5. *Short pause*

6. The third homecoming is community. Begin by reflecting about the communities, groups, and spaces where you experience love or the feeling of being accepted and supported in being happy. Moreover, what are the communities and groups not only where you feel loved but also where you feel as if you can love and return love back to others? Where do you feel safe to love? Where are you being loved? Invite those communities and groups into the space around you with your guides and wisdom texts. And if you don't feel as if there's a space like that for you, then you can invite the aspiration to be a part of a loving space into this space as well. Say welcome to your communities. Relax. Inhale. Exhale and come home to being held by your communities.

7. *Short pause*

8. The fourth homecoming is your ancestors. Begin by reflecting on those ancestors who have wanted the best for you, including wanting you to be happy and safe. You don't need to know who these ancestors are. All you have to do is contemplate that there have been those in your familial line who want you to be happy. Invite those beings into the circle as well. Also reflect on the lineages you feel connected to, like the lineage of your spiritual tradition, or tradition of art or activism. Invite your lineage into the circle as well. As you invite your ancestors, remember that you too are in the process of becoming an ancestor. As you invite your lineage, remember that you are in this moment a lineage holder. Say welcome to your ancestors and lineages. Relax. Inhale. Exhale and come home to being held by your ancestors and lineages.

9. *Short pause*

10. The fifth homecoming is the earth. Begin by reflecting on the importance of the earth under you and how it sustains your life and the lives of countless beings. Reflect on the energy of the earth, which is the energy of sustainability, stability, and foundation. The earth also represents the ground of your experience. So coming home to the earth means touching the earth, acknowledging the earth, surrendering to the earth, and allowing it to hold you and, as it holds you, understanding that it is loving you as well. Invite the energy of the earth into the circle. Say welcome to the earth. Relax. Inhale. Exhale and come home to being held by the earth.

11. *Short pause*

12. The sixth homecoming is silence. Begin by reflecting on the generosity of silence as something that helps you to have the space to be with yourself. Reflect on how important it is to lean into silence, allowing it to hold you, and reflect on how you can embrace silence as a friend and/or lover invested in your health and well-being. Silence helps you to understand how to use your language to benefit yourself and others. Allow the silence to be present, and accept it. Invite silence into the circle. Say welcome to the silence. Relax. Inhale. Exhale and come home to being held by the silence.

13. *Short pause*

14. Finally, the seventh homecoming is yourself. Begin by reflecting on your experiences of your mind and body. Consider how your experiences are valuable, important, and crucial. Invite all the parts of yourself into your awareness, including the parts of yourself that seem too ugly or overwhelming. Embracing yourself as a homecoming means you make sure that you are showing up to being held by the other homecomings. Allow yourself to be present. Accept that you are present. Say welcome to yourself. Relax. Inhale. Exhale and come home to yourself.

15. *Short pause*

16. Embrace all of your homecomings. You can see your guides, communities, ancestors, and lineages as your benefactors. You draw inspiration to open and be more vulnerable from your wisdom texts. You remember that the earth is under your feet and that there is silence offering you the space to be with yourself. And then finally there is yourself being held with this circle of care.

17. Just sit in this circle and imagine that your benefactors are sending care and kindness into the circle. Try to feel that care in any way that feels appropriate. What does that care feel like? Just sit and connect to the care from your benefactors.

18. *Short pause*

19. Now imagine that your circle of benefactors begins to dissolve into white light, and gather that white light into your heart center. Rest your mind and relax.

20. Finally, move through the ending practice sequence.

## Breathing Practices

*Breathe Honey.*

—LAMA ROD

*Feelings come and go like clouds in a windy sky. Conscious breathing is my anchor.*

—THICH NHAT HANH

*Only those who know how to breathe will survive.*

—SHRIRAM SHARMA

Pranayama is a tradition of breathing that helps to control our life force energy and has a direct impact on our mental and physical health. Often I call it life force breathing. This life force energy is called *prana,* and prana is said to ride the breath and anything in the body that flows or is fluid. Pranayama moves prana through our energetic body via channels called *nadis.*

Breath is an important tool for us, as in every yoga and *tantric* tradition. I relate to prana as energy that can feel both subtle and apparent. In my practice, I have noticed that my body acts as an antenna responding to energy in and around me, which my mind then labels. My sensitivity to energy was further refined after I completed my training as a Reiki practitioner.

Pranayama prepares us for meditation because a stable breath can stabilize the mind and prepare it to do the work of awareness, concentration, and mindfulness. If the breath is not stable, then we find ourselves diverting energy to stabilizing everything and away from awareness practice.

Most people do not really breathe. If we do not breathe, we will not be free. Breath is life. Breathing helps us to move intense emotional energy around like anger and sadness. For the rest of the book, I will refer to pranayama as breathing practice.

One important note here as I introduce breathing practices: if you have a history of trauma, breathing practice can feel ungrounded. I often teach breathing practice with earth touching practice in order to offer something that can ground you. Earth and breath practice will be introduced in the Bhumisparsha, or earth touching practices, section. Following are some basic breath practices to begin with.

——————— THE PRACTICES ———————

## THE BASIC BREATH

1. Start by moving through the beginning practice sequence.

2. Continue by bringing your attention to your breath. Start with breathing in and out through the nose. Slowly begin to elongate both the inhale and the exhale, making them very long and deep. Try to relax. Keep your attention on the breath. As other thoughts come up, keep your attention on the breath and use it to ground your attention.

3. Now shift your breathing to breathing in through the nose and out through the mouth. Again, ground your attention in the breath and relax, keeping the breath long and drawn out. Do this for as long as you want.

4. Move through the ending practice sequence.

## CALMING BREATH

Begin by breathing in through the nose and breathing out through the mouth. After breathing out through the mouth, breathe in through the mouth and out through the nose. After breathing out through the nose, breathe in through the nose and then out through the mouth, and then breathe in through the mouth. Keep this pattern of breath going while trying to relax and focus on the breath. Again, make the breaths long and drawn out. This breath is meant to calm you down, as it helps to open up space in your mind.

---

**CLEANSING BREATH**

I like to do this breath at the beginning of a longer practice. It helps to clear old breath from the body as well as any negative emotions. This breath involves some visualization.

Begin by noticing your breath. Breathe in and out through the nose to begin with. Keep the breaths long and deep. Now notice any discomfort in your mind and body. Imagine that as you inhale, the breath is dissolving sensations of discomfort in your experience, and imagine breathing this dissolved discomfort back out through the mouth. Keep repeating this process until you feel settled.

When you are ready to end the practice, inhale as deeply as you can, and then forcibly breathe out, imagining that you are releasing all the discomfort in your experience out through every opening in your body, including pores, mouth, nose, ears, eyes, everything. Do this three times and then relax.

---

## Tonglen

*Tonglen* comes from the Tibetan Buddhist tradition, and it means "taking and sending." It can also be described as replacing ourselves for others. It is one of the first practices I learned, and it is something that I like to often share with others.

Initially, the practice can seem very magical or mystical. It is not. Instead, I find it to be practical. I believe that tonglen is a practice of remembering our suffering and allowing ourselves to be in our experience and taken care of, as well as doing the work of holding space for others and their suffering. Tonglen rides the breath, it is the breath that guides us onto the ground of our discomfort, and it is the breath that begins to move us into the experience of suffering for others.

Our breath is perhaps the most magical aspect of the practice. The breath can bring us into a shared moment with our bodies and with everything else that is showing up. I don't have to like any part of the moment, nor am I being asked to. Tonglen is an expression of showing up for ourselves and for others who depend on us.

Traditionally, tonglen is taught as taking in another person's suffering in the form of dark smoke and sending out peace, joy, and deep well-being in the form of white and cooling light. In my revision of this practice, I like to think of the other person's suffering as white mist, because dark smoke seems a little intense for me to imagine breathing in. I also call the person I am supporting the recipient.

I like to think of tonglen as protection. It allows me to enter into and remain in situations of intense suffering, giving me a way to make this suffering workable and less of a burden. It takes some of the heaviness away. It also takes the edge off. This can be one of our core practices for holding space for ourselves and others.

Moreover, we protect ourselves from having negative energy needlessly reside in our bodies and minds. I often say that compassion is one of the strongest things we can possibly have as it is an inherent state of being that removes the focus from a sense of "I" or "me" who can experience fatigue or any negative impact of unresolved negative energy. When I am able to decenter this sense of "me," I begin to also disrupt the sense that there is an inherent "me" who can experience discomfort.

### Approaching the Practice

There are two ways in which we should approach this practice. I believe that most practices should begin with "on the cushion" work, or formal practice in which we set aside time to devote exclusively to a practice. This method strengthens our "off the cushion" or informal practice, which is what we would also call our "on the spot" practice that occurs simply by living our lives and working with things as they arise.

---

### THE PRACTICE

1. Start by moving through the beginning practice sequence.

2. Focus on the breath or another object, or simply let your mind rest within emptiness itself.

3. Move through a short practice of the Seven Homecomings, calling into the space your homecoming circle. After you have summoned the circle, imagine dissolving it into your heart center, and imagine the energy of care residing in your heart center.

4. Call to mind someone who is having a difficult time right now. Imagine them sitting in front of you. They are the recipient. Also imagine that around them forms a thin white mist like a fog or steam. This mist is the expression of this person's discomfort.

5. Turn your mind to your breath, noticing both the in breath and the out breath.

6. Generate or connect to the aspiration or instinct in you to alleviate their suffering. Imagine this desire strengthening the energy of care in your heart center.

7. Keeping your mind on your heart center, imagine breathing in and out of the heart center.

8. Imagine that you begin inhaling the white mist around your recipient into your heart center and that the mist of suffering is completely cleansed by the energy of care in the heart center.

9. Breathe out this purified energy as white light of peace and contentment. Continue the process of breathing in the mist of discomfort and breathing out the white energy of peace and contentment, and imagine that slowly the mist around the recipient decreases and is replaced by the white light of your purified energy.

10. Continue until you feel as if you have done enough practice for the session. Imagine that your recipient is experiencing peace and contentment. Now imagine that they dissolve into the white energy that you have shared. Next, dissolve that energy into your heart center. Rest your mind.

## Informal Practice

When you encounter situations with others outside of formal meditation sessions, bring to mind the care of your homecoming circle, and feel the energy of that care in your heart. Imagine breathing in whatever you are experiencing of another person's suffering as white mist, bringing it into the light of care in your heart center, and releasing the positive well-wishes as white light.

## *Bhumisparsha: Introductory Earth Touching Practices*

Upon his enlightenment, the Buddha reached down and touched the earth, essentially asking the earth to validate his enlightenment and to serve as a witness to his accomplishment. The Buddha was being harassed by Mara, the personification of doubt and distraction, who wanted to lead him off the path. The Buddha reached down to acknowledge the earth and to settle himself into this time and place. That settling was the validation itself that not only did he deserve to be enlightened, but he was claiming it without apology. In a way, when the Buddha touched the earth, he was telling Mara to fuck off. That gesture of touching the earth is called Bhumisparsha.

The Buddha was teaching us to touch into the ground of our basic experience in the world. For most of my life, I have never really been connected to the earth. The earth was something that seemed unimportant. When I began to engage in the work of embodiment, I was introduced to my body, which brought me into relationship with the energy of the earth itself. I started understanding that my disembodiment prevented me from being sensitive to the earth. When I am not in my body, I cannot be with the earth. It seemed to me that my body was an extension of the earth and that the earth was an extension of my body. This realization was startling. I had been missing vital teaching and experiences from the earth most of my life because of my disembodiment.

I knew for me that disembodiment was largely due to systems of power and oppression that kept me disembodied, because these systems would not operate with such disruption. Slavery and systematic racism emerging out of capitalism were ritualized systems of disembodiment forced on my ancestors, passed down through each generation through transhistorical trauma, and perpetuated by systematic oppressions like racism. By remaining disconnected from my body, I was remaining disconnected from knowing how oppression functions in my body. Further, I was alienated from ways that I could work to liberate myself. One of my primary paths of liberation was relying on the earth.

As my embodiment grew, my liberation experience deepened. I saw how our fundamental disconnect from the body made it almost impossible to understand the pain of the earth and the shifting of our climate. Because I was feeling aspects of my body for the first time, I was feeling how the earth was expressing itself in my body. I could feel the energetic instability of the earth under me and in me. I could feel the shift in the world around me. I discovered that the way we treated our bodies was the way that we were treating the earth. To love my body made it easier to love and care for the earth. If we are to mitigate the change in our climate, we must return to our bodies and do the work of caretaking the earth through our bodies.

The earth is always under us. The earth is always inside of us. The earth is always around us. The earth is always holding us, which means that the earth always loves us regardless of who we are. This is the most beautiful and intense gift of the earth, and it is something that we can evoke and rely on when we feel the most alone or unloved. The earth has been making profound offerings to our deep well-being and safety for as long as there has been life on the planet. I wanted to return that love by first learning to care more for my body and then extending that care to the earth in whatever way was possible.

My embodiment and deepening love for the earth also connected me more to my ancestors. I believe that the love I received from the earth was also an expression of the love that my ancestors were expressing to me. I believe ancestors are linked to the energetic expression of earth as a foundation that expresses itself not only in this realm, but in other nonphysical realms as well. The energy of earth can be something that keeps beings like our ancestors connected to the world, and the energy of earth in our bodies can be something that beings attach themselves to as well. I also believe that beings can have a karmic connection to the earth, especially if their lives were centered on the earth. Acknowledging and evoking the beings who have cared for the land that I am practicing on has become a common practice for me before a retreat or talk. There are still beings attached to the land that we dwell on each day, and if we were more embodied we would remember them and try to care for them.

And while the earth is caring for us, it is also helping us to hold our woundedness. It is easy to think that offering our trauma and other woundedness to the earth harms it. Earth energy is about grounding, holding, and transforming. What harms the earth is our abuse of the earth through impacting natural habitat, pollution, exhausting natural resources, and our addiction to paving over paradise. However, when we offer our trauma and woundedness, we are offering the energy of these struggles, which the earth just interprets as energy that should be held and transformed. One expression of love for the earth is trusting the earth to hold what we struggle with.

I believe that the Buddha realized all of this as he touched the earth. I think he was giving up something to be held by the earth, which was the suffering of his relationship to doubt. In the touching, he released himself from any ambiguity, and in return the earth touched him back. Bhumisparsha practices bring us into relation with both our bodies and the earth. When we are able to touch the earth with our minds, the energy of the earth can gently pull the rest of our awareness home into the body.

### Basic Earth Touching Practice

This meditation is a mindfulness-based practice using the energy of the earth to create a sense of stabilization.

---

## THE PRACTICE

1. Start by moving through the beginning practice sequence.

2. If you are seated, shift your attention to the floor under your seat. If you are sitting in a chair, notice your feet making contact with the ground. If you are sitting on a cushion, notice the sensation of your cushion on top of the ground. The ground is earth. Let your attention touch the earth.

3. Notice the energy of earth. Name the energy. The energy of the earth can express itself as the energy of stability, firmness, solidity, steadiness, sustainability, or others. Try to connect to the energy you most resonate with, and imagine that the energy begins to rise up into your body.

4. Imagine that this energy has filled up your body, and allow yourself to rest in the sensation of being held by this energy.

5. Reflect on how you are an extension of the earth and how the earth is an extension of your body.

6. Finally, offer gratitude for the earth as well as your body.

7. Move through the ending practice sequence.

---

## Earth and Breath Practice

This meditation is a mindfulness-based practice using breath to connect to the energy of the earth to create a sense of stabilization.

--------- THE PRACTICE ---------

1. Start by moving through the beginning practice sequence.

2. Now bring your attention to the sensation of your body on the seat. If you are standing, start with bringing your attention to the sensation of your feet on the floor; or if you are lying down, bring your attention to the sensation of your body on the floor. Just notice the sensations, including the weight of your body and the seat or floor under you.

   If you are seated, shift your attention to the floor under your seat. If you are sitting in a chair, notice your feet making contact with the ground. If you are sitting on a cushion, notice the sensation of your cushion on top of the ground. The ground is earth. Let your attention touch the earth.

3. Bring your attention to your breath. Notice both the in breath and the out breath. Taking your time, begin to slow your breathing down, elongating both breaths as much as you can. Relax.

4. Now imagine that when you inhale, you are breathing deep down into the body, all the way through your seat or down through your feet as if your breath is touching the earth. Try this breath a few times. When you are ready, imagine that when the in breath touches down to the earth, it pulls up the energy of the earth; and as you exhale, the breath carries this energy up through the body and even out of the body. Keep repeating this breath as much as you want.

5. When you are ready to finish, offer gratitude to the earth as well as your body.

6. Notice the energy of earth. Name the energy. The energy of the earth can express itself as the energy of stability, firmness, solidity, steadiness, sustainability, or others. Try to connect to the energy you most resonate with, and imagine that the energy begins to rise up into your body.

7. Imagine that this energy has filled up your body, and allow yourself to rest in the sensation of being held by this energy.

8. Reflect on how you are an extension of the earth and how the earth is an extension of your body.

9. Move through the ending practice sequence.

## Earth Gratitude Practice

This meditation is a mindfulness-based practice using the energy of the earth and the energy of gratitude to create a sense of openness and connectedness to the earth.

### THE PRACTICE

1. Start by moving through the beginning practice sequence.

2. Bring your attention to the sensation of your body on the seat. If you are standing, start with bringing your attention to the sensation of your feet on the floor; or if you are lying down, bring your attention to the sensation of your body on the floor. Just notice the sensations, including the weight of your body and the seat or floor under you.

   If you are seated, shift your attention to the floor under your seat. If you are sitting in a chair, notice your feet making contact with the ground. If you are sitting on a cushion, notice the sensation of your cushion on top of the ground. The ground is earth. Let your attention touch the earth.

3. Notice the energy of earth. Name the energy. The energy of the earth can express itself as the energy of stability, firmness, solidity, steadiness, sustainability, or others. Try to connect to the energy you most resonate with, and imagine that the energy begins to rise up into your body.

4. Imagine that this energy has filled up your body, and allow yourself to rest in the sensation of being held by this energy.

5. Reflect on how you are an extension of the earth and how the earth is an extension of your body.

6. Also reflect on how the earth is expressing love for you as it is holding you. Begin to generate gratitude for the earth. Imagine that the energy of gratitude begins to gather in your heart center in the form of warm energy.

When you have generated as much energy as you can, imagine that the energy begins to rain down through your body, down through your seat or feet, and out of your body into the earth, blessing the earth with your gratitude.

7. Move through the ending practice sequence.

## Earth Energy Invitation Practice

———————————— THE PRACTICE ————————————

1. Start by moving through the beginning practice sequence.

2. Allow yourself to relax and to be at ease. Beneath your seat is the ground. Notice the sensation of the ground. The earth is holding your body and the seat. What is that experience like for you, of being held by the earth? Are you trusting that the earth can really hold you right now? Are you fully relaxing? Are you easing into being held by the earth right now?

3. Allow your attention to float down beneath the seat one foot into the earth.

4. Allow your attention to settle right within the earth itself.

5. Now allow your attention to float another foot down into the earth.

6. Now allow your attention to drop yet another foot into the earth.

7. Now pull your attention up one foot.

8. Pull your attention up another foot.

9. As you pull your attention up for the last foot, imagine that with your attention, you're pulling up the energy of the earth, which is this sense of foundation, stability, and stillness. However you feel and resonate with the energy of the earth, begin to pull that up with your attention, and rest that energy at the very base of your spine. And now slowly begin to pull that energy up the spine, vertebrae by vertebrae, bit by bit, feeling that sense of earth, that energy of earth, slowly rising up the spine. And as you're moving that energy up into your neck, to the base of your brain, imagine that you're just allowing that energy to simply fill up your skull. And just allow yourself to relax.

10. Move through the ending practice sequence.

## Anger Practices

Anger is one of the most complex emotional states that we experience, and also one of the most destructive. Meditation as a strategy to work with anger helps us to diffuse the often-stifling experience of anger and helps to promote a sense of spaciousness. Anger arises out of tightness and contraction in our mental experience. It is very difficult to act in a way that limits violence when we have no mental spaciousness. The following practices help to introduce us to beginning to feel our anger, often for the first time.

---

——————— REFLECTION PRACTICE ———————

1. Start by moving through the beginning practice sequence.

2. Do you struggle with anger? What is the hardest aspect of working with anger? How have you hurt people with your anger? How have you hurt yourself? As you reflect, begin to notice how the energy of anger is initiated in your experience. Just notice it.

3. Now bring your attention to the weight of your body, feeling yourself held by the chair or cushion if you are seated; or if you are lying down, feeling the ground under your body; or if you are standing, feeling the ground under your feet.

4. Move through the ending practice sequence.

---

## Am I Really Angry?

Saying "I am angry" is such a suffocating phrase with no potential for growth, movement, or freedom. To say "I am angry" means that you *are* anger. You are not anger; you are experiencing anger, in the same way you experience sadness and happiness. You need space around anger and all of your emotions in order to be free. Instead of saying "I am angry," you can say instead, "I am experiencing anger." When you identify an experience, you are allowing there to be space, because you know an experience is not inherently who you are.

The following reflection practice can help you with this idea.

---

1. Start by moving through the beginning practice sequence.

2. Say to yourself, "I am angry." Reflect on what your experience is like of being angry. After a few minutes, or when you are ready, relax and let go of the contemplation.

3. Next, say to yourself, "I am experiencing anger." Reflect on your experience of experiencing anger. How does it feel in comparison to being angry? After a few minutes, or when you are ready, relax and let go of the contemplation.

4. Finally, say to yourself, "There is an experience of anger." Reflect on there being an experience of anger somewhere. After a few minutes, or when you are ready, relax and let go of the contemplation.

5. Move through the ending practice sequence.

---

## Anger in the Mind

As we continue to work with anger, we see that anger is an experience that is both a mental experience as well as a physical experience. Let's explore the mental experience of anger.

---

**THE PRACTICE**

1. Start by moving through the beginning practice sequence.

2. If you are not already angry, reflect on a time when you were. Notice what is happening in your mind.

3. What kind of thoughts are you having? Are there narratives about blaming others for being wronged or hurt?

4. Do you sense frustration? Do you feel helpless?

5. Do you feel powerful?

6. Do you feel spacious in your mind, or tight and contracted?

7. Is this a pleasant experience?

8. Allow yourself to relax.

9. Move through the ending practice sequence.

---

## Anger in the Body

Let's explore anger in the body.

---

**THE PRACTICE**

1. Start by moving through the beginning practice sequence.

2. Again, if you are not already angry, reflect on an experience of anger.

3. As you reflect, where are you in your body? Where do you feel sensation?

4. Focus on the sensation rather than the thoughts around the sensation. How does the sensation feel?

5. Where in the body is the sensation the strongest?

6. Can you relax around this sensation? Can you give it space to be there, instead of pushing it away?

7. Can you just experience it, instead of thinking about it?

8. Move through the ending practice sequence.

## Holding Space for Pain

Let's practice holding space for different aspects of anger.

### THE PRACTICE

1. Start by moving through the beginning practice sequence.

2. Again, reflect on a situation of anger if you are not already angry. Notice both the mental and physical experience of anger.

3. Often anger is covering up our experiences of being hurt or wounded. Explore your thoughts around your anger, and pay attention to the narrative of why you are angry.

4. You may find that anger is triggered by your being hurt or disappointed. This is an important experience. Allow yourself to sink through the anger into the hurt. As you do this, take care of yourself. As you open more to the hurt, try to relax and allow your awareness to expand around the hurt.

5. Allow the awareness to hold the experience of hurt as much as possible. Don't get distracted by thoughts. Keep returning to the awareness of the pain. This is called holding space.

6. Move through the ending practice sequence.

## Noticing the Energy of Anger

Now that we have worked some with noticing anger in the body and mind, let's bring our attention to the energy of anger itself. This is a complex practice, as it requires us to notice just the energy of anger, not sensations, not even the pain. We are trying to notice the force or power that we feel in anger, and how we center the needs of the ego in that energy, which makes the expression of that energy harmful for ourselves and others as the ego seeks to protect itself.

### THE PRACTICE

1. Start by moving through the beginning practice sequence.

2. Again, reflect on a situation of anger if you are not already angry. Notice both the mental and physical experience of anger.

3. In your mind, notice the tendency to tell yourself that you are angry. What we have discovered in the previous meditations is that anger is an experience that changes and that passes through the mind and body.

4. Tell yourself: "I am experiencing anger. I am not angry." Allow that statement to trigger an openness.

5. In that openness, notice this sense of ego or "I" that is experiencing anger. Turn your attention away from the "I" that is experiencing, and turn it into the experience of anger itself. In particular, notice the force of anger. Notice how it is pulling and pushing. Hold space for it, and just continue exploring the energetic force of anger.

6. Notice your tendency to add a narrative to this energy, and look at how this narrative forces you to channel the energy into supporting this narrative. Hold steady as much as possible.

7. Move through the ending practice sequence.

## Anger Breath Practice

In this practice, we are using the breath to reduce the amount of anger energy in our experience.

---------------------------- THE PRACTICE ----------------------------

1. Start by moving through the beginning practice sequence.

2. Ask yourself this question: Where does the energy of anger arise for me in this moment? Using your intention to scan the body, notice where you're holding this energy. If you are having a hard time looking for that, just think of something that triggers anger, and go right toward where it arises in the body. And again, be kind. Don't fall into the heaviest forms of this energy in the body, but whatever you can manage right now. Just gently notice it.

3. Rest a hand on that part of the body where you feel that energy, as a way to anchor your attention. Rest that hand gently.

4. Now bring your attention to the breath. Just notice the cycle of breath, the in breath, and the out breath, in and out. Feel the physical sensations of breathing and all the nuanced sensations of breath entering and leaving.

5. And now return your attention to wherever in the body you identified the holding of anger. Imagine breathing in, and inhaling into that part of the body. And as you're inhaling into that part of the body, imagine that part of the body beginning to relax and expand around the sensation, the experience of anger. Just breathe into that part of the body, noticing the expanding, and just breathe out for now. Breathing in, expanding, breathing out.

Notice how we get really tight. Allow yourself to relax. And if it gets too overwhelming, bring your attention back to the seat. Bring your attention back to the ground. And now as you're breathing out, imagine that you're releasing this anger with the out breath. You breathe in, expand, breathe out, releasing this energy, sending it out of the body. Breathing in, relaxing, opening, breathing out, sending out, sending the anger out. Allow as much space around the anger as possible.

6. As you breathe into this part of the body, say to yourself, "I am not this anger." As you breathe out, say to yourself, "This is just an experience." Breathe in: "I am not this anger." Breathe out: "This is just an experience."

7. Return your attention back down to the seat and to the weight of the body. Whatever you feel in terms of tension, and tightness, imagine that it begins to be dissolved into a white light, allowing that light to fall down through the body into the earth, surrendering that discomfort. Let the earth hold it, and trust that the earth can hold it.

8. Move through the ending practice sequence.

## Anger Offering Practice

This is a practice that combines all of the other practices in one way or another. The purpose of the practice is to begin to understand how to let go of our anger so that we may eventually do the work of connecting to our hurt beneath the anger. This practice is longer and a little more formal in nature, so make sure you set aside thirty to sixty minutes of time to complete it.

---

### THE PRACTICE

1. Start by moving through the beginning practice sequence.

2. Now choose an earth touching practice and move through it to act as a grounding practice.

3. Once you feel grounded, move into the earth and breath practice for a few minutes until you feel calmer and more relaxed.

4. Begin the Seven Homecomings practice, and end with having a strong sense of your homecoming circle around you. Try to have a strong sense that your guides, communities, and ancestors/lineages are holding you while the earth is supporting you, silence is wrapped around you, and your wisdom texts are inspiring you.

5. Imagine that your circle begins to radiate a sense of deep care for you. Feel that energy of care as a warmth that begins to fill up the inside of the circle around you. That warmth feels like a warm blanket wrapping around you on a cold day. Feel the warmth touch the skin all over your body. Relax.

6. Turn your attention inward, noticing your body and mind. Practice identifying where your anger is and the best way you are experiencing it. You may experience it mentally in the form of an emotion or as a physical sensation.

7. Return your attention back out to the care around you. Imagine that the warm energy care begins to slowly sink into your body through the skin, into your muscles, bones, organs, fat, and tissue. Imagine that this warmth is circulating everywhere in the body.

8. Imagine that this warmth begins to be drawn toward where you are experiencing anger, either in the mind, the body, or both. Imagine that this warmth begins to wrap itself around that experience of anger. Relax.

9. Imagine that you begin offering this anger out of your body into the space around you that is still being bordered by your care circle. You can imagine that the energy of care pulls that anger out of you into the circle, where it is being held and cared for by the circle. Practice giving up this anger, let it be held by your homecoming circle, and relax. Do this for as long as you can, or until you feel as if you are getting distracted or tired.

10. Move through the ending practice sequence.

# 5

# EMBODIMENT

*I shall not be moved. Just like a tree that's planted by the water, I shall not be moved.*

—NEGRO SPIRITUAL

*I am determined to be more than my body—what my body has endured, what my body has become. Determination, though, has not gotten me very far.*

—ROXANE GAY

*Dear Tony,*

*I wanted to write this letter to you because this is the only way I can talk about approaching my body. If I am to speak about what my body has meant, then I must speak it to you because you were the last person who reflected something valuable back to me about my body. And I need someone to write this chapter to in order for it to be held kindly and warmly, allowing all the ugliness as well as the beauty to surface.*

*I remember the night you held me and something in the evening or the warmth of your body offered me the permission to say how much I felt I didn't deserve your arms around me. I shared how I could not understand why you were attracted to me. How I confided in you the many times I have failed to love my body and all the times it has failed to love me in return. I assumed that you had no clue as to how to relate to my struggle until you looked at me and said how you were here with me now and there wasn't any other place you wanted to be. And then how you spoke of those many years of not being able to look in the mirror and those same years of loneliness believing that you did not deserve to be touched or held kindly in the same way you were holding me. Your disclosure was the moment I stopped feeling so alone.*

*I continued opening to you telling you how I both admired you and at the same time found myself terrified. You had earned a different relationship to your body. You told me how all of this was a misunderstanding and that you too still struggled with your flesh. I did not believe it, but you loved me in that moment and you held space for my vulnerability. In your eyes I could see the unfolding of many nights with other lovers struggling too with a clarification of thought and feeling that kept pointing you back to all the ways you could not trust the care you were receiving because you could not trust your body to receive it. Your eyes told me that you had been there and it was a place that you still cycled into when the doubt became too much.*

*What I need to say now are all the things that need to be articulated before I can move on to what is really on my mind. I need to say that I am a fat Black cisgender man who despite my imagination am firmly stepping into my middle-age years. I am no longer young. Neither are you.*

*My body, like yours, tells a certain story. It has its own narrative. It speaks in a clear, direct, and simple language, which is sensation. My body, like yours, like every body, does not lie. Though it does not lie, somehow I have been taught to distrust it. My oppression and the subsequent trauma are rooted in this fundamental distrust.*

*And because of this experience of distrust, I am mad. Angry. Anger lives in my body like a ghost haunting a house. To understand my anger I have to learn to understand my body, to return to it to ask the ghost to leave.*

## ——— WHAT IS EMBODIMENT? ———

In my practice, embodiment has two key components. The first is the practice of remembering my body as it is in this moment and context. Embodiment is the work of returning home to the body, which is also to say that my awareness returns back to dwelling in my body. Yet as my awareness returns back to my body, I must do the next work of seeing my body as an experience. If I can see my embodiment as an experience, I am much more able to practice a fluidity and lucidity that will make it much more possible for me to open to the spaciousness that allows freedom from habitually responding to everything.

This kind of embodiment is important, because nothing fragmented can ever be freed. The trauma of systematic reality, with its illusions, sufferings, and instability, has eroded our minds and bodies from each other. The body will always tell the story of our woundedness in a language so direct and simple that it can be too much to bear witness to. As protection, the mind pulls away and keeps itself isolated from the body. The most radical project we could ever engage in during our lives is the project of embodiment. This is the most radical act because there is no liberation without the union of body and mind.

I remember the story of the Buddha's awakening. The Buddha had been born a prince and lived a luxurious life. Eventually he left this life when it began to dawn on him that there was much more than pleasure and ease. He wanted to get completely free from the duality of pleasure and displeasure. After having studied with a few teachers, he settled in to meditate, vowing not to stop until he reached full awakening. After a few years, he took a break and discovered that his body was completely emaciated and weakened, though his mind was quite strong. He felt as if he could not proceed further into deeper levels of meditative absorption until he cared for his body. He was able to take some nourishment and started practicing awareness of his body along with his awareness of mind phenomena. This act was an expression of *yoga,* or union. These practices had been around for a while before the Buddha, but he had finally realized this union for himself on his own terms. I believe that this was his first profound teaching, that we must come to terms with the truth on our own terms in our own time.

To be embodied means to know both our joy and our pain. It is a means through which we return home to the truth of how we are and how this truth has been restricted for many of us. Embodiment is not fun times for me. It is a time of coming into my mourning for what my mind and body have had to endure, and intentionally offering gratitude for the union I am being called into. Union of body and mind through embodiment is not the liberation yet; but when union gives rise to the remembering of our wholeness, then we can move with our complete selves into the work of getting free. There is no freedom through fragmentation, though so many of us have tried to do that. At the end of the day, we find ourselves exhausted, because no matter how hard we try, it is difficult to haul one piece of ourselves at a time to freedom.

My lived experience of embodiment is this: When I move, I am with my body. When I eat, I am eating with my body. When I am sitting, I am sitting with my body. When I am making love, I am with my body in the process of lovemaking. And when I come to die, I am with my body dying and letting go to enter into a new experience of embodiment. These are all expressions of love for my body and what my body does. Ultimately, embodiment is learning to love everything, including what is unlovable.

## How Many Bodies Can We Serve?

There are several kinds of "bodies" that we can come home to that must be worked with if we want to get free. One thing that I have discerned from my practice is that all our different bodies are interconnected. The physical body is the central experience body for us, as it is the body that seems to be in the same time and place with us. Every other body links into our physical body, and we can work through our physical body to connect to and learn to embody our other bodies. The bodies that I identify and work with in my practice are the physical body, emotional body, subtle energy body, sexual body, spiritual body, collective body, social media body, and ego body.

## Anger and the Body

As I grew into my practice, I saw that disembodiment is the primary strategy through which oppression is maintained. When you condition a person to be disembodied or disconnected from their bodies, then that person moves through the world desensitized to how their bodies are responding to conditions around them through the production of physical sensation, which our minds may label as emotion. Being disembodied, it becomes difficult to know how we are feeling and why we are feeling it. An outcome of this is the potential to act out of unidentified emotions.

Yet at the beginning, my anger was unseen, unfelt, and thus not embodied. I was sashaying through life as if I had beat anger. I didn't want to be that angry Black man. So I was the nice Black guy. I was everyone's Black friend. I had no need to be that angry Black man. That role was overplayed and played out. I wanted to be liked.

I am a Black man. Like many people, I have a diverse and complex identity play. I understand identity as stories we create to describe who and what we are. The identities that have most shaped me are being Black, cisgender, queer, mixed-class, and fat. As a Black person in these United States, I have never been taught to use my anger in a constructive way. Matter of fact, I have learned that my anger can get me killed. My anger is the single greatest threat to my life.

Moreover, I am angry that my anger is not taken seriously. I have never been taught that I have a right to my anger, in the same way I have never been taught that I have a right to my body. If emotions arise out of the body as sensations, and if I am not embodied, how do I own and relate to that anger as mine? How do I hold it and take care of it if I am not at home when it comes knocking?

My unexamined anger and rage as a cisgender male is the cornerstone that perpetuates the violence of patriarchy. If I am disembodied, I am unaware of my anger; and if I am unaware, then it is likely that I begin to direct my anger toward you. On top of that, I may be unconsciously tuning into my own unmet needs and blaming others around me for those needs going unmet. Yet in terms of patriarchy, men are conditioned to be dominant and that they have a right to claim anything, to take up space, to be the center of attention, and to, essentially, be normal. What we are not told to do is claim our own bodies through an intimate knowing of our body and its sensations. To claim these sensations and to listen to them would tell us a more accurate story of what is happening around us. However, in patriarchal conditioning, this kind of knowingness of our bodies and experiences is labeled as feminine or weak.

My anger is also related to a sense of dominance. The ego, the collection of sensations and experiences we label as an autonomous existing self, is about both domination and submission.

It is about domination because part of how the ego maintains itself is through controlling things around it. It must subjugate and stabilize things in order to stabilize itself. Instability, fluctuation, ambiguity, and indirectness are the antithesis of ego maintenance. Another way to understand this is that the ego must have solid ground around it to stand firm.

## The Ego Body

When I teach about love, I talk about loving ourselves, including the ego. I define "ego" as a collection of beliefs, perceptions, thoughts, and feelings that are happening all together, creating an experience of a self-existing and autonomous self. This becomes a body for us. In Buddhist thought, we confuse this compilation as who we are, and we label it "I." Yet there is no "I" or "me" there. What is there is our consciousness, or this ability to be aware and knowing. This is often the most confusing aspect of Buddhism, especially for those of us coming from traditions that teach about the soul. Consciousness is not a soul. I understand the soul to be a self-existing expression of ourselves, which is the essence of who we are. Consciousness is awareness itself that is not limited or localized to the essence of who I am. It is much more expansive than that. Consciousness permeates all phenomena. Part of the enlightenment experience is learning to rest and remain in the energy of awareness, which is the essence of consciousness.

Right now we are having two experiences of consciousness. The first experience is that of ultimate consciousness, or the quality of awareness and knowingness that pervades everything. The second experience is the relative consciousness, or the limited knowingness that is attempting to merge with ultimate consciousness or knowingness. The relative consciousness is limited because it is attached to the ego and thus distracted by the illusionary realness of the ego. Attachment disrupts spaciousness, so relative consciousness is always struggling to expand into the naturally present ultimate consciousness. Another way of thinking about the experiences of consciousness is to look at ultimate consciousness as the mother and our relative consciousness as the child. Our goal in practice is to unite the mother and the child. Our relative consciousness is longing to be poured back into the ultimate consciousness.

When we examine this Buddhist perspective of ego, it is easy to believe that the ego should be avoided or erased. This kind of relationship to ego is dangerous. We are instead trying to see the ego for what it is, especially the illusion of ego. We still need to relate to ego in order to be in relationship with this reality and with others around us. The ego is the anchor that keeps us connected to others. Think of it as something like a common denominator through which we can communicate our shared experiences and perceptions. When we erase ego, then we lose connections to others and the world in general, and we call this condition insanity.

Our egos are fragmented, which means that we don't often see or experience the totality of ego. This also means that we are responding to and protecting different fragments, which gets overwhelming and exhausting. The practice to meet the challenge of our fragmented ego as well as the issue of ego in general is love. Love means that we accept the reality of ego, and in doing so we can start relaxing around ego, which helps us to connect to the inherent space around ego. That space and the distance we get with loving help to bring the totality of ego into perspective. This is called healing the ego, and this healing is based on allowing ego to be whole. Yet the truth of all of this on a relative level is that the ego is already whole and is wrapped in expansive space. We use love to recognize that reality. The more we practice like this, the more we begin to earn our experience of the ultimate nature of all of this, which is emptiness, along with a lucid potentiality saturated with awareness. We also call this the nature of our minds. To realize the nature of mind is to realize the truth of ego and all phenomena.

Yet when we give ego lots of space through the practice of love, we find that we become less reactionary in relation to our ego. We begin to understand that many of the ways we attempt to protect ourselves are also attempts at strengthening our fixation on ego or our fixation on the belief that there is a definite "I." One way I practice this is by reminding myself that everything isn't about me, for me, or even because of me. When I remind myself, I let myself relax into this acknowledgment.

Whereas ego is a compilation of experiences we label as "I," identity can be the ways that we attempt to describe the relative uniqueness of "I." Identities are just the stories we tell ourselves about who we are as well as the stories the world makes up about who it thinks we are. Identity and ego are not quite the same thing. Let's use this example: Our egos are really into drag. The world is a grand ball, and our identities are what our egos are using to play drag and sashay around the world in. And in the tradition of balls, we are walking to win prizes in categories. Some of us are going for realness as transgender, gender non-conforming, women, or men, as Black, Asian, queer, bisexual, rich, smart, handsome, beautiful, or an infinite range of other identities. We want to pass through the ball of the world having everyone believe in what we are serving. At the same time, the ball of the world is either helping us fulfill this performance by believing us and contributing to the performance, or it is not. The more the ball of the world believes or disbelieves, the more intense our experiences are.

The ego can be more than just individual as well. Like our different embodiments, we can have a social ego, social media ego, community ego, etc. Who we think we are and how we relate to our egos can be projected into any space, medium, or collective.

In the collective ego, we find ourselves dealing with not only our individual egos, but how our egos function together with other people's egos, creating a kind of unified ego, thus turning the "I" into "we" and "mine" into "ours." The collective ego can create, inform, and perpetuate systems. Identity expression is key here. The expression of identities can become collective experiences that are driven by the principal energy of ego, which is about believing that this expression of who I am is actually me and should be taken seriously at all costs.

Collective identities based on race or gender, for instance, intensify who we think we are as well as distribute the privilege and disprivilege across the collective, creating systems of power. The collective ego many white people in the United States participate in has yielded, and continues to yield, incredible privileges at the expense of Black and brown people, resulting in the system of white supremacy. The collective ego of cisgender men yields the social privileges of power over women, as well as transgender, gender nonconforming, and queer people, resulting in patriarchy. Yet, collective egos that are based on power and dominance also hurt those who gain privilege from the collective identity, because the collective ego is not adaptive; it is quite rigid and fixed. It is difficult for the individual to divest from this collective ego, because there seems to be no space to do so. This illusion of no space blurs the line between the personal ego and the collective ego. Moreover, both expressions of ego become normalized, which makes it difficult to even have a thought of divesting from the collective ego.

## The Physical Body and the Ego Body

The body is important in this discussion, because we have learned to equate our sense of self with the physical body. The physical body is also an anchor for how identities are created and expressed. We often think who we are is related to the body, or even that we are our bodies. In the work of embodiment, we are trying to bring our bodies into awareness, embracing all the sensations of our bodies. Our bodies are important, but they are just experiences of one way we show up in the relative world, just like our egos and identities. This identification with the physical body is seen at the moment of death. I believe that death is an experience of when our consciousness transitions from the body into a formless realm to journey into a new life taking form again in a body. It becomes hard for our relative consciousness to leave the body if it identifies with the body as who we are. And our relative consciousness will never be able to reunite with the ultimate consciousness if the ego and body limit it. It will be difficult for many of us to die if we are so attached to our bodies as who we are, instead of seeing our consciousness or even our souls as our most pure experience. We should be ready to let go when we need to in order to be free.

## Trauma and the Emotional Body

The body is significant, because unlike our mind, the body is always in the present. It does not have our mind's ability to be in the past or future, and when we are really fortunate, to be here in the present. It does not get distracted. Despite all of this, the body can still be confused. When I say confused, I mean that experiences of trauma can disrupt how our bodies can be in tune with the things happening around us. Trauma disrupts the body's equilibrium. For example, have you ever been in a conversation with someone, and you realize that for a while you both have been talking about different things, and then one of you goes, "Wait, what are you talking about?!" Or have you ever heard thunder and wind blowing outside, and it never ends up raining? This is how the body may respond to trauma: by expressing sensations that are responding to or pointing toward something we don't understand.

As someone descended from slaves, I acknowledge that my disembodiment is largely an expression of transhistorical trauma originating with my ancestors' initial emotional injury of being kidnapped, enduring the brutality of the Middle Passage, and landing in this country to be enslaved and further brutalized by systematic racism for centuries. Slavery disrupted my ancestors' right to their bodies, while physical and emotional violence took root in both the mind and the body as trauma that kept us from reclaiming an awareness of our bodies. So many Black folks today are walking around haunting themselves by occupying a psychic distance outside of their bodies because racial trauma has made their bodies unsafe for them to occupy.

The body tells the truth regardless of if we can speak its language or not. My body tells the truth of transhistorical trauma, most often experienced as a distrust of my body as well as a belief that I do not have a right to my body. Often my practice has focused on trying to meet my body where it is, instead of constantly trying to get it to meet me where I am. Meeting my body where it is has meant meeting it at a woundedness that I inherited and that has been exacerbated by a disembodiment that I am just learning how to address.

## The Spiritual Body

The practice of spirituality is the practice of remembering who we really are beyond our suffering by allowing the universe to point us back to our most basic, truest selves. Spiritual practitioners are consenting to be guided into communication with the most honest expression of ourselves, the world around us, as well as ultimate reality. To be a spiritual person means to be always willing to be in communication with things as they are, not as we wish them to be. I have often related to my spiritual practice as a deep listening to everything, and then allowing myself to be shaped by what I am hearing.

There is also my experience of spirit. Spirit has taken on various meanings. Here I understand spirit as the energetic expression of mind and body collaboration that projects an experience of solidity, directness, and nurturing into the world around us. It is what healing and being healed feel like as an experience happening in real time. One's mind and body are talking. They are practicing community together. Not only is there community, there is a kind of unshakability. Spirit is an expression of embodiment. It reminds me of growing up in church and singing "I Shall Not Be Moved." I didn't get the meaning of the song as a young person, but now I understand it as a declaration of wholeness and the promise that I will not be made unwhole again.

## EMOTIONAL LABOR

### What Is Emotional Labor?

To begin with, emotions are mental states originating in the body as sensations, which are labeled by the mind, resulting in experiences that are pleasurable, unpleasurable, or neutral. Emotional labor is both the seen and the unseen work of caring for, caretaking, and taking care of our emotional states or other people's emotional states. Currently we understand the expression of emotional labor as the many ways we attempt to make other people comfortable and happy. This includes actively listening to others, asking how people are feeling, checking in with them, letting them vent in front of you, and not reacting to someone when they are being rude or disrespectful. It is the work we do to help people process their emotions. If you are in a helping profession or customer service position, emotional labor is always having to smile and be pleasant, even when you don't feel like it and especially when someone is being a monster to you. More-over, it is how some of us sense imbalance in interactions and relationships, and the work we do to bring these relationships into balance, often without being asked to do so. I have strong empathic abilities, which means that I am very sensitive to other people's emotions and thus am also sensitive to imbalances in relationships. This fuels my work of doing emotional labor for others.

The idea of emotional labor comes out of 1970s feminist work, and since then has been instrumental in helping us to understand how emotional labor was a gendered expression where women were seen as carrying the bulk of emotional labor. Describing this work as labor frames it first as something that is offered and should be compensated for, and second as something that does take effort. I appreciate this framing not because of its reference to capitalism, but because it helps me to understand that emotional labor is work. If I am doing this labor for others without support, I will get burned out and resentful. When we are working through our anger and hurt, we need individuals and communities to support us in doing this labor while at the same time being aware of the effort others are putting in.

## Holding Space

Holding space is the work of being with ourselves and others in a nonreactive way. I am able to notice everything that comes up in my mind and body, and I can allow it to be there without having to react to it. Not reacting to the material in my experience means that I have the space to focus on other things as well while not losing awareness of this material. When I get distracted and start reacting to the material that is coming up for me, then I am not holding space for myself or anyone else. Authentic holding space means that first and foremost, I am holding space for myself.

## A Note for the Emotionally Mature

Emotional maturity doesn't mean you are always stable. It does mean that you have strategies that help you to manage fluctuations in your emotionality. Emotionally mature people I know express all kinds of emotions. They get pissed, they laugh, they are serious, playful, and sometimes sad. I consider them emotionally mature because they have a basic awareness of what they are experiencing; they can practice a lot of spaciousness around emotions.

If you are someone who is emotionally mature, then your emotional stability actually becomes a support for others who are experiencing emotional instability. You become the earth for others, and that holding can translate into an act of love and kindness.

I consider myself an emotionally mature person. This has come through my many years of meditation practice, as well as having to deal with systems of oppression my whole life. Though dealing with these systems alone does not make me or others emotionally mature, it has, however, lent itself to the development of emotional resilience, or the capacity to acknowledge difficult emotions like anger and despair and to experience them while still maintaining a degree of focus on and connectedness with what's happening around me. This emotional resiliency,

---

### REFLECTION

Think about people in your life you consider to be emotionally mature. What is it like to be around them? Does it seem that others like to be around them? How do you use folks like this for your own benefit? If you are someone who is emotionally mature, what is your experience? What does it feel like?

coupled with meditation practice, has deepened my emotional maturity. I still experience the whole range of emotions, but I also have the strategies to actively hold space for these emotions and cultivate spaciousness, which offers me the room to make choices as to how I wish to be in relationship to my emotions while decreasing my chances of getting distracted and potentially creating harm for myself and others.

## What Does Emotional Labor Look Like for Me?

Overall, my work as a spiritual teacher is to do emotional labor for anyone who needs support. I appreciate offering this support, because this is the support that I need as well. I need others to hold space for my struggle and confusion.

The work of emotional labor is all well and good until I find myself feeling emotionally fatigued, where I lose the capacity to be resilient. This is a sign that I am in need of self-care, which often for me means being alone and in silence to rest and relax back into the spaciousness. During these times, I have to set boundaries as part of my care. Sometimes my boundaries are tested, because people can come to expect that I am always on and there to do labor for them.

There are times when I am deeply frustrated with how others fail to hold space for me, like when people ask me how I'm doing but really aren't interested in how I'm doing. Or there are other times when I am attempting to be open and vulnerable, but that vulnerability is not seen or held. In those moments, I shut down and retreat into the strategies of offering myself support and losing trust in other people's ability to hold me. However, there are many ways that people do emotional processing for me. I have family and friends regularly checking in with me. My mother often calls and texts to see how I'm doing. I have several mentors who check in with me and make sure I am doing well. I have close friends I can call when I need someone to listen to me.

Sometimes I get triggered and need someone to help me process what I am struggling with.

## Getting Triggered and Doing Emotional Labor

When I started writing this section on emotional labor, I had an experience of getting really triggered after learning that an organization I thought considered me an ally was publicly stirring up animosity against me among the community they served. I was triggered because I felt as if the actions of the organization were unskillful, considering no effort had been made to contact me in person to talk and offer direct feedback about how they might be seeing me as not being in line with their values. I was pissed and hurt. When I am attacked, an old narrative engages, which is that no one is going to come to help defend me and that I have to protect myself. I know that this is not the truth, but it is an old narrative rooted in growing up and feeling alone and victimized as a Black gay boy.

Anything can be a trigger, and triggers are different for everyone. Triggers can change and shift over time. When I am speaking of triggers, I am speaking more of experiences that seem overwhelming when we need to really care for ourselves.

---

### REFLECTION

Take a few minutes to reflect on and make a list of the things that trigger anger for you. After you have made your list, look through it to see if there are patterns or ways that you can organize your triggers. Are there triggers that come from other people saying things? Are there triggers that are about seeing certain images? Are there triggers based on hearing certain sounds? There are no right or wrong answers.

Triggers are part of the normal emotional labor we end up doing each day. Anger triggers can be the most intense triggers to work with, along with trauma triggers. One of the ways that we can support ourselves is by reflecting on what triggers anger for us.

Another aspect of triggers is our physical and emotional response to them. I start to feel warm, especially in my chest and neck. I also experience tightness in my forehead. Then the first emotional response I notice is anger, and soon after I am able to shift my attention to the hurt. At that point, I am able to move through SNOELL and some other grounding practices that help me to hold space for the hurt.

The practice of using SNOELL is part of a strategy called compensation. Compensation is also an expression of emotional labor. In the moments when I am feeling a lot of response in my body and mind, it can become difficult to maintain focus, especially in a situation that I need to be engaged in. Compensation at that time means that I am going through SNOELL: noticing my breathing, resting on the earth, and getting as much space into my experience as possible. I try to ground myself back into what's happening around me.

I also use compensation to support me if I know I am moving into a situation that will be triggering. In this practice, I ask myself what I will need, and then I start putting together a support strategy to rely on. Many of us do this if we are preparing for a difficult conversation or other interaction. I am often asked to support spiritual communities that are going through some spiritual hardship; and before showing up, I do my compensation work, which includes prayers, chanting, meditation, silence, and rest. It almost feels like stocking up for a long journey into, well, drama. The drama is all the ways we get distracted and lose ourselves in the habitual reactions to the material coming up for us, and these reactions often increase harm. If I am well resourced through compensation, then I find that I am less likely to get tired and fall into the drama of the situation.

---

——————————— REFLECTION ———————————

In this exercise, reflect on your emotional and physical responses to triggering. Be as specific as you can. Notice if different triggers have different responses. Next, think about ways that you can support yourself or offer compensation as you are experiencing being triggered. Finally, think about ways that you can offer yourself compensation before getting into intense situations.

---

## Levels of Emotional Labor

I believe that emotional labor happens on three levels: the personal, interpersonal, and collective.

### 1. Emotional Labor for Ourselves

On the personal level, emotional labor is the work that I am doing for myself to be with my own emotions. Often when I give public talks, I offer the option of people submitting questions to me anonymously on slips of paper. Part of one talk was on self-care. I received a question from someone who wanted to know how to look at someone who appeared not to take care of themselves and yet to take them seriously concerning issues of self-care. Though the question did not name me specifically, I still took it personally. I am fat. That is obvious, and when I say "fat," it is not self-deprecating. It is my effort to reclaim this word. I appreciate my fatness. Yet when I received this question, I was livid. Beneath this anger was my hurt. This hurt felt like embarrassment, shame, and sadness. I read the question as someone basically saying, "You are fat and disgusting, and how dare you attempt to talk about self-care." So I went through my process of looking at what was coming up for me, including using SNOELL, and I called in my homecomings. After all of that, I was still pissed, but I was able to hold space for being pissed and hurt. I don't know if that question was about me. I made an assumption. Making an assumption is okay as long as I own that assumption and am willing for that assumption to be challenged. In my response, I was transparent about what I was experiencing in that moment. My anger underlined the directness of my response, but it was being held by my compassion. The spaciousness is what offered me the resources to be adaptive. I wasn't fixated on the emotions, and thus had the clarity to answer the question honestly and directly, being informed by the anger and hurt but coming from a place of compassion.

## 2. Emotional Labor for Others

We often find ourselves doing emotional labor without consciously consenting to it. It has become an important practice for me to offer consent for myself to engage in interactions that feel as if I am doing emotional labor. Of course, there are interactions where the focus is for me to hold space for others, and I fully consent to doing those. However, sometimes I may be having a casual conversation with someone, and at some point the conversation may start to bring up heavy material for the other person. At that point, I often check in with myself to see if I am resourced enough in the moment to hold space for the other person. Being resourced means I have what I need to do what needs to be done in the moment. I am often resourced enough to hold some space. When I reach my limit in the conversation, I can usually communicate that I'm hitting my edge and that it will be hard for me to continue holding space. Many of us also communicate this through nonverbal cues.

More often, I am finding myself in interactions where the other person is aware of what's coming up for them and may ask if it's okay for them to continue. If that doesn't happen, what also sometimes happens is after the conversation, the other person may thank me for listening and may apologize for going so deep into something. All of this is okay. We can't control what material may come up for us in an interaction. I want to provide as much support as I can for others. Besides, because of my training and practice, people tend to feel very comfortable around me, and they find themselves going deep into issues and topics that they normally wouldn't with others. People have told me that over and over again.

To hold space for others and to do emotional labor, we must keep a few things in mind.

1. Make sure you are able to hold space for yourself before engaging with others.

2. Set boundaries between yourself and the person you are supporting. Know when you are working on your edge, and communicate that to the other person.

3. The more we struggle with self-agency, the more we will struggle with boundaries. The more we struggle with boundaries, the more emotional labor we will do. Boundary setting is born directly from our ability to consider ourselves worth being cared for. When we value care for ourselves, we can understand what forms of emotional labor are appropriate for us in the given moment.

—— THINGS TO KEEP IN MIND WHEN NEEDING ——
EMOTIONAL LABOR FROM OTHERS

1. I see the use of emotional labor as something that can manipulate others into offering an emotional support that they are not resourced enough to provide. Then we blame this person for being emotionally shut down, when in reality they are just as emotionally drained and traumatized as we are. Sometimes we hold people hostage by our demands for them to do emotional labor for us. Often what we are needing is to seek professional support through therapy, instead of forcing others around us to do this work on our behalf.

2. Sometimes emotional labor can be manipulative. For instance, we accuse people of not doing emotional labor for us when people have not consented to doing this for us. We assume that someone is always available to us. A common practice within my professional and friend groups is to ask each other if it is okay that we talk about certain things that may require emotional labor. This is an act of asking for consent before confiding heavy emotional material.

3. Sometimes we are confused about the amount of emotional labor others are always doing for us. Once I was accused of not doing emotional labor for someone who for more than a year had been using me for emotional labor. In the moment of being accused, I reflected on how when we feel as if we are not getting the emotional labor we think we want, we accuse people of not doing the emotional labor at all.

4. Maybe part of what makes emotional labor so intense is how we attempt to force others into doing emotional labor for us. We say things like "I need you to do this for me" to people who often cannot even do the emotional labor for themselves. Resentment arises when our expectations are not met.

5. Sometimes what we mean by emotional labor is accountability and boundaries. I also feel that we should be clearer about what kind of labor it is. Not everything is emotional labor.

## 3. Collective Emotional Labor

Some of us are in a position in communities and collectives where we tend to be in the position of mediator, or what I like to sometimes call space holder. People who are fairly resourced and/or empathic often find themselves doing this work for the community. I believe that this is such an honor to have the capacity to hold space for others like this. When I think about collective emotional labor, I think about the scene from *Beloved* by Mother Toni Morrison where Baby Suggs, an elder Black woman and former slave, calls the Black community into the forest. She first asks the children to step forward to laugh. Then she asks the men to come forward to dance, and last she asks the women to cry, mourning for the living and the dead. By the end of the scene, everyone is doing a little bit of everything. Both Mother Toni's text as well as the film adaptation reveal the complex and beautiful work of a community elder and space holder supporting the community in profound emotional labor. The novel is set shortly after the Civil War in Cincinnati, Ohio, during a time when the

Black community still faced incredible obstacles and hardships. Baby Suggs offered a way for members of the community to connect to their emotions and to express those emotions within the safety of a container held by her, which manifested from her own deep connection to her emotions. She embodies so many leaders in our communities who model emotional labor and space holding for themselves, and who offer it as profound medicine for the community in a variety of creative ways.

I often reflect on Serena Williams when she took her stand during the final round of the 2018 US Open tournament. She felt as if she was being wrongly treated by the umpire. She expressed herself directly, vented her frustration, and was punished by the umpire and by the media. Watching clips right after it happened, I found myself cheering her on. She was mirroring all the frustration that I experience being in a place that was not meant for me. She reminded me that my anger and rage are justified responses to the ways systems attempt to police me into silence and consent. Her taking a stand was her doing emotional labor for many of us who are marginalized and feel emotionally shut down and powerless in the face of oppressive conditions. However, when we are confronting systems through our emotional expression, we can experience the weight of challenging something experienced by many, but addressed by only a few. Then the labor is not distributed fairly, and that labor becomes a burden. This may have been what Williams has often experienced being a Black woman and excelling in a field dominated by white folks. This may be what others feel who are underrepresented in a field they excel in. When I am speaking out against serious issues in my community that so many others are silent about, I feel the weight of the labor I am doing for so many others. This is the risk we take when standing up against systems that others feel so disempowered against. It seems we are both fighting the system while shouldering the emotional needs of others we are doing labor for.

# 6

# HAPPINESS

*Whatever happens, happens.*
*Whatever comes, comes.*
*I don't need anything at all.*

—LAMA NORLHA RINPOCHE

*Don't wait around for other people to be happy for you. Any*
*happiness you get you've got to make yourself.*

—ALICE WALKER

## ———————— WHAT IS HAPPINESS? ————————

I always say that I am not interested in people being Buddhist or
meditators or engaged in any spiritual path in general. But what
I am interested in is people living lives where they feel resourced
enough to limit violence against themselves and others and to
experience a sense of happiness. I am committed to supporting
people to be happy because it has been my experience that happy
people create less violence. I often think about the times when I
have been violent and how unhappy I have been in those times.

It is not a privilege to be happy. When we experience happiness, we are not taking it away from someone else. Happiness is the natural state of our minds, as it holds space for all the material of our minds and our experiences, both the comfortable experiences as well as the uncomfortable ones, and everything in between.

Happiness doesn't exist outside of ourselves. It is who we are. It is the essence of our minds. Many contemplative traditions seek to lead us to this essential truth about ourselves. In my practice, I often think about the metaphor of a cloudy day. Because the sky is overcast doesn't mean the sun is not shining. A really dramatic experience of this can be seen on a plane flight as the plane takes off and ascends above the cloud level, breaking through to the intensity of sun radiating in the clear sky. Happiness is always there, but often I have to be reminded of that.

In my practice, happiness is this experience of contentment, connectedness, and balance. When I say happiness, I'm not necessarily referring to this euphoric experience that's like being in a Disney cartoon where we're just skipping down the road and humming a melody, and the sun is out and it's raining candy. Euphoria is what most people think authentic happiness is; and thinking this, they feel barred from the experience, because this experience is so hard to bring about when their lives are so difficult. However, I'm not that interested in that kind of happiness. I'm interested in the level of happiness that is actually about us just being in our bodies or at least having an aspiration to be in our bodies, being connected, being sensitive, being in tune with the world around us despite how hard the world is.

Happiness doesn't mean we are forcing anything away. It is this profound and revolutionary practice of allowing and accepting. When I say "allow," it doesn't mean condoning or celebrating what's in your mind. It means that there is already material there, and how can I do the work of allowing it to be there? And when I do the work of allowing something to be there, then I begin to enter into a relationship with what is. I don't have to like what I am allowing either, but I have to let it be there.

Happiness can abide with other things. We can be happy and struggle at the same time. Often I can experience happiness while at the same time experiencing sadness. Often when people think about happiness, they think that happiness is an eradication of discomfort. Rather, it is the holding of our discomfort in a spaciousness that makes it less likely for us to fixate on the discomfort and exaggerate it. But, if we're really living our lives and being in tune with what we're experiencing, there's happiness that begins to surround the struggle.

Practicing happiness means that I am doing the work of trusting myself. When I am able to trust myself, I develop more wisdom in how to trust others. My happiness holds my suffering and the troubles of the world, and I can step out with compassion to confront the suffering of the world being held by my happiness. There is no magic here. It is staying with the truth of the relative while understanding that it is the liberation work with the relative that will help us earn our experience of the ultimate. None of this is comfortable or fun. Practicing dharma and revolution is not fun. It is complex and sometimes confusing.

## ASPECTS OF HAPPINESS

### Space

There is no happiness without mental spaciousness. Space is something that we do not need to create in our minds; it is naturally there if we can notice it. However, noticing space requires us to relax our fixation on the material in our minds. Relaxing the contracting opens up vision and sight, and we can notice that there has always been space around us. That space is the very heart of happiness. When we notice the space, the other material doesn't go away, but you realize that you can hold everything without fixating on it. I love using the language of dancing. I think of living as dancing with all of the bullshit that arises for us. The dance is the expression of adapting, and we can't do the dance of adapting without space. Happiness is the space in which we dance with even the toughest shit in our lives.

## Trust

When I speak of trust and confidence, I am talking about taking refuge in my basic experience of myself. I trust myself. I trust that I have the ability to experience and feel. I trust that I have the ability to empathize. I trust my ability to change. I trust my ability to embody agency. I trust that I can discern the positive and constructive things the world can offer me as feedback that can help me grow through my suffering. I also trust that I can discern through the bullshit what the world is trying to tell me about myself that has nothing to do with my benefit. This trust in myself doesn't mean that I'm okay all the time, but it does mean that when I am not okay, I can let myself not be okay and I can take care of that not-okayness. This trust is built upon a real acceptance of myself that is supported by intense gratitude. I have to let myself be sick in order to have the space to start working toward being well.

## Connectedness

Happiness is an expression of connectedness. This means that I feel a part of things and people around me because I have the mental space to relax and open. When I am feeling disconnected, I begin to experience fear and isolation, and these are experiences that can lead to us committing all kinds of violence. When I am feeling connected, I am also engaging in empathy for my basic experience, as well as for the experiences of others. I am drawing near to these experiences, and I draw closer to others. I then enter into sympathizing or abiding with everything that arises, and then there is a kind of intimacy that emerges. The intimacy is born from just having the courage to dwell with our experiences.

## Accepting

Acceptance is the energy of happiness. It is our work of allowing what is already present to be right where it is. Happiness isn't about bypassing anything. It is about acknowledging what is present and leaning into it. When I let go of the constant pushing away of things that are not comfortable, then I find myself reinvesting that energy of aversion into giving space to the material that is uncomfortable. Happiness is found in the space around the difficult material, and over time we begin to discover the space within the difficult material. The difficult material is like a natural sponge. When we are able to get close to it, we see all these little pores that allow things to move in and out of it. Our difficult material is porous, and we can use our awareness practice to explore the pores and rest within the space there to experience some happiness in difficult situations.

## ———————— HAPPINESS AND JOY ————————

I often use the words "happy" and "joy" interchangeably in the same way I may use "anger" and "rage" interchangeably. Happiness and joy rise from the same conditions. However, there is a difference between the two. Happiness is an experience that can be really subtle and somewhat nuanced. It's like turning on the heat in a cold room. Slowly the room will get warmer. You may not notice the growing warmth until you realize that you aren't as cold as you were a while ago. Joy, on the other hand, is being in a cold room, and instead of turning on the heat, you walk over to the fireplace, build a fire, and instantly have a lot of heat. The heat may get really strong and distracting, but it won't last, because the fire logs will burn down and the room will slowly get colder until you build another fire. Moreover, I understand joy as a natural state of my mind when I do the work of meditation to reveal that state. Happiness, on the other hand, is an emotion that I work to cultivate.

## Sympathetic Joy Practice

Sympathetic joy is the practice of energetically giving joy and happiness away, as well as taking part in other people's joy and happiness. Offering joy means that when I experience something pleasurable and feel happiness or joy, I imagine giving that experience away to others, especially people who could really use this energy. The happiness that I give away can come from any source. You can offer the happiness of anything from smelling a sweet-smelling flower to experiencing pleasure during good sex. Any experience of pleasure that increases our happiness can be offered.

A simple practice I do is noticing several times throughout the day when I feel happy or joyous. Noticing it, I make an aspiration in my mind that all beings may experience the happiness or joy that I am experiencing now. I can even offer it to someone specific as well. Even during sex, you can practice giving away the pleasure you are experiencing, which will begin transforming that experience into wisdom and compassion and will make sex less violent for you and your partners.

Taking part in other people's joy means that when I see other people happy, I open my mind to their energy by empathizing with them and experiencing what it may be like to have the causes of joy they have. This is the most edgy practice here, because we are called to take part in the happiness of people who receive things that we believe should be ours, or we believe that the person experiencing happiness does not deserve it. People tell me that it's challenging to share the happiness and joy of someone who is happy because they unfairly received something or got something that should have been ours, like a raise, a promotion, an award, etc. Matter of fact, this is my antidote to jealousy. When I see someone getting something that I want, I think about what it must feel like to get what they are getting and the work that they have put in to get what they have. I try to rest in the space that opens up through the empathy and abiding with everything that arises. Over time, you can shift more and more into this shared happiness, and you will have a deeper experience of happiness, because you are using the happiness of others around you to connect to your own inherent experience of happiness.

## RECOGNIZING MENTAL AND PHYSICAL SPACIOUSNESS

The following practice is my basic practice for recognizing the space that is naturally present in my experience. I don't have to create space. I only have to learn to turn my attention to it. Holding space means that I am noticing when I get distracted and start reacting to things and in doing so losing the sense of spaciousness in my mind and the capacity to allow everything to be. Without this training, it becomes very difficult to work with tough emotions like anger.

The breath can be an important tool that allows us to start connecting to the space that is naturally present. When we can calm and channel that energy with the breath, we can start to experience a settledness that makes it easier to focus on spaciousness.

## Type of Practice

This is a mindfulness-based practice.

---

——————————— THE PRACTICE ———————————

1. Start by moving through the beginning practice sequence, ending with a breath practice.

2. Continuing with the breath, breathe deeply in through the nose and out through the mouth. Try to make both the inhale and the exhale as deep as possible. After a few minutes, take a two-second pause after the inhale through the nose before releasing the exhale through the mouth. Gradually make that pause longer, up to five to ten seconds, or however long is comfortable for you. In the pause between the breaths, notice the space and stillness that that opens up. If you can, try to rest in between those breaths. As you continue resting in the pauses, try to start experiencing the breaths as well as the pauses. Let the breath breathe you, and while doing so allow it to move you into a deeper sense of spaciousness and calm. Practice with the breaths as long as you want to.

3. Now turn your attention to your mind, and notice all the material, like thoughts and emotions. Slowly imagine that this material is like clouds passing through the sky. In this case, it is material passing through the sky of your mind.

Let go of the material and try to rest, imagining that you are lying on the ground gazing up at the sky and the clouds passing overhead. As you do this, a sense of spaciousness begins opening up, and in this space you are allowing all the material in your mind to simply be there and float through your mind. Turn your attention to this sense of space. Try this for as long as you can.

4. Now turn your attention back to your body, and notice any physical sensations while keeping in mind the trauma support practices. Make sure you are able to return to the seat and the earth when you feel unstable. Imagine that you are inhaling and exhaling through every hole in your body, including mouth, nose, ears, eyes, pores, anus, and genitalia. Again, take a pause after the inhale, and let that pause extend as much as is comfortable before exhaling. Repeat the same method of resting and noticing the calm and spaciousness.

5. While keeping some attention on the seat and the earth, imagine that your body is like a large inflated balloon, while inside your body has this sense of openness and space. Practice with this for a while, trying to focus on the sensation of your body being open and spacious. Try to link the practice of mind spaciousness with the body spaciousness, and rest within this wide-open space where you are letting everything float through your complete experience.

**WORKING WITH ANGER**

6. As you are connecting with the sense of spaciousness, turn your attention to any experience of anger
   as either a mental experience or a physical experience
   or both. Let that experience of anger float within this
   spaciousness. When working with difficult energy
   like anger or even grief, it is important to notice the
   energy; but as we notice, we must be careful to not
   get fixated on the energy. To help with this, imagine
   that you are feeding these energies' space by relaxing
   and letting go. Keep doing this over and over again,
   and connect to the realization that these energies are
   just experiences and are not inherently who you are.

7. Once you feel as if you have practiced enough, move
   through the ending practice sequence.

# 7

# ACCEPTANCE

*God grant me the serenity*
*to accept the things I cannot change;*
*courage to change the things I can;*
*and wisdom to know the difference.*
*Living one day at a time;*
*Enjoying one moment at a time;*
*Accepting hardships as the pathway to peace.*

—SERENITY PRAYER

*I go where I am loved. I go where I am allowed to express*
*love. In loving, I have no expectations.*

—LAMA ROD OWENS, *Radical Dharma*

OVER THE PAST few years, I have been struggling to understand love in a simpler and more direct way. I am grateful for my Buddhist practice and tradition that has offered me a beautiful and realistic understanding and paradigm of loving and being loved. Yet the word "love" can still be loaded with ambiguity and indirectness in my practice. In my teaching and past writing, I try to offer as much detail as possible around how I understand love, yet I keep returning to the same question: But what is love really? Sitting with this question is important. It has led to another important question: What am I doing when I love? What is happening when I am receiving love? Over time, I came to an important new consideration of love. When I am loving, I am practicing acceptance; and when I am being loved, I am being accepted. Acceptance is the key to my understanding of love.

Acceptance means simply allowing the thing to be there, whatever the thing is. It is a practice of no judgment. We are not interested in the quality or nature of the thing at the time. We are just interested in letting the thing be there. Of course this brings us back to our work of holding space, which is still defined as allowing the thing to be there. Holding space means that we are both allowing and accepting something. Accepting without judgment means we are not celebrating or denying the thing.

For example, I hurt my foot when I started writing this chapter. Though there was pain, the real inconvenience was losing full mobility of my foot. The thing was the pain I was experiencing. That was the basic experience of a sensation that was not pleasurable. The suffering of the situation was the added layer of resisting feeling this pain. My work was to hold space for the pain, which was again to accept the pain. When I was able to do this, then the pain became more ordinary and less of a distraction. I found myself less distracted and had the spaciousness to consider remedies like taking aspirin, icing my foot, staying off it, and massaging it. Acceptance offers us the space to develop wisdom, and it's from that wisdom space that we can decide how to address what we are holding space for.

I often say that if we want to change something, we must first begin to love it; what I am actually communicating is that we must accept the reality of something before we begin to change it. If we do not accept something before trying to change it, the process becomes like trying to walk without your feet being on the ground. There has to be contact with what it is, because we need to see and know something before we do something about it. This teaching is particularly hard for addressing the difficult stuff in our lives. This teaching can be a hard thing to hear when we are being asked to accept forms of violence or harm happening to us or others. I tell activists often that if we want to change systems of violence and inequity, we must accept the reality of these systems. Again, accepting doesn't mean celebrating or condoning; it only means that we allow the reality to be present so we can see it and really figure out how to change it. We cannot walk unless our feet are on the ground.

## ———— ACCEPTING QUEERNESS ————

There are many things that I have struggled to accept. However, something that has been important for me has been accepting my sexuality.

Growing up, I was homophobic. It was an expression not of hate but of a deep shame in response to my own insecurities around noticing my ever present gayness.

I grew up being terrified of sex, and this terror extended from a fear of my body. Growing up in a Christian community, I was never taught how to have a healthy relationship to my body or to anyone else's. The message I got as a young boy was that my body was dirty and that the solution to the filth of my body was to deny its natural urges. In denying its natural urges, I could achieve and maintain a kind of bodily purity that I was taught was a reflection of the divine. Later I would discover that this messaging happened to coincide with high rates of teenage pregnancy and STD contraction in my home community.

In my early teens when I learned how to masturbate and ejaculated for the first time, I felt the simultaneous feeling of liberatory bliss along with the thought that I was doing something terribly harmful and would die. Soon I started getting access to straight pornography through videos and magazines. While the sex between men and women in the scenes was stimulating, over time I found myself being obsessed with men's penises, along with the rest of their body. Discovering that, I started getting access to gay pornography, which slowly began to confirm my gayness. However, my being gay was something I refused to admit to myself for the obvious reason of my still deeply held beliefs at the time that homosexuality was punishable by eternal damnation. Yet even before my exposure to pornography, I had had erotic encounters with other boys my age that consisted of touching, fondling, and nude play. I never initiated these experiences, and while part of me loved it, another part of me was horrified at the part of me that loved it. The horrified part won, and I learned how to avoid being in situations where this could happen with other boys. However, my private relationship with pornography continued, as it served as a way for me to explore my sexuality through imagination and exploration of my own young body. I cannot argue that pornography is good for everyone or that there is no harm in the industry and in the private consumption of the material, but what I do feel strongly about is how I needed these videos and magazines to understand my sexuality and body within the context of eroticism and pleasure. I didn't have other gay friends, boyfriends, or mentors. I did not have the skills, conditioning, or safety to express my attraction to other boys publicly. There was no internet back then to connect with others like me. There was pornography that opened the door into a world that had been previously barred from me. Yet as long as I didn't call myself gay and resisted sexual contact with other boys, I was not gay.

As I headed into middle school in the early '90s, most of my male friends started dating girls. This coincided with my being attracted to these same friends. There was one student in middle school who was out and very effeminate. We were not friends. I remember our having spoken to each other maybe once in our two years there together, but I do remember him often sashaying around between classes surrounded by other girls. I never remember being sexually attracted to him but do remember an urge to be his friend. He was the only boy in school who would occasionally wear finger waves. He was not attempting to hide. Looking back, he was nothing but fabulous and fierce. Yet for me back then, he was neither of these. He was dangerous and endangered. He was dangerous because he kept showing me and other boys who we could be if we just chose to be it; and by doing so, he reminded us of our despair of being caught in the brutal conditioning of heterosexual patriarchy where we compromised our happiness and sanity. This is what made him endangered as well, because we were instructed that no one could escape this path, and so it was our duty by any means to suppress the threat that he presented. Deep down, I wanted to be like him and others like him, because they seemed to be free. I still want to be like him.

I do not remember participating in the communal rituals of suppression that the boys (and some girls as well) enacted on him. I do not remember being a part of the vicious, mean comments. I do not remember calling him faggot and making him the punchline of jokes or using him as a threat among us to keep each other in line when we noticed one of us dressing nice or being kind or soft: "Oh, I see you trying to be like him. I guess we need to start calling you _____." I know there were other things that happened to him that were even more violent. Though I do not remember being a part of this communal violence, I was. I chose not to disrupt how others were talking about him. I chose not to befriend him and to be seen with him publicly. I was afraid, and that fear kept me from disrupting the violence against someone who was doing emotional labor for me by simply being in the world and choosing to be himself regardless of the violence he experienced. This work and sacrifice that members of marginalized groups do to be in the world in a way that doesn't compromise their integrity are how the rest of us understand being as free as possible regardless of the cost. They help show the rest of us still gathering our courage and resiliency how to eventually be in the world and to survive the world and its brutality. Though I did not have the courage and resiliency to be out, he still showed me what it could mean being myself. However, at the time, what I was most afraid of was how he kept reminding me of what I was becoming, and because of that, I secretly needed him to be erased as well.

This is the suffering I carried into high school. This is the same suffering I expressed outwardly as homophobia, because by high school, I was openly participating in community rituals of violence against other queer and gay students. In my mind, I had no choice, or I could become as othered as them. My expression of homophobia was first and foremost an expression of emotional violence toward myself. It was a fear of myself and how I could not hold space for my body or my sexuality. It was also an intense recognition, and a severe bypassing of the realization, that I did not love myself. The way that I judged other perceived gay people around me and on TV was an expression of the pain that I was experiencing feeling unloved. So much of the violence we enact on others emerges from our experience of being unloved and unhappy.

Throughout my time in high school I started experiencing some shifts in how I related to my sexuality. There were a few factors that contributed to this. The first was my growing interest in radical political history. In retrospect, I was feeling helpless and trapped within the intersection of queerness and Blackness within a social system that disprivileged both severely. I needed to experience my own agency and a sense of empowerment.

On my twelfth birthday, my father gave me copies of the auto-
biographies of W. E. B. Du Bois's *The Souls of Black Folks* and
Booker T. Washington's *Up From Slavery*. Soon after he gave
me the screenplay to Spike Lee's movie *Malcolm X*. These texts
ignited my interest in radical Black thought and led me to further study on my own the life of Malcolm X and moving into
studying the Haitian Revolution and the Black Panther Party in
high school. I felt empowered studying this history that was so
absent from the regular school curriculum. I learned that there
were Black queer people working to liberate others, especially
within the Black Power Movement. My study of the history
worked to expand my understanding of what freedom meant
and how people, systems, and institutions worked to impede
people living freely.

A second factor was seeking out Black queer literature such
as the work of James Earl Hardy and his *B-Boy Blues* series.
The books gifted me such an intense sense of self-worth reading
about other Black queer men expressing love for one another.
The series also helped me to evolve my relationship to sex and
helped me to understand what sex meant in the context of relationships and emotional needs, moving away from the emotion-
less portrayal of sex in pornography. I loved the series, as it gave
me language to start articulating my reality as a Black gay man.

A third factor was my growing relationship with the few gay
students who were out in my high school. I didn't have relationships with other gay males but with lesbians. It has been
mostly lesbians and later transgender and gender nonconforming friends who have been so healing in my journey toward self-
love as it relates to sexuality and gender. Yet, in high school,
developing real relationships with lesbian students helped me
to experience community in the form of affinity with other gay
folks, and this felt like an important support for me that started
convincing me that it was safe to start coming out.

One last factor was that overall, I was getting older and moving through my development into later adolescence. I was developing a stronger sense of who I was; and even more importantly, I was developing a sense of who I wanted to be. I knew what suffering and unhappiness were, and all I wanted was to be free of those experiences. Not really having a spiritual practice or strong faith in my root religion of Christianity, my primary belief was in the potential to change my reality of oppression and marginalization through study, critical thought, and strategic action.

All these factors culminated one evening in a moment of acceptance. One thing that is very common with me is how great things that happen to me are often registered as being anticlimactic. It is very exciting thinking about the prospect of something; and then it happens, and I'm basically like, "Oh, that's wonderful," and move on. I am past the wonderful thing even before it happens. In any case, I was lying in bed one night, and suddenly a thought slid through my mind that I had been resisting throughout high school. "I'm gay," I thought to myself. It was very basic and ordinary. My life shifted drastically in that one moment, and that was it. That was the first time I had experienced acceptance like that. There was more work to do to fully open to this reality—and make no mistake, I am still doing this work of accepting myself—but that night lying in bed was important and profound.

This basic acceptance of my gayness was the first time I experienced a conscious moment of self-love. At the time, it didn't register as love; but as I look back, informed by my present spiritual and contemplative practice, it was the first time that I had spoken to myself and said this is what's up and it's time to deal with it. At the heart of acceptance is telling the truth. This truth begins with ourselves and acknowledges what is happening for us.

Then again, what all these factors coming together meant was that I was beginning to experience enough safety to start telling myself the truth and feeling all the discomfort around that truth. The truth of my gayness was not the issue. The issue was my relationship to my gayness, which was informed by how the world around me told me I should relate to that gayness. Part of my feeling of safety started to help me let go of the messages that I was being fed about my gayness. I had to start trusting in my own experience of gayness, which felt normal and natural. And as my gayness deepened, it gave way to queerness, which was and is an identity location that articulates not just my expanded attraction to different bodies and gender presentations, but also articulates my radical sexual politics.

## ———————— LOVING OUR ANGER ————————

This book is a love song to my anger. This love song charts the effort that I have undergone to love something that seemed unlovable. It has not been an easy tune. This song is not, as the young folks say, a bop. My anger is intense and fierce. It is a boundless source of energy that I have believed has been invaluable, especially when used as a force to confront all the ways that I have been victimized and hurt. It has been my anger that has been there to right all the wrongs done against me. I have called this anger righteous, but it is still anger, and it has been there for me more times than any other person has.

My anger is like a living being that I am in partnership with. My anger has been precious to me ever since I realized through the practice of meditation that, like any other person or thing, it too deserved to be loved. Before this realization, my anger was sad and lonely. It felt forgotten and ignored. It acted out like anyone who has felt ignored or even taken for granted. I had to learn how to be in relationship to it.

I started practicing loving anger because I wanted to be liberated from it. When I say liberated, I do not mean the erasure of my anger, but to no longer be caught up in a compulsory relationship with it. When I talk about loving anger, I am not saying that I love what it does or what it helps me to do or how it makes me feel. I don't love it because of what it gives me. I love my anger because it is mine. Loving my anger means that I allow it to be there without judgment and without shame. I accept it. Moreover, loving anger disrupts its power over me and allows space for me to be in power over my anger.

Anger and love can exist together. Matter of fact, this love song is a duet between anger and love. Part of this duet means singing about the practice of love for ourselves and the love of wanting others to be happy. This practice can actually hold the space for the anger to be there, and this frees up my compulsory relationship to it, which results in reducing violence against myself and others. Anger is telling me something important about me and about how I am out of balance. But beneath that, the love is helping me to move beneath the anger to sit with my basic woundedness or heartbreak and all that's complex and nuanced and in general very uncomfortable.

But I have to admit that loving my anger is dangerous. This kind of love only breaks my heart over and over again. My anger is always telling the truth about things that I don't want to deal with. It is telling me that there are things that are out of balance. It is telling me that I am hurt. When I love my anger in this way, I am also exposing myself to the truth about myself and about the world.

To love my anger means that I must love myself. This is what a loving and liberatory relationship with anger demands, and these demands must be met fully without reserve or aversion, because the consequences mean that my love of anger alone turns to an abuse where I begin to demand of my anger to annihilate what I believe the root of my hurt to be.

We need to own our anger, but we don't have to operate from that anger. We can operate from the love while anger continues to inform what's going on. But it also continues to direct us back to our hurt, and to let the hurt connect us to others, and to let the broken heart remind us that we're not the only one in the world struggling. We are all experiencing broken hearts. None of this is working out the way we wanted. I find this realization to be incredibly important for me. It continually reminds me that I am not special because I am hurting. I am basically just like everyone else: basically basic.

As Mother Audre Lorde has taught us, there is a lot of data in anger. That data is there to help us learn from it. Anger is teaching us how to be free, how to live dynamic and rich lives, cultivating, embracing, and expressing our self-agency, setting boundaries, and reducing the harm we experience as individuals and collectives. To allow anger to do this, we have to love it and, in loving it, let it show us what it really is. In loving it, it shows us where the hurt is.

Loving our anger invites it into a transformative space where it emerges as the teacher. If we bypass this precious opportunity to enter into this transformative space, which is the space of tension, anxiety, and sometimes terror, then we're missing something. The most important times of teaching for me are the times of complete and utter disruption and loneliness. My pain emerges to teach me how to love it and to develop a different relationship to it. If we don't show up to work with that data, then we miss the teaching. And then we keep stumbling back into our old ways of being that actually never serve anyone.

That keep us perpetually traumatizing ourselves over and over again, because we can't get the teachings, because we can't show up, because we can't understand that it is within our discomfort that we're being taught how to make different choices about how to take care of ourselves.

# 8

# #METOO AND THE GURU

*And what everyone overlooks is that in order to do it—when the book comes out it may hurt you—but in order for me to do it, it had to hurt me first.*

—JAMES BALDWIN

*Compassion is caring and from there you trust yourself to make the right decision.*

—KARMA WANGMO

I BEGIN THIS reflection by admitting that I do not want to do this reflection. A part of me does not consent to this disclosure. Then again, another part of me knows that I have no choice but to consent. If I am interested in healing, I must also be interested in articulating what I have been avoiding. I don't want to do this, but I have to.

We are now living in the apocalypse. It is a time of things falling apart while other things seem to be falling together. In Buddhism, it is a time when our emotions seem stronger and coarser, and we believe them above any other data we may have about the truth of what is really happening around us. You may think that the apocalypse is about the end of the world. It is not. That is too easy. The universe does not do easy. It is, however, about the ending of delusion and the birth of truth. Denying the truth and pushing away from it create a tension from which violence always emerges. The violence will be mostly against ourselves if we are avoiding the truth, and may likely be expressed toward those embracing truth, as they will remind us of the violence we engage in to stay ignorant.

I know that the truth can be subjective. I suppose at this time the truth I am interested in is the truth of how I feel and how I relate to something that is complex. It's a hard road, especially when we are faced with the truth of love and rage living together.

To engage in the spiritual path that I have chosen in this life (or rather, the path that has chosen me), I need teachers. My first root or primary teacher in my main path of Tibetan Buddhism was the Venerable Lama Norlha Rinpoche. He was a monk and also the founder and abbot of Kagyu Thubten Chöling Monastery (KTC) north of New York City where I lived and trained to become a teacher. He was a realized master in his late sixties or early seventies when I met him. Though he was not my first teacher, he was the first teacher who I knew could help me become a teacher. He was revered and honored, and I saw in him everything that I wanted and needed to become.

After I moved to the monastery, I remember hearing a rumor that Rinpoche once had a sexual affair with a female student. It was spoken in a small group of residents at the monastery. Another very important teacher in our lineage was also mentioned as having affairs with female students. This was a bizarre experience, because I didn't even think about the rumors. I heard them, they passed through my mind, and then they went out again as fast as they came in. At no point did I think about the rumors. When we hear serious things about people we love, we tend to have some kind of reaction or thinking about the news.

I had nothing, not even a thought denying the truth of the allegations. Nothing. It was as if I had heard nothing disconcerting about my teacher. Yet it should have been disconcerting, as he was a monk with vows of celibacy.

Several years after that incident, after I had completed my training and was living away from the monastery, a friend disclosed to me that she had been one of several women who had been in a sexual relationship with our teacher. That was the disclosure that stuck in my head, because it wasn't a vague rumor. It was a disclosure from someone I loved and trusted about someone else I loved and trusted. Because of my years as a sexual assault victim advocate in my early twenties, I had come to understand how important it is to believe anyone who disclosed sexual-based harm committed against them. My teacher held the power in his relationship with her and in all the relationships he had with his students, and it was his primary responsibility to maintain boundaries. He didn't, and so there was harm against my friend and others who had been in sexual relationships with him. Moreover, because of the power my teacher held, he influenced my community against her when she ended the relationship. Though all this had happened years before I moved to the monastery, I had firsthand experience of that community's campaign to marginalize and silence her as I moved into an environment that still held openly negative attitudes toward her.

This disclosure left me pissed, confused, and sad for both myself and my friend.

This issue is tough and complex. The relationship between student and teacher in tantric traditions is not ordinary and is outside of anything that I had ever experienced before. Rinpoche was the first teacher I committed to being vulnerable with in order to facilitate my interpersonal transformation using the dharma as a vehicle. This strategy of personal vulnerability with one person whom I believed to be realized and accomplished within this particular spiritual path saved my life. This level of vulnerability is extremely delicate; and if the teacher is not mature enough, then boundaries are crossed and violence happens, resulting in trauma.

After the disclosure, my feelings evolved further from anger, confusion, and sadness into anxiety, shame, fear, and often experiences of numbness. I believe that this numbness was an expression of trauma. Sexual and all other ethical misconduct happen in all religious and spiritual traditions and especially in Buddhist communities. It is especially rampant in Tibetan Buddhist communities in monasteries in Asia, where young monastics are abused by older monastics, and where young reincarnate lamas are identified, confiscated, and subjected to years of emotional, physical, and sexual abuse as part of their religious training. Here in Western countries, we experience the sexual, physical, and emotional abuse of female, male, transgender, and gender expansive practitioners by mostly male Asian and Western teachers, as well as other ethical misconduct around money management, racism, ableism, misogyny, and others. This is not the practice of dharma, religion, or spirituality. It is the practice of humans struggling to relate to their own suffering and how we act out of our suffering often in ways that are very unskillful and that end up creating suffering for others.

At the time, I had taken on the responsibility of drafting a code of ethics for the teachers in my community. This seemed simple enough. Though I was still struggling with my friend's disclosure, I hadn't decided what my role in all this was. I was a junior lay teacher living outside of the monastery, and it seemed like a good step forward to explore ethics with the teachers of the community, most of whom were resident ordained monastics as well as trained teachers. I thought this was going well until I had a conversation with one of the senior teachers responsible for Rinpoche's personal care. She reached out to inform me that she knew that I knew about the affairs, and that I shouldn't talk about them, because she had made sure that nothing like this was happening anymore. She explained that our teacher was too old to engage like this any longer. She felt that the revelation would upset the community, since a majority of both the residential and extended lay community had no idea any of this had been happening. My feelings went from not just being angry to being enraged and deeply hurt. I was being told to be quiet.

After that conversation, I confided in one of my mentors about the situation and being asked to be quiet. I was so overwhelmed and fighting numbness that I was feeling immobile. I was hovering on the edge of just doing nothing and trying to forget about it. My mentor helped me to see the complexity of what was happening and challenged me to make a conscious decision about what I should do next. I had a responsibility to recognize everything that was happening and to make a wise and skillful decision, even though that decision may be to do nothing. I decided to believe what the senior teacher had told me about how my teacher was no longer engaging in this misconduct. I also took my friend's position into consideration, as she had never given me consent to act on her disclosure. In the end, I decided to continue working on the ethics statement, but over time I noticed that I was beginning to pull away from the community.

Very strange family dynamics became apparent. I was someone in the family who knew that our dad was not as amazing as his performance revealed. I was keeping a secret of harm in the family. I did this intentionally, because I wanted to protect people. I rested this resolution on the fact that my teacher was not sleeping with any students anymore. I was encouraged to believe that our teacher was this kind old man now who just wanted to continue teaching and guiding students. No one forced me into this belief. I didn't want to confront the reality of how the person who had saved my life had at the same time harmed others.

This all dramatically shifted when my friend contacted me again, needing to talk. In our conversation, she ushered me into a real personal apocalypse. I had been lied to. Our teacher was still having sexual relationships with students, and had been since my friend had first disclosed to me. She asked for my support as she prepared to enter into disclosure meetings with administrators of our monastery. I was numb again.

I believe that my numbness was an expression of not just the trauma that I was experiencing, but also the frustration at my trauma. The trauma that I was experiencing was a vicarious trauma, or a trauma that I absorbed from the others who had been hurt. Regardless, I took on this woundedness, and it merged with my own hurt. The frustration with the trauma was read as anger and at some points rage. The trauma along with the anger associated with it would kick me out of my body, and this disembodiment made it almost impossible to be aware of my physical sensations, and that made it difficult to have a relationship to my emotions and how I was actually feeling. In trauma studies, this is also called dissociation. I have often experienced the relationship between trauma and anger as the tension between feeling wounded and needing to take care of myself, and how frustration as anger arises out of that tension and gets stronger when I do not know how to care for myself. The resulting numbness can be understood as fragility. This fragility is not about being weak, but rather about needing to develop the resiliency to meet the challenge of a complex and painful psychophysical experience.

The disclosure meetings eventually led to a community-wide disclosure meeting at the monastery, facilitated by a third-party organization specializing in clergy sexual misconduct. The meeting was on a Wednesday, which I was upset about because I felt that a midweek community meeting made it very difficult for many of us needing reconciliation to be there. I believed at the time that this was done on purpose to keep more people from being able to attend. One of the agreements for the meeting was that no one was to share details about the day with anyone not at the meeting; and since I was not there, I was not able to learn the extent of what happened outside of larger details. I was told that Rinpoche did offer a video apology that was played at the meeting. I felt that this was bullshit, inappropriate, and a failure to take responsibility for the harm he had caused.

I understand how significant Rinpoche's work had been in helping countless beings in ways that I will never be able to do in this life. I am so grateful for that work and sacrifice. However, I also understand the responsibility of spiritual leadership. Spiritual leaders make mistakes; and because of the authority a spiritual leader exercises, any mistake or ethical misconduct can translate into significant harm for the community. Regardless of the mistake and the resultant harm, we have to show up in person to be held accountable by our community. Being upset with how the disclosure meeting was scheduled, along with being disappointed with Rinpoche's video apology, on top of believing how ridiculous the monastery maintaining the same authority structure that had concealed years of sexual misconduct was, I could no longer trust the monastery. It was no longer safe for me.

Several months later, when I was co-teaching a weekend retreat close to my monastery, I had started having an intense urge to see my teacher. I asked my co-teachers for leave to go and visit with him. I knew Rinpoche was not long for this world. By then his health was failing, and he was walking around on oxygen. I arrived at the monastery and noticed the intensity of my anxiety. I walked around the grounds for a bit before going into one of the buildings to seek people out. I was greeted

kindly and asked to wait for Rinpoche. He finally appeared
with a small entourage of monastics I had known and loved
for years. We all sat together outside to talk. I was not bothered
to have to meet with my teacher surrounded by others whom
I assume were there to monitor the session. I have no problem
saying what I need to say, with or without an audience. But sitting there watching this being that had saved my life, watching
him perform the greatest teaching he could ever offer me, which
was the lesson that he too was human, complex, and occupying
a failing body that I knew he was preparing to vacate, suddenly something inside of me shifted. I realized that I had to
start letting myself mourn all the contradictions. I had to let
myself mourn my loss of belief in perfection. I let myself question enlightenment. He was teaching me that I was just like
him: imperfect and complex. This realization did not excuse
any harm that we had ever done. Our complexity never excuses
harm. And though we are all complex, when that complexity
creates harm it is also calling for accountability.

I sat heavy and worn, not knowing till later that I was absorbing another kind of vicarious trauma, the trauma of a place that
for many months had been impacted by the emotional instability of people and their struggle to make sense of our teacher's
actions on top of all the ways they were being blamed by so
many others for the violence. I looked at Rinpoche, thanked him
for his teaching, and said the one thing that I did not know I
was going to say, which was that I prayed that I would meet him
again in another life. Maybe the next time around would end
less dramatically.

There is a teaching that the Buddha gave called the Heart
Sūtra. It was given at a place in India called Vultures Peak. My
teacher recited the *sūtra* at Vultures Peak several years ago when
many of us were on pilgrimage with him. The sūtra expresses
one of the most complex doctrines in Buddhist philosophy as it

proclaims that "form is emptiness, emptiness is form." There is something and nothing at the same time. Buddhist philosophy claims that though there is a reality that we experience, this reality is an expression of emptiness. This reality is relative truth, while emptiness is ultimate truth. Both are true, yet are even more true together. So while we dwell in this reality, we must also understand that this reality is an illusion. The point of the teaching is to live in the middle, where both extremes intersect. This is where I try to live, and this is where I take my relationship with my teacher. At one extreme he changed my life, and at the other extreme he harmed other people. Both are true, and they are much more true together. Rinpoche saved my life while he ruined other lives.

I don't believe in evil people. Nor do I believe in crazy people. I think evil and crazy are things we label people when we are too lazy to deal with their complexity or our own complexity. When we fail to relate to our own complexity, we fail to see the complexity of other people, especially the ones who cause a lot of harm. To step into the middle as the Heart Sūtra asks us to do is to step away from the extremes of black and white into the discomfort of the many shades of gray. The gray is where we head to the edge of our practice where our hearts break and we are forced to sit with both the love and the rage.

My teacher passed away six months after my last meeting with him. Even in his death, my teacher keeps teaching me that this shit is complex and it will always be complex. I must make a home in the complexity, because there is nowhere else to live if I am interested in decreasing violence against myself and others. In the gray middle is where I begin to articulate my hurt. In the gray middle my pain is a mirror for myself so that I begin to know what I need to do to get free from suffering.

I continue to love my teacher and my community, though I am hurt and angry at the same time. I continue to love all those my teacher hurt and all victims of harm from spiritual leaders. My love is how my utter disappointment and anger are being taken care of right now. I love because despite the violence rampant in my tradition, there is a core spiritual practice that has completely transformed my life. I love because there are many good teachers and practitioners who are authentic and who are working to transform the tradition. I love because love is the only way I can take responsibility for my part in this violence and disrupt it.

Since becoming more public about teacher misconduct over the years, there have been three basic arguments from others challenging my stance. First, in Buddhist tantra, we are encouraged to see the teacher as a Buddha; and their action, no matter how extreme, as enlightened action benefiting us and all beings. This is an example of what we call pure view. I believe this view to be often misunderstood. Pure view means that I see and relate to my own complexity and hold space for that complexity with honesty and compassion. If I am able to do that, then I develop a sensitivity to how the actions of others, especially my teacher, either help or harm me. In this practice, pure view becomes about tuning into reality as it really is, not as I am pretending it to be.

The second argument is that criticizing your teacher creates negative karma that will impact your future rebirths. In situations of confronting ethical misconduct, our criticism is an act of love that limits more violence from happening, as well as making space for there to be more truth and transparency in our relationship to the teacher. Regardless of relationship, we have a right to ask what's happening, and we have a right to set boundaries. With boundaries, we can experience a deeper connection to our teachers and the work teachers are attempting to do with us, because we feel safer and more trusting.

And the third argument is that sexual relationships between a teacher and a student have historical precedent in tantra. This is true. Tantric sex rituals are meant to trigger higher states of consciousness and experiences of egolessness. These rituals are meant to take pleasure as a path into these higher states. Pleasure is not the goal nor the motivation. However, the issue we must confront is that we are not living in the same cultural or historical context in which these practices emerged. Also I am not convinced that there are many teachers who have the capacity to engage in tantric sex solely for the benefit of the student. I am not realized and will not consider a sexual relationship with a student. Yes, tantra is a tradition of uncommon means to experience uncommon goals; however, if my uncommon means traumatized a student and left them with PTSD, then the truth is I failed in the means. My teacher failed in his means. You could argue that the greater impact of my teacher's actions may end up being positive. However, I must trust what I see in the present, with all the harm that has been caused, and judge this for what it is now, not for what it could become down the road.

This is the beauty and the struggle at the intersection of love and rage. Sometimes love and rage can take us into some hopeless places. However, as long as love is present, we will not stay in that hopelessness forever.

## THE PRACTICE OF LOVING OUR ANGER

This practice is a love and kindness bathing practice. Here, the energy of love from your circle of care will be channeled into your experience of anger.

### Type of Practice

This practice uses mindfulness, breath practice, and visualization.

——————————— THE PRACTICE ———————————

1. Start by moving through the beginning practice sequence, ending with a breath practice.

2. Continuing with the breath, breathe deeply in through the nose and out through the mouth. Try to make both the inhale and the exhale as deep as possible. After a few minutes, take a two-second pause after the inhale through the nose before releasing the exhale through the mouth. Gradually make that pause longer, up to five to ten seconds, or however long is comfortable for you. In the pause between the breaths, notice the space and stillness that that opens up. If you can, try to rest in between those breaths. As you continue resting in the pauses, try to start experiencing the breaths as well as the pauses. Let the breath breathe you, and while doing so allow it to move you into a deeper sense of spaciousness and calm. Practice with the breaths as long as you want to.

3. Now move into evoking the Seven Homecomings and your circle of care.

4. Imagine that your circle begins to generate the energy of love for you, and feel that energy filling the space around you as warmth. Feel that warmth gently hold you, and wrap you; and slowly begin to feel that energy of love, this warmth from your benefactors, slowly begin to sink into the body beneath the layer of skin into the muscles, the bones, and the organs as if you're being marinated in this energy of love.

As you're breathing, imagine that you're breathing this love into your body and lungs; and when that love gets into your lungs, imagine this energy begins to circulate throughout the whole body in the same way oxygen is taken in by the lungs and distributed throughout all the cells in the body. Imagine the same thing is happening with this energy of love, that every cell gets fed by this energy. In the same way that you are being held by the energy of the earth, allow yourself to be held by the energy of love from your benefactors. Relax, open, and continue breathing.

5. Now shift your attention to your breath, and imagine breathing in and out from your heart center. Imagine that you are breathing in the energy of love around you, which intensifies the energy of compassion in the heart center. Imagine that even more energy of love circulates throughout the body from the heart center.

6. At this point, notice any experience of anger in your mind or body. Imagine channeling the love from your care circle into this experience of anger. Keep channeling that energy, and relax around the experience of anger.

7. As you continue channeling love into the anger, begin directly sending a wish to the anger that it experiences happiness and ease, and that it chills out. Keep making this wish for as long as you want.

8. You may experience some discomfort coming up. Whatever you may feel, allow your circle of care to hold it. If you are having a hard time feeling anything, just relax, and don't force anything to happen.

9. Continue for as long as you can. At the end of the practice, imagine dissolving your homecoming circle into your heart center, and rest in the residual energy of love for as long as you want.

10. Move through the ending practice sequence.

# 9

# KINDNESS

The problem with becoming myself was that, no matter how nice I had learned to be, no matter how smart or accommodating, sitting with myself meant I was becoming more myself, more Black. As soon as I started getting good at being human I was increasingly seen as a threat.

—DR. JASMINE SYEDULLAH, *Radical Dharma*

My goal is to always come from a place of love . . . but sometimes you just have to break it down for a motherfucker.

—RUPAUL

You are your best thing.

—TONI MORRISON

MY UNDERSTANDING OF KINDNESS is the expression of the compassion I have for myself that helps me move in the world in a way that is gentle, soft, and aware, but direct at the same time. In the same ways vicarious trauma is experienced by being around people who themselves are experiencing trauma that we energetically absorb, compassionate energy is absorbed by us in the form of kindness, and this kindness is naturally benefiting. It is like the feeling of the sun on our skin on a cold day. The sun isn't intentionally trying to warm us up, but we just happen to be warmed by the sun being its natural self.

There are realized spiritual teachers that I have had the fortune of spending time with and learning from. One of the qualities of sitting with these beings is how they radiate this field of gentle kindness around them. I do not think that they are doing it on purpose—it seems as if it's just a natural expression of the compassion they have for themselves. Once I was at a talk given by a well-known spiritual teacher. At the end of the talk, many of us started jostling to get close to him to have a few words with him and maybe have a picture taken. It was mayhem. Finally I got my chance to step into his personal space; and when I did, it was like entering into the eye of a hurricane. While there was mayhem around us, being next to him felt calming and relaxed. In that moment, I began to understand what this kind of vicarious kindness is all about. This kindness isn't personal. It had nothing to do with me or anyone else stepping into his space. This field of kindness and the peace that I felt in this field was all about how he was practicing compassion for himself.

## ——— KINDNESS AND WHITE PEOPLE ———

Sometimes I do struggle with the word "kindness." Frankly, it reminds me of all the white people in my life who have been kind to me but have hurt me when that kindness gives way to these old historical and habitual allegiances to whiteness and its dominance over my body and mind. My relationship to kindness has been mostly informed by my spiritual tradition and within communities of white practitioners in my tradition who have weaponized the teaching and practice of kindness. When I say weaponize, I mean to convey that kindness is not an expression of compassion, but rather a strategy we use to manipulate others or bypass discomfort in a situation. Often in my relationship with white people, kindness can be used to bypass or distract me from the reality that white supremacy is functioning in the relationship. This weaponizing of kindness also functions to further make unconscious not only their allegiance to white supremacy but also their terror of confronting their identity as white people. I have met a lot of white people who are attached to their identity of being good or kind, which makes it difficult to see the parts of their experience that are violent. Ultimately, weaponized kindness is a kindness that may feel good initially but will hurt me down the road.

I reflect on growing up in the South and how we were raised to "speak" to everyone. This meant that I had to essentially say hey to anyone I encountered in a public space regardless of race. We even had to speak to people we didn't like! I especially had to speak to other Black folks because if I didn't, word would get to my mother and there would end up being a "stern talking to" that would go something like this: "So and so called and told me that they had seen you at such and such a place and you didn't speak to them. Boy, you better say hey to people when you see them. I don't know why you think you are too good to speak!" To not speak to other Black folks reflected on your upbringing and may convey that you weren't "raised right" by your parents, guardians, and other family members. I struggled to speak to other Black folks for two reasons. The first was that I actually did think that I was too good to speak to other people (something I think I have grown out of). And second, I was and still am an introvert. I have a deep need to be left alone! It was a joy to move to the northeast in my twenties and be able to walk down a sidewalk not having to bother acknowledging anyone.

I was raised to speak to white people as well. I recognize that speaking to Black people was a method that we used to cultivate a sense of belonging. We needed to always identify one another to feel safe and to communicate the reality that we were not alone in this ocean of racism. But I feel I was taught to speak to white people out of the ways we, as Black people, were conditioned during slavery and into the Jim Crow era to acknowledge white people. This speaking to white people was not something we did to belong or to strengthen group membership. We spoke to white people because it was demanded that we acknowledge and see them in the world, because they deserved to be in the world taking up space. They were, still are, the ruling class. For my ancestors, not speaking to white people could cost them their lives. This fear lives as a transhistorical offering in my nervous system that jumps a little when I pass a white person in a public space. And my nervous system whispers to me, "If you do not acknowledge them, they could kill you."

But my question is this: How authentically kind can white people be to me or any other Black or brown person if they lack the compassion to acknowledge their conditioning as white supremacists? How kind can they be when at the end of the day, this lack of acknowledgment perpetuates their dominance over my body?

Like myself, many Black and brown people still find themselves in situations where kindness is demanded from us in order to stay safe around white people. This is a demand of emotional labor. I continue to wonder what this means for those of us invested in white-dominated spaces where we have come to distrust the kindness of white people because of the labor we are called to do to feel safe enough. I wonder about the spiritual communities I found myself in and all the ways I feel angry and frustrated at being shown kindness that struggles to be authentic given the cultural and historical power dynamics.

I have struggled most often with white women and kindness. Growing up with white women, I would often experience a subtle distrust of them. When I was assigned *To Kill a Mockingbird* in high school to read, I was introduced to a cultural dynamic that I knew was far from fictional. My white female friends were wonderful, and I had lots of fun with them, but there was a sense that I was disposable in the face of white supremacist loyalty. It was only with white female friends who were doing anti-racism work or trying to disrupt racism in some way that I developed more trusting relationships. White women have for me functioned as doorkeepers maintaining both white supremacy and patriarchy. It has been tricky, because I want to trust that being female-identified in a white supremacist culture is enough for them to devote themselves to seeing and understanding the complexity and interconnectedness of all oppressions across all identity locations. But sadly, I keep getting disappointed.

Once I was driving a car with some good white female friends of mine. We were on our way to a club. One of my friends, who sat in the front, wanted to get the party started early, sipping out of a bottle of vodka. I was okay with that. Then she pulls out a blunt, and I flipped out! No way was that gonna happen in my car with me being a Black man on a Southern highway at night. If we were pulled over and the cop found that, I would be off to prison. The other women, sensing the urgency, jumped in; my friend submitted and tucked everything away out of sight. It ended up not being a big deal. A few weeks later, I was cleaning out my car and found my friend's blunt, and I hit the fucking roof again! Nothing but rage. It dawned on me how her irresponsibility had been putting my well-being at risk for weeks. There was such a lack of consideration around how her privilege put my life in danger. Most of the direct experiences of discrimination, including being profiled and harassed in stores, to having cops called on me, have been from white women.

These experiences have resulted in a deepening compassion for myself. When I am a victim of racism or other forms of discrimination, I have trained myself to take care of my needs in the moment. So many of us who are victims of violence like this get distracted by the anger or this need to get back at the person who hurt us. It is much more sustainable and beneficial to offer ourselves what we need in the moment. Once we do that, we can feel more resourced to address the situation that created the harm for us.

## ———— NICENESS AND KINDNESS ————

Niceness is a tough word for me. It conjures up memories of people smiling at me and saying pleasant things while talking shit behind my back. I was raised to be nice; but as I got older, niceness gave way to my anger and disappointment, and I had to let go of this valuing of being nice. Being nice felt too superficial and inauthentic. When I started being introduced to kindness and compassion, I knew that these were the expressions that felt solid, real, and very honest. Being nice felt like being disconnected from my experiences and attempting to bypass them in order to center a performance for someone so they wouldn't think negatively about me. It felt as if being nice was about just trying to get through an interaction. When I started studying compassion and kindness, it felt like a shift toward acknowledging what I needed in the moment, being aware of those needs, and holding space. When I started taking care of myself in that way, it became much easier to practice actual compassion for others on the spot.

### On the Train

Once I was waiting for a train on the subway platform. I was standing behind a group of young people as the train approached. The etiquette of boarding any form of public transportation is to wait for people to first get off before getting on. When the train stopped and the doors opened, the young people rushed inside before letting the handful of people get off first. After the young folks rushed on, the rest of us waited for folks to get off before we ourselves boarded and took seats. As I sat down close to the small group of young folks who had rushed in, a woman who had just exited stepped into the closing doors, using one hand to keep them wedged open. She looked straight at the young folks with a certain directness in her eyes that I knew was caused by anger. I thought, "Uh-oh! She is fixing to cuss these kids out!"

Everyone in our part of the subway car looked intently back and forth between her and the young folks, bracing themselves. My anxiety was heightened for a few reasons.

First, both the young folks and the woman were people of color, and I dreaded seeing people of color go after each other in a public space, because we continually play into seeing each other as targets for our unexpressed and unmetabolized trauma, which would be expressed, in that moment on the train, as rage.

Second, before my training in meditation, I had a habit of absorbing tension and negative emotions within a space. I knew that I would be absorbing the energy in this exchange. This energy would flood the space from the emotional reactions of everyone involved in the exchange, manifesting as tightness and heaviness in my body.

Third, I knew that I would fall into my old patterns of relating to the young people and wanting to protect them.

Finally the woman spoke to the young folks: "Listen, I just want to let you know that I didn't appreciate you all running in here all over me. I thought that was really ignorant. I wanna let you know that you need to watch out for that stuff because next

time someone may react in a way that won't be good for you."
Her voice came out even, strong, solid, and pointed. There was
anger, but that anger was being mediated by what I felt to be an
empathy for the teens. The young people sat staring in different
directions, and at times laughing nervously, but I knew that they
were listening.

She continued: "You can laugh all you want, but I'm just
trying to let you know what happened, because it wasn't right."
The exchange took less than thirty seconds; and as she finished
the last statement, she backed out of the doors, allowing them to
close. The train got under way. The young people started laughing and joking about the woman. The rest of us just sat quietly. I
sat, noticing how I didn't feel tense or heavy. Yet what I felt was
a mixture of awe and relief.

I have never forgotten that situation because of how it
helped to register the expression of compassion and anger
in dialogue. I could tell that the woman was pissed, but she
decided to return back to the train to not only express how she
felt but also somehow impact the future behavior of the young
people she was addressing. We were all being taught not just to
follow the etiquette but how to hold others accountable when
we are pissed.

As I reflected on the experience and how it has impacted my
own relationship to anger and compassion, I began to see how
much emotional labor it takes to hold this tension of holding
space for anger in general as well as holding it in dialogue with
any other emotion. This tension is the resistance we feel against
reacting to anger itself in ways that could further create harm. It
is the space that we are offering our anger that helps other emotions to be there, and it helps us to have the space to experience
anger as well.

Also, what the woman was doing was emotional labor
for others who felt hurt by the young people rushing in. She

was doing labor for the young people as well, who were not responding with attentiveness and respect and not taking responsibility for the harm they had caused. She had to hold space for her own hurt she was feeling due to not being heard, or maybe for the embarrassment of speaking out, or even for the resentment we offered her as she held up the train. She had, to hold the space for our negative projections on her as another pissed-off woman of color. All of this she held and still somehow held the young people accountable with a wish for them to be free from pain.

Many people struggle with needing to be liked. This can be a form of suffering and can prevent us from taking risks or telling the truth. Sometimes this need to be liked takes the form of avoiding conflicts. My experience of needing to be liked stems from how I was raised to experience being liked and loved as the same thing. If you loved me then you liked me and vice versa. They are not the same. Loving is a liberatory practice that advocates for happiness for myself and others, whereas liking is temporary and is subject to someone keeping us comfortable or fulfilling another valuable service.

## PRACTICE: KINDNESS BATHING WITH YOUR HOMECOMING CIRCLE

This practice is about resting in and allowing ourselves to be held by the energy of kindness. The energy of kindness in the practice is a composite energy that is mixed with compassion, love, patience, and attention.

### Type of Practice

This practice uses mindfulness, breath practice, and visualization.

--- THE PRACTICE ---

1. Start by moving through the beginning practice sequence, ending with a breath practice.

2. Continuing with the breath, breathe deeply in through the nose and out through the mouth. Try to make both the inhale and the exhale as deep as possible. After a few minutes, take a two-second pause after the inhale through the nose before releasing the exhale through the mouth. Gradually make that pause longer, up to five to ten seconds, or however long is comfortable for you. In the pause between the breaths, notice the space and stillness that that opens up. If you can, try to rest in between those breaths. As you continue resting in the pauses, try to start experiencing the breaths as well as the pauses. Let the breath breathe you, and while doing so allow it to move you into a deeper sense of spaciousness and calm. Practice with the breaths as long as you want to.

3. Now move into evoking the Seven Homecomings and your circle of care.

4. Imagine that your circle begins to generate the energy of care for you, and feel that energy filling the space around you as warmth. Feel that warmth gently hold you and wrap you; and slowly begin to feel that energy of kindness, this warmth from your benefactors, slowly begin to sink into the body beneath the layer of skin into the muscles, the bones, and the organs as if you're being marinated in this energy of kindness.

As you're breathing, imagine that you're breathing this kindness into your body and lungs; and when that kindness gets into your lungs, imagine this energy begins to circulate throughout the whole body in the same way oxygen is taken in by the lungs and distributed throughout all the cells in the body. Imagine the same thing is happening with this energy of kindness, that every cell gets fed by this energy. In the same way that you are being held by the energy of the earth, allow yourself to be held by the energy of kindness from your benefactors. Relax, open, and continue breathing.

5. Now shift your attention to your breath, and imagine breathing in and out from your heart center. Imagine that you are breathing in the energy of kindness around you, which intensifies the energy of compassion in the heart center. Imagine that even more energy of kindness circulates throughout the body from the heart center.

6. Continue for as long as you can. At the end of the practice, imagine dissolving your homecoming circle into your heart center, and rest in the residual energy of kindness for as long as you want.

7. You may experience some discomfort coming up. Whatever you may feel, allow your circle of care to hold it. If you are having a hard time feeling anything, just relax and don't force anything to happen.

8. Move through the ending practice sequence.

# 10

# LET'S TALK ABOUT SEX

Partially adopted from "Conscious Sex: An Interview with Lama Rod Owens" by Leslee Goodman appearing in The MOON magazine

*I was like, Am I gay? Am I straight? And I realized . . . I'm just slutty. Where's my parade?*

—MARGARET CHO

*We will not go away with our issues of sexuality. We are coming home. It is not enough to tell us that one was a brilliant poet, scientist, educator, or rebel. Whom did he love? It makes a difference. I can't become a whole man simply on what is fed to me: watered-down versions of Black life in America. I need the ass-splitting truth to be told, so I will have something pure to emulate, a reason to remain loyal.*

—ESSEX HEMPHILL

OFTEN PEOPLE ASK me what lama means. *Lama* is the Tibetan word for the Sanskrit word *guru*. So lama in the Tibetan tradition means "teacher." It connotes a certain spiritual weight, or gravitas, usually conferred after completing a three-year retreat by the teacher who guided you through the retreat. I practiced through my retreat time as a novice monk or renunciate.

People think becoming a renunciate is somehow avoiding the world, along with our instincts, appetites, and desires. That's not the case. You're actually moving deeper into the nature of these instincts and desires. So going into retreat, I came face-to-face with my sexuality. Tantric Buddhism is a tradition that confronts ideas of gender and sexuality through practices that help you to realize that these attributes, and identity in general, are quite fluid, and actually quite illusionary. You're brought into that realization very intimately and told to sit and experience what fluidity feels like. You come face-to-face with the ways in which you struggle to solidify sexuality and gender, and the ways in which you believe in it so earnestly.

Fluidity challenges all of that. The rug keeps being pulled from under you. The message you keep getting and the experiences you keep receiving are that no, this is just an illusion. You're actually not this idea of a man; you're much more than that. Your suffering sometimes comes from the ways in which you're desperately trying to plant yourself somewhere so that you can have an identity. It can be easier to be in the world if you can just name yourself.

Tantric traditions are not about sex, yet pleasure certainly becomes something that is used to imagine and experience freedom from dualistic and binary thinking. We are attempting to disrupt how binary thinking contributes to ego formation and fixation. One way is to use the energy of pleasure to disrupt this dualism. Another prominent way was through deity practice, or imagining that I was certain deities and attempting to embody their enlightened qualities. You can become various deities. Sometimes the deity is female, so you become a female deity. The point is to disrupt the ego; to realize that you're not who you think you are, so you pretend to be something else, even for a second. Soon it starts dissolving your fixation on this self that you think you are.

When you associate with a deity and ask to take on the qualities of the deity—be they compassion, love, kindness, fierceness, equanimity, or whatever—your own essential fluidity becomes quite apparent. Even coming out of the retreat, I noticed how my attraction, my sexuality, was wider. My own self-love was also deepening. As you get more and more glimpses of the vastness of your true ultimate nature, you realize, "Oh, all this shit I've been believing about what people said I was is actually a lie." Then you start having a direct, deeper experience with your true nature. I realized that my attraction was so much broader and wider after leaving retreat because I loved myself enough and trusted myself enough to appreciate how everyone around me was attractive in certain ways.

I also think that the self-love I experienced in retreat began to decolonize my sexuality and my sexual desire. For many years prior, I didn't see people like me as attractive. I often found myself very much attracted to white men and to slim, muscular men, rather than to heavier-bodied Black men like myself. That was something I was ashamed of. But in retreat I realized that idealizing this one masculine form was just another aspect of my cultural conditioning; it didn't have any inherent reality for me. For the first time, I really began to love and value my own body and my own sexuality.

## SEX AND ANGER

Some of us practice a lot of anger in our expression of sexuality. We attempt to practice our sexuality in the pursuit of pleasure, but that practice turns into bypassing our woundedness. When we are not doing work to take care of our woundedness, our sexual expression becomes a vehicle through which our aggression is expressed. This results in violence against ourselves and others.

I consider myself sex positive and enjoy sexual relationships that are based on consent and clarity. I am not often bothered by being labeled promiscuous. However, I try to be honest with myself in periods of being more sexually active. I ask myself, Am I using my sexuality to avoid something, or am I genuinely using it to experience freedom? I believe that it is always okay to have fun as long as we understand how we can become attached to having fun.

During sex, I am practicing being open, clear, and spacious. I am trying to rest within my experience of pleasure while at the same time being an agent of my partner's pleasure. I am attempting to send the energy of happiness, peace, comfort, and ease to my partner. I like to ask my partner during an experience if they are enjoying themselves or if there is something we can do if they are not having fun. I feel especially seen when my partner also checks in with me.

Promiscuousness and sex positivity are not inherently liberating either. For them to be liberating, sex positivity must become an attitude that sees sex and sexuality as doors into experiences of freedom, using the pleasure of sex to unlock those higher levels of consciousness. Sex and sexual expression become a method to achieve higher states of mind, which will help to reduce dualistic thinking as well as the violence that comes with it. If we are not trying to free ourselves, we will return to repetitive experiences of pleasure that keep getting wasted and not used to move into other experiences.

To be free, everything must be loved, even what is unlovable. If we are really serious about freedom, we must learn to love both our pleasure as well as our displeasure. To take sexual pleasure as the path of liberation, we must begin to love our pleasure. Loving it means we accept it, and that acceptance invites us into being in relationship with its true essence. To love my pleasure is not the same as being attached to my pleasure. Loving pleasure means that I allow it to be itself. I enjoy it when it arises, and I let it go when it leaves. When we are in relationship with our pleasure in this way, then it can direct us into the experience of spaciousness, and that spaciousness is the basis of happiness, joy, and bliss.

When I experienced my first intentional orgasm from masturbation in my early teens, it was such an intense experience. I had never experienced anything like the pleasure that came with my ejaculation. As I continued experimenting with myself, I discovered various ways to intensify the experience, including having sex with other men. I learned over the years that orgasm is one of the most profound experiences because for many of us it will be one of the few experiences of bliss we will ever experience. From my perspective, the experience of bliss is a moment when everything falls away and we find ourselves face-to-face with the nature of our own minds, which is clear and wide open. Then after that second, we come back to our dualistic mind with all of its clinging and storylines. Part of sex addiction is about chasing the dragon of orgasm bliss over and over again. When we cultivate an authentic spiritual practice, we will be creating a foundation of contentment that we can rise above into bliss during an orgasm and then fall back after orgasm to be held by the firm foundation of contentment. Spiritual practice helps us to moderate extremes in our experiences, and it helps to hold any experience that we might have.

## ATTRACTION

I've come to consider embodiment to be one of the primary benefits of my time in retreat—and perhaps it is the radical revolutionary practice of our time. Though I would say that I am not 100 percent at home in my body, I am further along the path of coming home to my body than I have ever been. My body and mind are beginning to partner; I try to bring both of them together into every interaction and situation. This definitely slows me down, but it also keeps me grounded and healthy. I now listen to my body as much as to my mind, because my body has its own wisdom, which is just as important as that of my mind.

My retreat training and the embodiment that continues to grow from my practice have enabled me to see beauty in all kinds of bodies—in all races, in all body types, and in different gender expressions and performances. But ultimately, what I have to deal with, too, is that I am attracted to masculinity—to this basic, raw expression of masculinity, which can be performed in all kinds of bodies: cisgender men, masculine-performing women, transgender men. I also love and am attracted to femininity. However, I find masculinity often erotic, which is to say that I find it sexually desirable and arousing. Wherever masculine energy is expressed, I find myself attracted to it. But to be clear, this attraction isn't always sexual.

I think it's really important to admit that we're attracted to people. As a spiritual teacher, my practice is first and foremost acknowledging and accepting that I do have physical, sexual attractions to many people. However, as a spiritual teacher, there is an ethic concerning how I relate to bodies that I'm attracted to. As a Buddhist, my basic ethic is to do no harm; to limit the violence that I commit toward myself and others. Consent is an important practice. So as a teacher, I cannot engage in any kind of sexual relationship with a student or a mentee because there is a power differential in my relationship with students, which makes authentic consent very difficult if not impossible. So when I seek sexual relationships, it's always outside of my spiritual communities. This, actually, is a big part of how I maintain boundaries with my students—by having a satisfying personal life with others.

I think attraction is complex and multilayered. I can initially be attracted to someone whose values and ethics don't line up with mine, but it's not going to last very long. If I am just hooking up, I'm not so concerned with that. I will strive to do no harm in the experience and have fun and help my partner have fun. Yet in longer-term relationships, what's most important is alignment in ethics and in the vision for one's life. For me, being in a conscious relationship means that I'm not spending a lot of time fighting you or educating you. We have to share a commitment to living a just life and working toward just communities. If that's not there, then I can't communicate safely; and if I can't communicate safely, then I can't be with you.

Some people believe that we can't always bring our politics into relationships. I think we absolutely have to. If our politics are really important to us, we have to be with people who understand our politics and share them. Otherwise, there will be ethical conflicts. Ultimately, I think that if you can invest in being embodied, and you listen to both the mind and the body together, you begin to discern a kind of truth about people, or about a relationship. The earlier you're able to listen to your mind and body together, the less likely you will find yourself in a relationship that is unsuitable for you. And the sexual expression within a relationship is even more fulfilling when we are with people who align with our politics, our ethics, and so forth.

My retreat experience has also helped me relate to stop seeing sexuality and sexual expression as being outside of my spiritual practice, even if it's outside my spiritual community. All of my relationships become a container where compassion and care can be practiced—even if the relationship is short term and primarily sexual. That's how I understand sexual relationships—as an expression of compassion and care. I am concerned for the pleasure of my partner as much as I am concerned with my own pleasure. Part of my contract is to ensure that my partner enjoys the experience as much as I want to enjoy the experience.

Sex is important for me, but not imperative. Sexual expression is a profound way that we can connect with someone and share an experience of body and mind. But it's not the only way I experience intimacy in the world. I think when we come together in communities, we're ideally building a kind of intimacy, because it involves vulnerability. Sexual expression is also based on vulnerability; about opening up to someone and showing parts of yourself, both physically and emotionally, that you don't show to everyone.

## HOOKUP APPS

I appreciate hookup and dating apps. I get strange reactions from people when I say that. The idea of a hookup and dating app was fascinating after my three-year retreat. During my time away, smartphone technology grew by leaps and bounds. The day I finished retreat, I was sitting with some friends and family. They were so eager to show me their phones and everything that could be done. My gay friends showed me my first hookup app that day, and I was so confused! First, I didn't know what an app was or what it did. Second, I couldn't figure out how it revealed all the gay men around me! It seemed like magic. I wondered if I was on the app as well. After a little time, I chilled out and understood that the app used GPS to detect other people around me who also had the app and a profile. There was something so radical and liberating about this, while at the same time I was feeling unsettled about the whole thing.

What seemed radical was the creation of a space where all kinds of people could gather across identity locations to engage in dating and sex. Access to technology seemed to be the only restrictive barrier. If you had a phone and the app, then you could enter into the marketplace to be seen and to engage in getting your needs met. Yet what was and is unsettling is the marketplace itself and how bodies are valued and devalued. This valuing and devaluing is a commodification of our bodies, where younger fit bodies are valued and bought, while other bodies are ignored. Sometimes I feel as if I am at a slave market where I am both the slave and the slave master. Though I willingly enter onto the stage, I am expected often to offer my body through endless nude photos, and where others do the same with me, and maybe at the end we decide to buy each other. There is an intense sense of loneliness that has arisen out of the ways that my intimacy with other men has been impacted by this system of exchange. This kind of sexual capitalism tells me that I can bypass my humanness and can objectify others to meet my sexual needs. I crave the intimacy of conversations and dating, trying to relate to my humanness so I can relate to another's. I love sex and plea- sure, but I know that what really gets me off now is arriving in a dynamic space through understanding that this person I want to experience pleasure with is a real person with joy and fear, who loves and who is loved, and who also wants to be safe and be free from harm.

There are other forms of violence as well, related to how the marketplace continues to perpetuate hierarchies and systems of power based on race, class, body type, ability, and especially one's HIV serostatus. These apps can be quite racist, ableist, and misogynistic, as expressions of femininity are marginalized. However, STI status is used as a symbol of purity, reinforcing the stigma of living with disease, compounding the hurt that many people living with HIV and other STIs must experience. What this reality shows me is even in queer and gay male spaces, virtual or not, the intersection of whiteness and patriarchy still thrives, in making us never good enough to receive the affection, pleasure, and even love that we can get from others.

What becomes harder for me is trying to manage the space after sex, when the tenderness that opens for me is not held and I am left alone, feeling ashamed for being vulnerable. Regardless, I continue to remain on the apps, because there is a community there that I want to be a part of. I like the space where sex and sexuality are present and being engaged with. I think that it is important for gay and queer men like me to claim spaces to explore our sexuality in a way that has been denied us in other spaces. I believe that pleasure can be an act of personal and collective liberation when done in collaboration with our humanness. Overall, I want to convey that when our whole selves are brought into lovemaking, then our whole selves can be made love to.

## COMMUNITY

I advise people all the time to "go where you're loved." For most of us, there aren't a lot of places that qualify. That's why so much of my work in the world is helping to create these communities of authentic love and vulnerability. To do that, I have to model what it looks like to be loving, to be in love with myself, to be in love with others around me, and to be vulnerable. Most of all, I have to model what it means to hold the vulnerability of others around me. I have to do this for communities as well as for my sexual and intimate partners.

The questions I am most interested in are: How can we be radically open? How can we take risks? How do we have the conversations that begin to build communities where we can actually be ourselves? And how do we leave communities where we're being hurt over and over? If you don't have a community where this kind of radical openness and vulnerability is being practiced, then you leave, and you may have to create your own.

It's the same thing that we have to do in intimate relationships too: stop settling for all the bullshit. If you keep getting hurt, then leave. I realize this is really easy to say and not so easy to practice, given in certain cases how powerless we can feel, particularly in abusive relationships. In these cases, we have to strengthen our sense of "I" and work to feel that we deserve to be happy and free from harm. If we can do this work, the next time we seek partnership, it's with people who are able to meet us where we are. It's not impossible, but is difficult. And sometimes it means you have to be alone. I have learned the most when people have stopped putting up with my own bullshit and have walked. The walking throws it back in my face as work I need to do.

I try to be radical even if I have a one-time sexual hookup. I'm always going to communicate as much as possible, I'm going to practice love and compassion as much as possible, and I'm going to have fun. If I can't express compassion, love, and vulnerability, then it's not fun and I can't go through with it. Because it's not just about sex; it's actually about experiencing this kind of intimate exchange.

Holding each other's vulnerability in a community setting or in a sexual relationship of any kind means that we're witnessing, we're being present to someone's opening. We're not flinching, we're not arguing, we're not judging; we're just witnessing. Basically, if someone starts sharing something, then you start listening. You're not planning an argument, but you're inviting the opening to continue by being interested in what they have to say. That's where we need to get to: where everyone feels as if they're safe enough to share something and not get marginalized, judged, or criticized. This is not to say that people can't offer feedback; but first and foremost, they have to allow space for someone to present their experience. Once that has happened, others can share their experience, and there doesn't have to be conflict if the experiences differ. It can just be people sharing the same space together.

## ——————— EMBODYING SEX ———————

The body doesn't lie. It always tells the truth. So as I move through the world, I use my body to pick up cues that my thinking mind can't discern. What is my gut telling me? What is my intuition telling me that I feel in my body? I listen to that information. If I feel relaxed in my body when I'm with someone, that's a really good sign. If I feel tension in my body, especially in my gut, when I'm around someone, then maybe that's a clue that something's not right for me.

When I started listening to my body, I started actually learning what partners I should be with and which ones I shouldn't. The relationships that have been really important for me have started off with us talking about how we feel about the world, about justice, about gender, about the work we're doing in our lives to be better people. During that period of discernment, my body and my mind were really relaxing into the experience. And the physical attraction deepened as I realized how aligned we were in other parts of our lives. I think so many of us are settling, because we feel as if "this is the best I can do." I used to feel that because of the body I was born into and other circumstances, I could only have certain kinds of relationships and I had to be okay with what I was given. That came from a severe lack of self-esteem and depleted self-love and self-compassion. I had this energetic mentality that no matter how out-of-sync someone was with me, if they were attracted to me I had to be grateful for that, because so many other people weren't attracted to me.

As I began practicing, and moving through retreat, and coming back out into the world, I learned to really challenge that mentality and to assert that I deserve to be with someone I'm compatible with. Maybe I'll have to be really patient, but that's okay, because I've also taken on some of the tasks people often rely on their partners for—like appreciating myself, and loving myself more and more. Of course, it's wonderful when someone else shows up and appreciates me; but I'm not in need of it, because I can give it to myself. So now I seek relationships because I want to take care of someone and I also want to be taken care of. I want there to be a balance of care.

As a teacher, it's easy to fall into the role of giving. It can become my default setting, which gets in the way of being cared for myself. It's easy to minimize my own need for care. I've noticed, however, that it's my mind that tells me, "Oh, you don't need help," but my body is more likely to say, "Actually, you could use some."

Another edge for me is being in a relationship where a partner offers support and care that I don't usually get, and then we fall into roles. I do all my caregiving in the world and then rely on my intimate relationship to replenish what I have given to others.

So then it might become a practice for me to be conscious of how I accept generosity from a partner. That can be such an incredible lesson. The flip side of it is to learn how to be really attentive to the ways that I return care. In conscious relationships, we should be asking, "What do I need, and what does my partner need?" And you communicate with one another. Maybe you're in a situation where you can't possibly give what your partner needs, and then you have to discern together whether certain needs can be met beyond this particular relationship. All of it—communicating and listening to our bodies—becomes a space for discernment to happen.

I think non-monogamous relationships are important for me. For me, there is a recognition that I may have needs and desires that are important to me that maybe are not met in my primary relationship. So I may have to create ways to honor and explore my connections to other people while protecting my primary relationship. To engage in healthy non-monogamy, we have to communicate what our needs are, what the boundaries might be, so that other relationships can be protected.

It's incredibly important to have these conversations if indeed people have these desires. I'm not saying everyone should be in a non-monogamous relationship. They take an incredible amount of maturity, and there has to be mutuality; it can't just be the interest of one partner. Multiple significant relationships take time and communication. They require openness, vulnerability, and processing, all of which take a lot of energy. You have to be honest with what you need, and you have to be honest with what you're willing to give.

If you are not in a relationship but just enjoy sex with different partners, it's still important to have some clarity about how you define being safe. This is different for everyone. We also have to be honest about our reasons for engaging in this kind of practice. Does it stem from sexual trauma or sexual addiction? No matter what choices you're making in terms of expressing your sexuality, you have to be honest. You have to ask yourself why you're doing what you're doing. Sex can then become a profound way that we shape our character and our moral selves. My sexual relationships have helped me develop a sense of what's healthy for me, how I have valued or devalued myself, and how I can make choices to protect and value myself and others.

Sex positivity is important too. The United States where I grew up is not a sex positive nation at all, even though sex is everywhere. We're sex saturated but not sex positive. That comes from a lot of sexual trauma and a lot of body shame. The dharma has helped me to critically examine my own body shame, as well as my shame around sexuality, and to do some healing work around both. And of course this led me to teaching and providing resources for other people doing the same work for themselves.

Sometimes I can be judgmental toward people who aren't thinking about non-monogamous relationships. It is easy for me to dismiss people by saying something like, "Well, you've just been colonized by the white supremacist, hetero, able-bodied, monogamous culture, and you need to break out of that." That's judgmental. Instead, as a spiritual teacher, I try to help people make the best decisions for them at this point in time. I want those decisions to be supportive of their ethics, and I hope that their ethic is about getting free. I can't tell you what to do, or what choices to make, but I can help you develop a meditation practice, an awareness practice, and through it you will begin to discern what's right for you.

## —— SERMON ON MY SEXUAL BODY ——

To offer voice to this experience of my sexual body, I must give voice to memories and experiences that may not be ready to be revealed, but I reveal them in order to facilitate further liberation for all beings. As I do this, I am calling on my ancestors to hold me, and I am calling on the earth under me to remain sturdy. I am calling on the love of any being that has loved me and continues to love me. May I be caught as I fall.

I identify as a queer man who practices non-monogamy. However, that's a long way from where I started. I grew up in the Southern United States, north of Atlanta, Georgia, in a small community called Rome, Georgia. I grew up in a very religious community. My mother was and is a minister. My grandfather was a minister, so I grew up in church. I grew up, particularly, in the Black Church. And that's important to point out. Because I, in reflection, noticed growing up that I was taught to be in relationship to my body in a very different way than my white friends.

I grew up as a Black person who descends from slaves. So, the institution of slavery was this institution that robbed Black people of agency over their bodies. And that was a kind of trauma that was passed from generation to generation as a disembodiment.

So, when I was growing up in my community in the church, one of the things that kept being reinforced was that I had no right to my body, that my body was still in the possession of others, particularly white people. And that was communicated through the ways in which we were taught to make white people comfortable, to always accommodate white folks around us. I was trained not to do anything to upset them, because the consequences would be violence. And whatever I did with my body, it was something that I had to get permission for. Maybe it was permission from my family, but also, I had to be very sensitive to how white people considered and felt about the use of my body.

And so, there were so many things that I saw growing up that came from this kind of disembodiment. And one of the things, particularly in my community, was the presence of certain medical conditions such as high cholesterol, hypertension, heart disease, and diabetes. There was also a high pregnancy rate among young women. There was this kind of fear of the medical establishment, and also a fear of the mental health services.

And again, all this was kind of based back in slavery, where slaves were abused by doctors and researchers. There were experiments run on slaves that gave rise to modern fields of medicine that many people benefit from. There were early experiments run on slave women that gave rise to modern gynecology. There was the Tuskegee experiment that began in the 1930s and ran through the 1970s. There arose a really legitimate fear of anything that had to do with our bodies, checking in on our bodies, or taking care of our bodies. I inherited a lot of fear of my body.

I don't ever remember getting any formal training or advice around my sexuality. Sex was something that had no language for me. I learned that sex was something that we shouldn't be thinking about, when in fact, so many people were engaging in sexual relationships. In church, I felt I was expected to ignore my growing attraction to experience pleasure with other bodies, and I was especially encouraged by the silence of my community to ignore my growing appetite to experience the bodies of other boys like me.

In school, it wasn't any better. We really weren't taught to be in a healthy relationship with our bodies. Sex Ed was more of a scare tactic to keep us from having sex. The dominant message was to save ourselves, to preserve ourselves until marriage, and marriage was the time in which we were allowed to engage sexually.

Of course, that message was a double standard because, though we didn't talk about it, I discovered that many of my male friends were sexually active and it seemed to be okay, whereas young women around me were actually told to be celibate and abstain from sex until they were married and that their celibacy was an expression of their purity, which would be offered one day to men. And so, there are a lot of contradictions and ambiguities around our relationship to the body.

As I moved into my later adolescence, I was scared to death of my sexuality. And what made it even more intense was this recognition that I was gay and attracted to other boys. And that really complicated everything, particularly my relationship to religion and to my faith. Mostly, I just felt as if this was something that I would definitely have to struggle with my whole life if I chose to remain as a Christian within the church.

As I entered into my young adult years, I went off to college. There I started pulling away from church, which was fantastic, because finally I could engage in the brunch culture on Sunday mornings, which was lovely and something I enjoy to this day. (It could be argued that Sunday brunch is a natural habitat for me!) But that distance I had from church actually gave me a lot of space to start working through a lot of emotional issues I had around sexuality.

I remember one evening I was sitting with two women who would become good friends of mine, and they were fabulous and fierce. They would be like many straight-identified women I would later come to befriend who were deeply loyal to their gay and queer friends. One evening we were sitting in a public lounge, and just kind of watching other students walk past. And I saw this guy that I found very attractive. Before I knew it, I was saying something about how hot he was.

And then, as that phrase slipped out of my mouth, I froze, because I had never in my life articulated my desire for another man out loud, particularly in front of other people. There was so much terror that built up, and I felt so much shame. And the shame that I felt was this fear of being found out and being told to go away.

I was just really afraid that my two friends would look at me and think I was out of control and would feel embarrassed and attempt to shame me back into silence. But one of them looked at me and could see the struggle that I was going through, and the fear and the terror that I was experiencing. And she looked at me, and she said, "No, Rod. It's okay. You can say whatever you want. You can be yourself around us. It's okay." I remember in that second, something hard and crusty around my heart center began to melt. I suddenly began to experience a glimpse of what it would be like to feel comfortable in this body.

And what I learned from that experience was that part of our liberation is first, articulating the things that we have been taught never to articulate. Second, I recognized the importance of being in relationship with people who can love and nurture these parts of ourselves that need loving and nurturing. To this day, they're benefactors for me, and their example is something that I credit being a foundation of how I was able to continue to do the work of being out and proud.

So that began this whole intense, beautiful path during my time in college, where I moved from being really closeted and shut down to being very open and public. By the end of my college years, I was an activist and an organizer around LGBTQ+ issues, including identity and education and HIV and AIDS education and awareness.

And what was also important was how I began to distance myself even more from the label of Christian. Not only was I not going to church regularly, I was actually not even identifying as a Christian, because I felt that, basically, God was cruel, and I wanted to be a part of a practice, and a path, that was about love, and not shaming, marginalizing, or criticizing. And so I broke up with God. I felt also that God had already broken up with me. So, I felt as if I was simply having the courage to acknowledge something that was already happening. And that started giving me so much space to be myself.

And one of the things that I committed to in that moment was a path of service, activism, and advocacy to follow my heart, to practice kindness, to practice compassion, and to try to help as many people in this life as possible.

And after that, I didn't give a shit if I was going to "go to hell" because I was gay—it didn't make sense anymore. This helped me enter into this more loving, nurturing experience of who I was.

After graduation, I moved to Boston and lived as a completely out person. It was healing to be in a space where I wasn't fighting to get space to be gay. I had to start working with and negotiating my struggle around body shame. This shame came from being a larger-bodied person and feeling deeply unattractive and ugly, not sexy, and not erotic. And confronting that suffering within myself was really challenging.

I also began to notice these experiences of vicarious trauma that I carried from the AIDS epidemic. Back then, I carried a lot of deep, intense fear of HIV and AIDS, and I had inherited that as a kind of transhistorical trauma from other gay men around me and the gay community as a whole, and from the media. I was dealing with a fear of being infected on top of feelings of being deeply unattractive.

So now I had this amazing freedom to be in the world and to be myself, but all of a sudden, I had to deal with these heavy realities. And again, when I speak of liberation, I speak of spaciousness, and I had no space back then. But what I did have was a really important community of friends who believed in me and who loved me. I had audacity, I had a will, I had a work ethic, and I just refused to be beaten by anything. That really began my path into dharma.

That eventually led into learning how to meditate from a healer I knew in my community, and that meditation practice led into the formal study of Buddhism, and particularly Tibetan Buddhism. And that was something that was almost preordained. When I came into dharma practice officially, it was as if the red carpet rolled out, as if I'd always been a Buddhist.

And then, at that moment of starting to practice Buddhism, I acknowledged that I had always been a Buddhist. And that began this wide opening that led me into working with my experience of depression head-on. Not just through meditation, but through a whole spectrum of modalities, including nutrition and exercise, and limiting the kinds of violence and toxic material that I was on and absorbing in my life, and I was able to do that work without having to go on medication or anything like that. Which, again—I say this over and over again—we all have to figure out what our modalities are. And sometimes that does include medication. And so, we have to figure out what that looks like for ourselves.

I didn't have to start medication, but other people have to. And if you do take medications, that still makes you a good person, still makes you a meditator, still makes you a mindfulness practitioner, and still makes you a Buddhist. What that means ultimately is that you're wise, and you're doing something that's skillful to take care of yourself. This is really important to understand.

But what my early Buddhist practice introduced me to was the practice of love and kindness, of mettā, of self-compassion and self-love. And that was the beginning of this intense path to liberation. Actually, it was the beginning of something that super fueled me along this path, to do the work of turning back and looking at all the self-hate, and how the self-hate manifested itself through fear of my body, through fear of disease, through fear of sexuality. I began to look directly at these fears, but I began to do so being deeply wrapped in love.

I had made the commitment to enter into a three-year retreat at my monastery, and that was something that brought me into a deeper relationship with tantric practice. And the part of tantric practice that was so important for me was that of deity practice. And so, deity practice is the work of becoming the deity, imagining that you are the deity. And then, imagining that you are the deity, you actually begin to disrupt the ways in which you fixate on ego in general, as well as certain parts of ego.

And so as I was engaging in this tantric deity practice, I began to disrupt all the ways in which I was clinging to my identities. I was clinging to my disembodiment, I was clinging to that fear, I was clinging to my fear of HIV and AIDS, and so forth. And that clinging began to dissolve bit by bit. And as it dissolved, the sense of space began to open up in my experience. That space was actually where I began to experience the sense of happiness or contentment. And that contentment began to hold all these experiences that have been a source of suffering for me in my life.

However, not all of that stuff went away, but I had this increased space. And the space, it had always been there, but now I could see it and rest within that space, and I could actually use the space to hold everything. And so, everything became less intense, my body became less intense, my fear of disease became less intense, my fear of the world became less intense, and I began to relax. And I began to open up, and I began to rest in this energy of self-love, self-kindness, and self-compassion.

After I completed my three-year retreat, coming back into the world felt like a new beginning, but I still had a lot of work to do. So in my post-retreat practice, it was really about continuing to confront the ways in which I was deeply wounded by sexuality, the ways in which I was still kind of disembodied in certain parts of my life. But it was coming into contact also with the development of a true liberatory sex positivity.

And for me, it was so important to understand the value and the importance of sexual relationships, but also, to recognize the potential reality of harm and abuse within sexuality. When I say I am sex positive, I mean that we have a right to do with our bodies what we will, but we also have an ethical responsibility to limit the harm, to decrease harm that we do against ourselves and others. Being sex positive for me means that I am a practitioner and a believer of authentic, enthusiastic consent. I am also a believer that we have a right to define for ourselves what safety means, and to be clear and to be direct about that for ourselves.

Sex positivity also means that I am always checking in around my intentionality, and my reasons for engaging in sexual relationships, and that I commit to an ethic of reducing harm, which specifically means for me that I am committed to the expression of compassion, love, and respect in any sexual relationship that I find myself in, be it a hookup or a long-term relationship.

Working with trauma and imagining freedom from trauma mean that I also have to even love the trauma. One of the things that I practice is loving even what is unlovable. When I say I'm loving my trauma, it means that I am accepting my experiences of trauma and then allowing it to be there, accepting it, giving it space. And by giving it space, I have room to relate to the trauma in different ways and to engage in methods of releasing that trauma. This has been really important for me.

And of course, part of my path around freedom from sex and body shame has also meant teaching and talking about sexuality, body, and gender as much as I can. And as a teacher and as a clergyperson, this is incredibly important. As clergy, I know that I can be an agent of intense shame and emotional violence for people. I am really sensitive to that. And so, I want to give voice to the things that many teachers and ministers choose not to talk about. I do this because I wish my spiritual leaders would have talked more about this when I was lost and suffering the most. And so, when I work with people now on the path, so much of my work is modeling: it's being myself. I commit to an ethic of reducing harm.

And in my relationships as a teacher, I have an ethical responsibility never to be in relationship with other students or to use my position as a teacher to create sexual relationships. And I do that by, first and foremost, having relationships outside of my spiritual communities, outside of sanghas. What that means is that not all of my friends are Buddhists. I hang out with other people, some of whom don't give a shit about Buddhism, which I love. I think it's important, particularly for teachers, to have an identity outside of dharma where they can have their needs met.

I think for me, what has been most difficult in the past is believing that all of my needs will be met by the sangha and by the spiritual community. That can lead me down a path where harm can potentially happen, because there are things that I need to engage in that are not appropriate to do within the sangha. And because of my positionality as a person of authority who holds power within the sangha, it becomes easier for me to get certain needs met, even if it is not appropriate, even if it's not ethical.

So first and foremost, I have the responsibility to make sure that I am not perpetuating harm in the sangha, and with my students, by asking for certain needs to be met. That is not appropriate. So, I have relationships outside of sangha. I have friends who aren't practitioners. I have sexual relationships with other partners who are not within Buddhist sanghas that are based upon consent, and openness, and communication and dialogue. And that's really important.

And I can bring my ethic of nonharm into any sexual relationship, especially if I'm clear and aware, and practicing from a place of wanting someone to experience the reduction of harm as much as I want to experience a reduction of harm. This is how sex positivity shapes my life. My ethics around sex positivity are an expression of freedom for me.

I try to be as open as possible. I really encourage folks within various communities to be in dialogue with me. I am in dialogue with folks who are Buddhist practitioners as well as members of transgressive sexual communities, kink communities, BDSM communities, group sex communities, and fetish communities. I know practitioners who engage in various forms of sex work as well. I think that there is a narrative that people are not engaged in certain things when, in fact, there are vibrant, dynamic communities of practitioners who are very much invested in other sexual practices, and who are wanting and needing dharma and Buddhism to help them to do the things that they love in a way that reduces harm and violence. I think that is within the project of a contemporary radical Buddhism and dharma.

And another point of liberation that I will mention last is the path of pleasure, and that Tantric Buddhism has been important for me in developing an open relationship to pleasure and how to experience a liberatory pleasure that I am not attaching to, but allowing it to be in my experience. A spacious experience of pleasure reflects our true selves back to us. I believe that everything must be loved, including pleasure and including suffering. It's easier to love pleasure over suffering.

Again, what I mean by love is that we accept everything, and by accepting it, we find that we don't have to be so fixated on things, that we can allow things to be there. And for me, pleasure is something that I can be easily fixated on. But when I love my pleasure, that means I simply allow it to be there, I accept it, I get a space to be there, and it is within the space that I'm able to relax and to hold the experience of pleasure. And that experience of pleasure can lead me into deeper expressions of consciousness. And that leads us, essentially, into our true natures. So, I don't have to get stuck with a reproduction of pleasure as something that I'm using to avoid discomfort. But I use it as a step into experiencing who and what I really am.

# 11

# APOCALYPSE RIGHT NOW

A DIALOGUE WITH Ravi Mishra for the Awaken app

**Ravi Mishra:** *Let's talk about the apocalypse.*

**Lama Rod Owens:** *People ask me all the time about what's going on. And I really think about how a lot of major religions and spiritual paths have literature and prophecy that helps us to understand this kind of period that we're entering into. In Christian theology we call it the apocalypse; in Hindu tantric traditions we call it Kali Yuga; and Buddhism, we refer to it as the Dark Ages, the ages where the teachings of the Buddha begin to die away. When we think about the apocalypse, and particularly also with Kali Yuga, they mean a breaking away, an unveiling, where on one hand truth is being unveiled, but on the other hand, we're facing the limitations of our being able to handle the truth. It reminds me of that famous line from* A Few Good Men: *"You can't handle the truth." I think that's exactly what we're saying: that a lot of people can't handle the truth. This is the truth. Like this is how we have been living together, this is how we've covered up so many issues, and now we can't cover them up anymore. And that* *everything that we've not done in the past is actually calling us to task now, be it social issues, be it the environment.*

**RM:** *Do you want to dive into a few of these specific areas where you see this idea of the apocalypse playing out?*

**LRO:** *Obviously for me it's politics. I think the election of Donald Trump is really a good sign of that falling apart! It's the entrance of chaos and the dismantling, the disruption of things that we felt were safe and stable. And we're seeing that it's actually not that stable, because what we understand to be the American government was in truth built with a lot of corruption, a lot of instability. And now we're seeing that up close and personal. We see that with climate change as well. We see that with the increase of a lot of natural disasters around the world, the increase of temperatures in the climate. We see it with the extinction of a lot of species of plants and animals, the melting of the polar ice caps, the overcrowding of certain places around the world, environmental pollution. I've been revisiting the work of Octavia Butler, and particularly her two novels the* Parable of the Sower *and the* Parable of the Talents. *They speak so directly to what we're experiencing right now. In the books, Butler explores the end of capitalism. So she looks at the breakdown of the economy, the breakdown of politics, the breakdown of social relationships. She has a Trump-like character in the book who has the phrase "Make America Great Again." She describes how people rise up around this man. And she talks about what it's like for people having to experience the rise of a right-wing fundamental movement and how that puts so many people in jeopardy. And we see that really clearly happening now. And so that's really scary.*

*When we look at the Buddhist framework of the Dark Ages, what we understand is that this is a time where our emotions get seemingly very strong. Our emotions actually begin to create a reality for us, particularly what we call the inflictive emotions, the emotions of anger and lust, desire, hatred. So those get really strong, and we start indulging in them. So hate becomes this way that we mediate relationships with one another, that drives our unwillingness to communicate, and to create boundaries with one another. It is an intense othering. Within our own experience, we're experiencing such intense suffering, and that suffering is just a very general blanket term for us to describe deep discomfort.*

*And we experience discomfort in a myriad of ways, from fear and hate to anger, despair, sadness, depression, terror. It's different for all of us. And so we lose the ability to hold a space for that suffering and therefore our anger and our rage, which helps us to identify that we are hurt—that anger and that same rage actually just becomes energy that we respond to habitually and that starts creating harm and violence for ourselves and for others. To work with what's happening for us in this moment, we have to actually return back to our deep hurts.*

*The Satipatthāna is important to mention here. The Satipatthāna, or the four foundations of mindfulness, is the discourse that the Buddha offered to introduce a basic way of developing awareness and attention. When you look at the discourse, you're able to actually practice these strategies of paying attention to what's arising in our natures, what's arising in our emotions, what's arising in our bodies, and what's arising in our minds. We're losing that basic capacity to be with what arises, and we're beginning to be very afraid of our emotional body and our emotional reality. The more we are afraid of our emotional reality, the more disembodied we get; the more disembodied we get, the more out of control that we are. So we get lost in the anger and the lust and the desire, and we begin to do things that are really super indulgent, and that begins to take a certain toll on our bodies and our minds and in our relationships. That aspect actually ties directly back into Kali Yuga, where people begin to deeply engage in these emotions, these mental experiences, at our detriment. It begins to be okay to just engage in any kind of lust-based activity that you want without any concerns for the consequences. We begin to objectify others. We begin to lose empathy with one another. Empathy begins with ourselves. It begins with touching into our basic experience, which gives us insight to touch into the experiences of others. So when all of that begins to break down, you begin to experience chaos.*

RM: *When it comes to feeling these strong emotions, how do we know when to indulge and when not to indulge?*

LRO: *We have to start with a basic acceptance of saying, Okay, yeah, things are out of control. You take a breath, return to the breath, return to the body, and begin to watch and to look at everything happening for you internally. And once you have some clarity about what's happening in your own experience, then you can move back into the world in a way that's much more stable and much more sustainable.*

*But even if you do that, that doesn't mean you're going to save anyone. It doesn't mean you're gonna stop anything, and that's the part of the apocalypse, too: that everyone isn't going to survive. With all this apocalypse talk, people think it's about the end of the world. It's not about the end of the world—it's about the end of a way of thinking, a way of believing, and that's painful to let go of. That's where the fire and brimstone and the end of the world metaphor comes from. It's from that basic tension and fear of letting go of the ways that we used to be, in order to make space for what's happening next. What's happening next is terrifying, because we don't know what that is. It's a mystery. We know we're comfortable with our silliness and our messiness right now. But when you ask us to let that go and to think about a new way of being, that's really terrifying. And it's particularly terrifying to the sense of ego, because the ego survives through stability, through hegemony, through comfort. Everything has to be in its place for the ego to survive. The ego doesn't know how to deal with the mystery. Also, we have this American ego: This is who we are as America. That's not who we are. How do we actually create the space to redefine who and what we are?*

*Our work together is trying to help us understand that what we do for ourselves, we're ethically obligated to do for others. That love and compassion is bullshit unless we actually do something to benefit the lives of others. So we're not talking about just going off and sitting in the corner and doing loving-kindness practice or compassion practice for yourself and just trying to feel really good.*

**RM:** *I'm curious to get your sense of the different areas of power that we're reclaiming, or we're learning to define differently.*

**LRO:** *We're learning how to actually develop an experience of who we are, and then to tell the world who we are. And I see so many people who actually don't have that basic agency. For example, I'm a cisgender man, and so patriarchy has told me who I am, and I'm not cool with that. In order to dismantle patriarchy as a cisgender man, I have to take that power of defining away from the patriarchy and to redefine who and what I am in a way that is actually less violent and less harming for myself and others. It's like these systems are on autopilot, and we just kind of hop in the car and just go wherever.*

**RM:** *I guess one question I have is: How do we get out of this situation individually and collectively? And you talked about* *some practices, but coming back to the big view of what's going on in the world.*

**LRO:** *I think we're goners! But the brilliant thing about these prophecies of apocalypse is that it won't last forever. This is just a stage that we're going through, and as the Bible says, there is a season for everything. So this is our season to wallow through the darkness. And it's hard to do that. It's supposed to be challenging. Everyone isn't supposed to survive. There is a basic reality that we need to accept. And that basic reality is that not all of us are gonna get to heaven. I don't know of any spiritual or religious tradition that says everyone's gonna end up in the same place. And so you have to . . . accept that. But in accepting that, you're also cultivating what's called* bodhicitta, *which is an aspiration to free beings from the suffering as we ourselves are doing the work to get free. So that doesn't mean we're gonna free everyone. It means that we're trying to take responsibility for the people around us. And if those people that we're responsible for make a commitment to be responsible for other people that are around them, that creates this chain reaction. I think it's really beautiful and powerful to think about. So I don't have to get lost in this anxiety about how am I gonna free countless beings. You become a catalyst for great change around you because you did the work of woke.*

**RM:** *Any last thoughts on the apocalypse?*

**LRO:** *Well, I don't think the apocalypse is a negative word or a negative idea. I think it's really exciting, because it's the breaking away of shit that we don't need.*

*I think what we're seeing is so many people getting it now. People are asking these questions they never asked before. So many people have a vocabulary to talk about social injustice that they never had. So many people are really uncomfortable in a way that they've never been uncomfortable before. And I think that's really amazing to see. But also what's really despairing is all the people who still don't give a shit. Which is a lot of people. There's that cognitive dissociation that's arising for us where it's like, no matter what people see, no matter what people understand or witness, they'll always revert back to their uninformed belief systems.*

*That's the physical violence that will arise when that tension becomes too much between those who believe and those who don't believe.*

**RM:** *And to vision into the post-apocalypse and vision into what might define a world in which all beings, or as many as we can imagine, are able to create a society and a world that works for everyone or that creates radically less harm: What does that look like for you?*

**LRO:** *I think it looks like an end to capitalism. And it takes us having to dream and imagine a different way of being in a relationship to one another that isn't mediated by a system of valuing and devaluing. And that takes turning attention back to ourselves and saying, Okay, how do I develop a sense of self-love for myself, because that's the key for me, this sense of self-love, a sense that I am enough, that I deserve to be happy, that I deserve to be safe. How do we dream past this sense of depravity, this sense that I don't have enough, the sense that I have to keep consuming over and over again as much as possible, because I keep being told that I'm not enough, that I don't have enough. Until we do the practices to take care of that, we're going to rely on these external systems to give us our sense of value.*

**RM:** *I love the way that's framed. Until we do that work, we will rely on these systems to do that work for us. And that reliance, that addiction, is one of the deep causes of suffering.*

**LRO:** *I think about mass incarceration. It's like, okay, we're just gonna rely on prisons to do this work for us. Instead of us establishing for ourselves a sense of restorative justice, which means that we actually have to take responsibility for love, compassion, forgiveness, and dialogue with people that hurt us. Because we can't do that work for ourselves, and because there aren't people supporting us to do that work, then we're just gonna push everything into the criminal justice system, which is not working at all. Again, a system isn't going to fix something about us that we need to handle for ourselves.*

**RM:** *Right. What kinds of practices do you think this moment, this recognition of the apocalypse, call for? I know you mentioned a few of them. Are there others that are coming to mind or that you want to emphasize?*

**LRO:** *It's so important that we learn to relate to discomfort instead of always bypassing it. There is trauma in our experiences which is really tough to sit with, but we can learn how to develop a more open relationship to that trauma by developing the muscle or the strength to learn how to be with it more over time. Of course loving-kindness, or mettā practice, which is a way of wishing ourselves this deep sense of well-being, is a basic practice. Mindfulness is also a really basic practice because it helps us to see what we habitually avoid and to learn how to get spacious around what we continually label as uncomfortable. And then more practical things like needing to surround ourselves with people who help us remember our goodness in the world—that we're not what the world tells us we are. We need to be with people who are advocates for our self-care and our self-love, advocates for reducing violence for ourselves and reducing violence in our relationships to others.*

*For me in my practice, I do work with ancestors, so I was remembering my ancestors, remembering the positive qualities that have passed from generation to generation in my family, deeply trying to embody these characteristics of resiliency, community focus, and self-care. We need rituals of self-care and self-preservation. Many of us don't actually know how to take care of ourselves. We know how to be super self-indulgent. But self-care (and in the way that Audre Lorde speaks of self-care in terms of self-preservation) is about supporting ourselves and doing the work to eventually lean back into engagement with others around us. Self-indulgence is self-isolating. The social justice understanding of self-care is about needing to sustain ourselves in order to sustain our communities. So self-indulgence and self-preservation may actually look very much alike. They may actually be the same practices. But it's the intention of those practices which differentiates them.*

*So I love to go to the nail spa. I love to get my nails done. I love a little shopping. I lean a little into capitalism. That's very complex, but I do that because I know that it provides a way for me to have space in order to come back and do the work of creating just communities.*

# 12

# HEARTBROKENNESS

In truth, we have to integrate our wounds into our understanding of who we are and what we are really capable of
so that we can be whole human beings. Only from there can
we begin the process of healing the brokenness, the broken-
heartedness within ourselves that is then the foundation for
beginning to heal that in our larger society.

—REV. ANGEL KYODO WILLIAMS, *Radical Dharma*

Am I capable of enduring suffering, facing martyrdom? And
   alone?
Again the long loneliness to be faced.

—DOROTHY DAY

You think your pain and your heartbreak are unprecedented in
the history of the world, but then you read.

—JAMES BALDWIN

TO BEGIN WITH, I have to confess that I didn't want to write
this chapter. I didn't want to write my suffering into words,
because to do so means that I have to acknowledge it. I will

give them much more of a life than they already have, and can I really afford more suffering? Can anyone? A voice in my head keeps telling me that I am the teacher, and all that is a trap for me. None of this is safe. This is not appropriate.

Then I think that this lack of acknowledging my suffering is how systems of power and abuse are maintained. There is great violence when we avoid our pain, because we become trapped in reacting to it as we target others as the reason for our hurt. This is why our anger and rage are dangerous. It is not the experience of anger itself, but our intense reaction to it. The reaction is also the avoidance of experiencing the experience of anger. But am I avoiding my pain? I really don't want to write this.

My anger feels like a warm blanket keeping me secure and comfortable above the ice-coldness of the pain below it. My anger has been so helpful. It has been like a big brother, keeping me from stepping into this territory of discomfort, while at the same time taunting me to react and do something stupid.

These are some of the questions that haunt me: When do I get good enough so that my despair goes away? Who will love me enough when they see who I really am? And then what of these hours sitting with the shadows and memories that are the hardest to stay present with? Who will hold me? Why do I keep running everyone away? Will I survive another night alone? Will I suffocate in the silence that sometimes feels violent for me? Are there any more uses to tears than just crying?

How will I choose to avoid this breaking heart tonight? Another Beyoncé song? A drink? A few swipes ön Grindr? Or do I wander the streets like I used to when the depression was the hardest, in the middle of the night, wanting the shadows to swallow me whole?

Despair is hopelessness. Often, in my tradition of Buddhism, we don't like to talk about hope, as it is something that takes us out of the present moment into the future. But for those of us who survive present moments of deep pain and despair, our hope is the only thing we have. To look forward to a future that is a little less dark, a little more happy and liberated, to dream new ways of being not what I am now. This is possible because of the tenet of impermanence. Everything is shifting and turning around and bouncing here and there; everything is movement, shuffling, a dynamic jostling base beat pounding out the vibrancy of breath and life.

## —— HOW DO I TALK ABOUT SUFFERING? ——

Pain. Suffering. Woundedness. Hurt. Trauma. Heartbrokenness. These are all words that I have used interchangeably to talk about my deep discomfort as I move through the world in this body. I want to offer clearer insights into how I use these terms.

When I say pain, I am speaking of either the bare sensation of physical pain that I have an aversion to or emotional discomfort I don't want to deal with. Pain is not a choice. I will experience plenty of things that will be uncomfortable. For example, when I have a headache, there is the basic sensation of the pain of the headache. It is unpleasant, and I would rather not have to deal with it. When I say unpleasant, I mean that it disturbs my attempts to feel at ease or to be chill. My chilling is the expression of my fixation on pleasant experiences. The headache disrupts my chill, and therefore I am unhappy.

So when I am unhappy, I want to be happy again and get caught up in trying to avoid the headache; I start using all kinds of strategies to distance myself from the painful sensation. I may take some medicine or try other ways to relieve the pain, but these methods may take some time to start working. Until then, anger becomes one of these strategies. Anger arises from the tension we feel needing to end this painful sensation but not actually being able to get away from it. We get wrapped up in the anger, and it feels as if we are avoiding the pain. In a way, we are; but we have to understand that the anger is being fueled by the tension we experience trying to get away from the pain itself. Therefore, I actually begin to feel much worse than I did just having the headache. This new experience is called suffering. Suffering is the mental layer of aversion on top of the physical and emotional pain.

So maybe the headache eventually goes away. I am still left with the memories of the headache, as well as my relationship to those memories. I will dread getting a headache again, but know that this is inevitable. More than likely, I will experience a suffering of suffering where I will dread the suffering that I will experience because of the pain of a future headache. Without even having the headache in the moment, I will still feel bad thinking about the future headache. This fixation on the possibility of future suffering is called anxiety. This is an example of being wounded or hurt. Woundedness and hurt are very similar words in my practice. What I mean to convey is a sense that because of the things that I have had to deal with that have caused the pain I have experienced, the suffering that has come with that feels as if it has dug something out of me. It feels as if there is a scar left. This scarring is the woundedness or the hurt.

## HEARTBROKENNESS

In my experience, there is also an experience of aching, which is a vibrant, active kind of energy that seems like the life force of my suffering. The aching feels slow, heavy, gray/bluish, the color of an autumn storm. However, inside this aching is something that is hard for me to explain. I call it heartbrokenness.

I define heartbrokenness as a disembodied expression of a severe disappointment that longs to be cared for. In this understanding of being heartbroken, I am not talking about a sorrow or sadness I feel due to a breakup or a disappointment of some kind. I am speaking about something that feels much more ancient and primordial. I am speaking of how both my body and my mind are the sum of suffering passed down to me from my ancestors and family, which is compounded by my own suffering in this world. This compounded suffering has resulted in being displaced from my body, because I have never had the tools to metabolize this suffering. What I long for and need above all is to return to my body, to my suffering, to take care of it, as I need to be taken care of to do this work. Outside of my body, I experience a severe disappointment that is hard for me to name or see.

I am so disappointed. Perhaps this is the emotion that has always been present for me. I have never not been disappointed. I remember growing up in church and being taught that this world is not our home, that this world that holds millions of Black bodies is cruel. We were taught that the world didn't want us. We were taught that we were like the ancient Hebrews, the Children of Israel, who wandered in the desert for forty years until they were allowed to enter into the promised land. God was testing them. What I was taught in church was that the whole world is the desert and that we would be tested our whole lives. Heaven is our promised land. By my late teens, I couldn't stand this bullshit anymore. I deserve to have my promised land now.

Anger permeates this heartbrokenness in the form of resentment. I ask myself: Why do I have to deal with this? I left the church resentful, asking myself if this was the best we could do. Why did it seem like white people got to enjoy their heaven right here and now? As I sat in church listening to how we must endure this life to reach heaven, I slowly began to understand that I was being taught to let white people have their way. I couldn't help but feel as if our religion was conditioning us to be better victims of systematic racism. And it seemed as if there were white people who were only staunch supporters of Black church communities because of how the Black Church was teaching us to internalize racism. This created a dilemma for me. On one hand the Black Church was how I and many other Black folks survived systematic racism, while on the other hand I began to feel that Black Christianity was a tool offered to Black folks to keep us from confronting the totality of white supremacy.

## Love and Heartbrokenness

We must learn to love even our broken hearts. That doesn't mean that we celebrate or are happy with the experience of discomfort. It means that we have to accept the reality of our broken hearts. We have to love and accept our pain in order to set it free. Growing up in the Black community, one of the things we are taught is that our lives will be hard. Systematic racism has created the conditions for us to struggle with senseless violence. For me, it was the conditioning for me to self-identify with the suffering of being Black, until I came to believe that being Black meant suffering. One of the things that led me onto the contemplative path was the fatigue of being so heavily associated with suffering. This association was an expression of deep grasping to suffering. I needed to break this identification, because I knew that I was not going to survive it. I began to break this identification by loving the suffering and the Blackness, and in doing so I found myself relaxing and tuning in to the spaciousness around the discomfort. That space helped me to relax and let go of the identification and offered me the agency to redefine what Blackness could be.

## Leading with an Open Heart

I have had to learn to invite my broken heart to dine with me at the table. It is meaningless to run now. My broken heart is not a judgment or a crime. It is a detailed record of how I have tried to meet the violence of the world with as much openness as possible. It is a testament to how I have succeeded and failed at this attempt, and it is an indicator that I will continue moving on.

I must learn to lead with my heart. But when I do that, I am always hurt.

For some time now, I have known that I have been misunderstanding love. Love has been a word used to distance myself from my own heart. Love has been a word that has helped me to bypass the work of allowing myself to notice that my heart is broken.

I turn my mind to my breath and notice I am inhaling in the present and breathing into the future. As long as I am not obliviated on the spot, each in breath will end in an out breath. I may or may not be conscious of it or be there to meet this beautiful out breath, but it will be there and it is something I can rejoice in. Somehow my teachers and ancestors have collaborated to bless me with the celebration of my breath.

All this seems small, but to notice this breath is to remind myself that my teachers and ancestors are breathing with me. And when I am crying, they are crying with me. It only takes the birth of one thought to call my people to me. It only takes a split second of remembering.

And who will see me and love me for who I am, not for who I seem to be in public or on social media? So many people love the lama, but who really loves Rod? Who would be attracted to Rod without the lama? Who will see me as a sometimes flailing person trying to overcome their violence to themselves and others? Who will let me be human, and who will let me be human while realizing that it is within my relationship to my own humanity that I can best show you how to be free? Who will hold me at night?

My emotional pain is important because it is mine, and I need it to tell me how to heal.

———————— DEPRESSION AND ANGER ————————

I have been interested in the relationship between depression and anger for a while. I connected to the experience of depression several months before my twenty-fifth birthday. I had been in therapy the year before, not for depression, but for support around anxiety. For me, anxiety was an expression of fear and worry about the future. My life as a poor Black activist was very worrisome! However, I did not identify as being depressed.

It wasn't until the following year when I returned from a few months of traveling abroad that I noticed that I could not quite get out of bed as much as I wanted to. I noticed that the joy and happiness that I would experience were completely depleted. Looking back at that time, it was as if life had faded into shades of gray. I self-isolated more and had no motivation to do anything besides stay in my bedroom listening to sad songs. At some point, my mind turned to a painful realization: I was depressed. Fuck!

I believe that my depression originated from a few things, including biochemical and energetic imbalances. I think it also had something to do with anger. Someone at the time had spoken of how anger directed inward facilitated depression. My inability to be in an open, expressive relationship with my anger, and the lack of being in touch with the hurt underneath the anger, frustrated and blocked the energy of anger. When anger is blocked, it stays put in our minds and bodies, making it difficult to feel much emotional fluidity, and that can start to impact our sense of self-worth.

Depression is more than just being sad—it is an extended period of feeling depleted, isolated, worn down, and distant from a sense of happiness, patience, and contentment. When I was growing up, we never talked about depression or any other kind of mental illness that I can remember. There was one man in our community who was always wandering around on the street. Looking back, I think that he was schizophrenic, but we just called him crazy and said he was acting a fool to collect a disability check each month. "Crazy" was the extent of our acknowledgment of variant mental health realities in our community. You were either "in your right mind" or crazy. There was no such thing as being depressed. White people were depressed. We were Black, as if Blackness was an expression of perpetual fatigue and rage. If you were sad, it was only because your Black ass was Black. There was no such thing as mental health therapy. Prayer and endurance were our therapy.

I decided to start therapy because so many people around me were seeing therapists and seemed to really benefit from the work. I lived in Boston at the time, and there were services and programs that made therapy accessible for people like me with very few resources. It was an incredibly hard decision for me. I realized how distrustful I was of therapy. I was afraid of my mental health, because I knew that there was so much woundedness in my experiences, and I felt as if I had no way to work with it without exploring the modalities that I was raised to distrust. This distrust came from how Black folks have been abused and manipulated in the health care system in the United States.

When it came to my family, I found myself much more secretive about therapy than I was about my sexuality. When I started therapy, I was not out to my family, but with the help of my therapist I started the coming out process, first with my mother. Looking back, I could see that being in therapy felt like an admission that I wasn't strong enough to endure. The one thing that I was taught to value the most and to embrace enthusiastically was resiliency. The message seemed to be that resiliency was the cornerstone of Blackness. It was the ability to keep going despite the violence and brutality of systematic racism. Therapy was seen as giving up and letting white people talk you out of the thing that made you Black, that established our sense of belonging in the community. Moreover, because I had left the church by then, I was afraid that my therapy would be read as a sign that I did indeed need the church and that my unstable mental health was due to my rejecting it. I decided to enter into therapy because I wanted to learn how to be resilient and healthy at the same time.

I stayed in therapy for four months. I left therapy because I was leaving the country for a few months and because I felt that the goals of reducing anxiety had been met. That few months actually taught me how to practice a self-inquiry that supported me in addressing my depression and opening the door to contemplative and spiritual practice. I didn't have to just struggle and endure violence and hope that when I died I would go to heaven. I could practice modalities of liberation right here and now that could help me meet and transform systematic violence through wisdom and compassion. That aspiration opened my mind to receiving support from others who taught me to understand my mind, and that was my liberation.

As I reflect on my path with depression, it is so important that I point out that we all must be skillful with how we understand our liberation. My path relied heavily on lifestyle changes, meditation, and other spiritual practices to work with my mental illness. For many folks, medication and other forms of therapy are crucial. We have to figure this out for ourselves. Everyone is different, and so we all must take different paths.

## ———— REFLECTIONS ON NIGGER ————

I was casually chatting with a white guy on one of the hookup apps. We exchanged pictures. Though I was attracted to him, I was not interested in meeting up at the time. He got frustrated and more than likely felt rejected. When I apologized for disappointing him, he texted back, "That's okay. You're nothing but a nigger."

Once I returned back home from a ten-day intensive meditation retreat. One of the possible effects of the experience is a kind of high. I call it a honeymoon period. My heart is open, and I feel inspired and ready to meet the world with compassion and love. I was living in an intentional community. One of the collective projects was running a soup kitchen. I had gotten back the previous evening and had headed down to our kitchen space at the end of our breakfast service. At the main door of the kitchen, I noticed an older white man standing, and I decided to go over to see if he needed anything. I opened the door, and he stood there not seeming to notice me. But he did. He began mumbling something under his breath. I didn't get it initially; but as I paid more attention, the mumbling soon realized itself to be a stream of racial slurs. I remember only two of the slurs: monkey and nigger.

I worked off and on for a few years at a preschool. The population was mostly white three- to five-year-olds. I loved the work because of the direct honesty of the kids. We were in the South. There were two little blond, blue-eyed boys who were brothers. The younger boy was a rambunctious ball of adorable mischievousness and charm, which meant he got away with a lot of shit. One day I found him sitting alone mumbling something under his breath. He was staring at me intently. I moved closer and caught what he was mumbling: nigger.

Once as a teen traveling in London, I was sharing an elevator with a German couple. Standing in front of them, I was casually trying to follow their conversation, as I had studied German a little and found the language interesting. It was no more than a thirty-second ride, but it took only thirty seconds to be called a nigger.

At one point in my life, I believed I was a nigger. I believed I was born a nigger and that my middle name was nigger and that

I would naturally die a nigger. The word was the embodiment of many centuries of pure degradation seething with a trauma that choked my belief in light, joy, and freedom. The word was both the prison and the executioner, both the rope and the strangler.

I never talk about this with other Black people. I never talk about the crippling effect of this word when it is particularly evoked by white people. We never talk about the reality that for many of us, deep down in places we were taught never to go, we believe we are niggers. There aren't many words that have been created that so effectively shut such a large group of people out of the world.

Each time that I was called a nigger, I was forced to face everything that I had been running away from, which was the trauma of being hurt over and over again by a word only created to steal my humanity away. In the absence of my humanity, the rage came to live. To keep white people from finding out that I was angry, I learned to hate myself; and in hating myself, I learned to shame myself, because that was the most efficient way to make sure I kept my anger hidden. Then I began to hate anyone who looked like me, because every Black person only reflected back my basic heartbrokenness. The trauma of believing that I was a nigger meant that I offered the worst to Black folks, because my hurting forced me to offer the best to white people, those who hurt me the most, believing that my best would somehow disrupt their violence. This was the heartbrokenness that my meditation practice was kind enough to help me understand. This is ultimately the secret that I needed to reveal, first to myself, and then to other Black folks.

Nor am I a fan of how Black folks have attempted to reclaim nigger as an endearment or a moniker for one another in the form of nigga. While I do believe in the power and necessity of reclaiming and purifying language, especially terms that were once used to degrade and shame, I also believe that the best way to neutralize the violence of certain terms is by getting rid of the terms altogether. Nigga can be reclaimed only when we stop believing that we are niggers in the way that white supremacist culture uses and maintains the term to suppress our humanity. I remember as early as the late '90s hearing the phrase "my nigga." It always bothered me, because my reaction was always that I was no one's nigga. I am not convinced that when we call each other nigga as an endearment we are not subtly weaponizing our trauma and calling it a ritual of affection or community belonging. Certainly when we use the term out of anger, we are rehearsing and weaponizing our trauma against one another. No matter how it is used, the term is violent from anyone who does not identify as Black or of African descent.

And here is my healing: When you call me nigger, I don't know what you mean anymore. I glance from side to side trying to figure out who you could be talking to. The word is not in my vocabulary anymore. It is as if you are trying to remember the name of something you heard once, or are retelling an old story that was old when you heard it, and you retell it because that is the only story you know and you don't have the courage to create a new one, because that would mean that you will have to face the painful narrative about yourself.

# 13

## TRAUMA

*We cannot have a healed society, we cannot have change, we cannot have justice if we do not reclaim and repair the human spirit.*

—REV. ANGEL KYODO WILLIAMS, *Radical Dharma*

*Remember your name. Remember that you and I are brothers, are the children of trans-Atlantic rape. Remember the broader consciousness that comes with that. Remember that this consciousness can never ultimately be racial; it must be cosmic.*

—TA-NEHISI COATES

*I hope in 2020 we can discard the "I am not my ancestors" line. If our ancestors were that weak, our Black asses wouldn't be here.*

—MORGAN JERKINS

WHEN I SPEAK OF TRAUMA, I am speaking of a violent or stressful experience that disrupts our mental, emotional, and physical equilibrium. When this disruption continues with our returning back to an appropriate equilibrium, we are experiencing post-traumatic stress disorder, or PTSD. "Trauma" and "PTSD" are often misused terms, especially trauma, as we attempt to describe some form of suffering. A traumatic event disrupts how we may relate to ourselves and thus may establish a pattern of modified behaviors when encountering the experience that triggered the original disruption. Trauma can be either physical or emotional. A traumatic experience can knock us out of our body and make it difficult to return back to our body, making the body and its sensations unsafe because they remind us of the original traumatic event.

*I never believed that I was someone who struggled with trauma until the summer of 2014 when Michael Brown was killed and his body lay in the street for hours. Those images were triggering. That was also the summer when Israel was heavily bombing the Gaza Strip. The images of Michael Brown and of bombs raining down on Palestinians sent me into a period of disequilibrium. I was hyper-paranoid, often exhausted, and angry. I felt a heavy despair that I actually couldn't understand. I was wandering around and never feeling like my feet were touching the earth.*

There are different kinds of trauma. I am often thinking about, as well as struggling with, transhistorical trauma. Transhistorical trauma recurs from generation to generation until it is disrupted and released from the ancestral or collective line. For most Black Americans, the root of transhistorical intergenerational trauma is traced back to the grueling and brutal transatlantic slave trade called the Middle Passage. The Middle Passage has been widely taught as, and studied from the perspective of it being, a historical artifact safely tucked away in the past.

## TRANSHISTORICAL RAGE

For many Black folks, anger is one thing, yet rage is another thing altogether. My experience of rage has been one of struggling with transhistorical rage, which is the shadow of transhistorical intergenerational trauma. Or another way to think about it is that Black rage rides the breath of transhistorical trauma. Both ride together as a highly functional and destructive pair. Both trauma and rage have been a part of how I have come to relate to Blackness. While I do believe that Blackness is full of great joy, I also admit that it is full of a potent sorrow. Trauma and rage live in the heart of this potent sorrow.

I define "Black rage" as a disembodied expression of deep disappointment that longs to be cared for. This deep disappointment is not just my suffering in this life, but the suffering of all my ancestors. The path of healing is the practice of embodiment, to return home to all of our bodies and to do the very hard work of loving the trauma, and in loving it beginning to set it free from our bodies. The rage is the anger that has compounded generation after generation of struggling to be well in racism, patriarchy, and capitalism that robs not just Black folks but all people of vitality, vision, breath, and space. The rage is also the frustration of never feeling as if there is enough, when there are others who have much more than they could possibly ever need.

*I have had a difficult time with the police for most of my life. I was never raised to trust law enforcement, and this distrust came from my personal observation. When the police got involved with anything, it always seemed to hurt me or someone I loved, from being pulled over on the road to being heavily monitored in stores or while walking down the street. When I pass an officer, my anxiety sharpens, my anger spikes, and I try hard to remember that this person is a person just like me. They are not bad people, but they represent something that I only associate with harm. Meanwhile, the images of violent cops march through my mind, from all the images of violence against peaceful protesters during the civil rights movement, to Rodney King being beaten, to*

*Eric Garner being choked, even all the times my friends and I have been harassed by police.*

*I am particularly judgmental of Black and brown officers, especially women of color officers. My practice is to see the humanity of officers and to try to believe that people are doing the work for a reason that is not related to wanting to exert power over others or to maintain a system that disproportionately punishes people who look like them. I want to believe that they have not betrayed me, that I can trust them. I want to trust them, because I can't deal with more brown and Black skinned secret agents of white supremacy. This is difficult for me. I was taught to trust Black folks. But I cannot trust all Black folks.*

*Anytime I am walking near police or driving by police cars or even hear police sirens, my body lets me know how I feel—my chest and throat tighten, my eyes and forehead get tense, and I begin to feel the anger. I know that I see law enforcement as echoes of slave masters and overseers and as people who are also protecting the interests of those who are more powerful and resourced. And there is the trauma here, something old from generations past who have never felt protected, even by those who claim to protect everyone. Not only is there the transhistorical experience, there are also my experiences in this life.*

Transhistorical rage is the rage that is gifted from generation to generation rooted at the historical time and place of the first major trauma and the rage that emerged from that impact. Whereas anger emerges from the tension between being wounded and struggling to address the woundedness, rage is the loss of self and the loss of agency over that anger that in turn impacts our sense of worth. Yet what I see from a lot of Black folks is that our anger is not just our own. While I believe that love can be gifted from generation to generation as an experience that connects us to our ancestors, the same can be said of rage.

*Another time, I was eighteen, the summer before I started college. This particular afternoon I left work early and decided to stop at a gas station to buy a drink. I remember walking into the store and smiling at the cashier (a white woman), who reluctantly smiled back. Ten minutes passed as I wandered the store deciding on something to pick up. A line had formed at the cash register, so I didn't hurry. Looking up several times, I found the cashier averting her eyes quickly. I thought little of it. The last time I looked up, she was on the phone. I still thought little of it.*

*Finally, I grabbed some juice and walked up to the cashier to pay. She was cordial and polite. I glanced at the glass doors as she handed me my change to see two policemen standing solid, blocking the doors. I looked back at the cashier. She was no longer smiling.*

*I don't remember much except meeting the white male officers outside. I know there were questions and obvious accusations like why was I there, did I steal anything, and "You match the description of . . ." "Where do you live?" "Where do you work?" "Where's your car?" After a while I could not look them in the eyes because my eyes had become blurred with something, maybe tears. I was desperate to run away, leaving my car, leaving the city. But I couldn't. Eventually, they told me to stay out of trouble. I barely mumbled okay before they were gone.*

*I drove home not really remembering the drive, only finally getting there. I remember getting into my house and locking every door and window, finally finding myself locked in my room sitting by the door waiting for someone to find fault with me hiding in my home and call the police.*

*Perhaps the greatest benefit of retrospection is the revelation of truth not evident at the instant of an experience. At the time, I had no idea what was happening. Now I know that I was literally scared to death, shaking uncontrollably, confused, and distraught. I know that I was paranoid that every policeman in the city believed that I had committed some crime in that gas station and would come to arrest me.*

*Later that day, I finally rose from the floor, realizing that something had been decided for me that I had absolutely no say in. Something was assumed about my actions and character that I had no opportunity to counter. Of all the people at that gas station, I was the only person of color; therefore, I was judged to be the most suspicious.*

*I am tired of telling this story. But this story refuses to leave me.*

When I experience rage, I understand that I am experiencing the rage of all of my ancestors. When I experience love, I am also experiencing the love of all of my ancestors. It is the transhistorical love that is often felt as resilience that keeps me and many of us alive; and when we fall deeply into the love that we are being gifted, then we begin to thrive, and it is that thriving that begins to disrupt systems of violence that were only created to annihilate us. We disrupt these systems because we survive the system, summon our joy, and dance into our thriving. A system of violence that does not kill us has failed. I am my ancestors' wildest dreams because I thrive.

Our trauma and its rage began with the forced capture, bondage, and transportation of what historians believe to be between ten million and fifteen million Africans, with several million dying during some part of the experience. My ancestors were chained and packed in the bowels of cargo ships, where they experienced an overwhelming variety of physical and mental ailments. Those who survived the trauma of the passage were introduced into what was to be centuries of forced enslavement, resulting in a deep and brutal impact on the Black body and mind. Yet the Middle Passage represented much more than the transport of Black bodies across an ocean—it was and still is the unexamined and unmitigated trauma of decisions made without consent. It is the creation of a context that does not privilege one's deepest desire to return home and inhabit one's own agency and body, but instead triggers disembodiment, making certain meanings out of Black bodies, minds, and spirits that fulfill the intentions of racist capitalist imagination. Thus trauma in this context becomes a cyclical experience of continuous movement through places without consent as it perpetuates terror, despair, hopelessness, and disconnection. It is a voyage that never docks at any port, but is suspended, unexamined.

> *I grew up in a Black United Methodist church. A lot of the Black folks in my hometown were Baptist, African Methodist Episcopal (AME), Church of God in Christ, Holiness, or heathen. Everyone in my family was Baptist except for me and my mother. My mother became a United Methodist minister in my early teens. I loved going to church not because of learning about God or Jesus or hearing the sermon, but because it was how I was raised to experience community and belonging. I loved singing and being in the choir, and frankly what little gay and queer boys didn't love to sing (or fool around with other boys in the church basement)! Choir was where we could show off and show out!*

> *My church didn't seem to be the kind of church where people "caught the spirit" or "got happy." Sometimes I even thought that this was looked down upon. Once an elder got happy during a choir song and stood up calmly but loudly shouting, "Amen! Thank ya Jesus!" That was probably all that we could bear in our reserved congregation. Our ushers weren't trained to contain high-energy shouting or praise dancing. It just seemed like we weren't that kind of Black church.*

> *Then I would go to other Black churches where the Holy Ghost was moving. To be frank, I was afraid of all this carrying on. It looked intense and embarrassing. Once while visiting another church, I was sitting beside a family friend who caught the spirit—she jumped up out of her seat and started waving her hands around, and I sat there praying that she*

*wouldn't hit me! After that experience, I appreciated our little reserved congregation, and I suppose this is why I gravitate toward the silence of group meditation practice.*

*I was taught that catching the spirit was how we opened to the divine joy and grace of God as expressed through the Holy Ghost, His animating energy. Catching the spirit was our embodiment and our expression of that embodiment. Once an elder told me that she thought our shouting was a way that we remembered how our African ancestors worshipped in their practice with drumming and music. I found this theory evocative, and it stayed with me for many years. As I grew older and developed more understanding of the intersection of spiritual practice and trauma, I began to see another theory for shouting: It seemed that Black folks accrued significant amounts of trauma as well as rage trying to survive and attempting to thrive in a brutally racist culture. We didn't understand what trauma was, but we intuitively understood how to release trauma. I slowly began to see our shouting as informal yet ritualized releases of trauma through movement and the practice of sympathetic joy. Traditionally, sympathetic joy is a Buddhist practice of experiencing joy or happiness and imagining intentionally giving it away. However, I believe that in shouting, we are unconsciously turning our minds to joy that is buried in our experience. This understanding fits into the field of somatic-based trauma practice, or the practice of engaging the body to release trauma from being trapped in the nervous system. Although this is just a theory, it has helped me to appreciate and celebrate this important part of my culture and root religion.*

This trauma that Africans experienced was passed to successive generations through the practice of storytelling, belief and value transfers, and behavior that in turn impacted the manner in which each generation related to their own bodies, to their own minds, and to other groups. Thus, transhistorical intergenerational trauma can be described as a forest wildfire. The Middle Passage is the trauma spark that is lost in the past; the fire is PTSD; Black Americans are the forest; the dry materials are retraumatizing factors (e.g., Jim Crow, lynch culture, police brutality, and microaggressions); and systemized oppression and racism are the wind keeping the fire spreading.

*When I was young, in my hometown, I remember taking two field trips to the county jail. It wasn't until I was older that I realized that field trips to correctional facilities were fucked up, to say the least. I remember on both instances walking through these open areas where male inmates were separated from us by large glass walls. Most of the men were Black, and because my town was small, some of my friends on both trips recognized and knew several of the men. For some of us, it was more like a family reunion! I was expecting to see one of my uncles, who seemed to often be in and out of jail during that period. Those visits stayed with me, and I knew that the mass incarceration industry specialized in targeting Black men like me.*

*Another time, I remember being with my dad when he was pulled over by the police. The officer was an older white man, and my dad was in his early thirties. I remember this incident only because I was so struck by how condescending the officer was, as if he were talking to a teenager. Even then, I felt as if there was something that was supposed to be natural, that it was supposed to be okay for this white officer to speak to my dad with such a lack of respect.*

Moreover, disembodiment is the failure to develop an integrated awareness of one's emotional reality and its effect on the physical body. Another term we use for disembodiment is "dissociation," which, like disembodiment, means that our body becomes unsafe, because sensations can remind us of a traumatic experience. For African slaves and their descendants like me, survival strategies emerged and continue to do so by inhabiting psychic space outside of the body of experience, a body of experience riddled by the emotional trauma of slavery and systematic oppression. To return to the body with a sense of choice in how to relate to the body, coupled with spaciousness, is at the heart of how we can begin to manage the process of healing.

> *I have a fear of walking alone in public because I am afraid that someone will call the cops on me for just being Black in public.*

> *I recently passed a white man on the sidewalk. It was dark, and as usual I was in all black. I said hello. He just looked at me; and out of the corner of my eye, I saw he looked at me strange. A quick glance showed me that he had slowed down behind me. My first thought was that maybe he was trying to cruise me or pick me up. Then the second, less comfortable thought: maybe he is calling the cops on me.*

> *I work with fear like I work with any other experience that seems to be limiting and potentially overwhelming. I try to love it; and in at least attempting to love it, I can offer it a little space so that I can make different choices as to how to respond to it.*

> *When I think a white person is calling the police on me, I am no longer afraid. Just as my teacher taught me, I let whatever happens, happen. I now have the spaciousness and love to meet the burden of living Black in the world.*

This is my trauma:

> *When Trayvon Martin was murdered, I stopped wearing black hoodies. When Tamir Rice was murdered, I thought about how to give up my hands so I wouldn't be mistaken for holding onto anything. When Renisha McBride was murdered, I vowed never to knock on any stranger's door again. When Sandra Bland and Walter Scott were murdered, I became hypervigilant about following every fucking driving*

*law. When Eric Garner was choked to death, I realized that we all had been choking. After Akai Gurley was killed, I tried to figure out how to always make noise so no one would ever be surprised by me. After Freddie Gray was murdered, I thought there was surely a way not to be Black any longer. After Charles Kinsey was shot, I began questioning why I would help anyone if the cops would simply show up and shoot me anyway.*

And this is my trauma:

*I am the little girl at the bottom of the ocean. I am the teenage boy in the belly of the ship. I am the young girl displayed on the auction block. I am the grandmother singing songs about someone else's god. I am the father in the fields with tobacco and cotton. I am the woman raped by my master. I am the baby born from the violence. I am the husband forced to watch. I am the same husband, who will be raped by his master's wife. I am the boy raped by the slave master. I am the mother who will never see her children again. I am the grandfather who will never know he was a grandfather. I am the one buried in an unmarked grave. I am the one hunting me.*

## USING THE SEVEN HOMECOMINGS TO WORK WITH TRAUMA

This practice again uses the Seven Homecomings to create a loving container that we can rely on to process through difficult experiences of trauma.

### Type of Practice

This practice uses breath practice and visualization.

--- THE PRACTICE ---

1. Start by moving through the beginning practice sequence.

2. Continue by evoking your homecoming circle.

3. Follow the practice just through imagining the energy of care radiating from your benefactors, and move through the stages of that care seeping into your body and letting yourself float in that energy.

4. Now turn your attention to the experiences of trauma. Remember, when intentionally looking at trauma, do not force yourself to look at sensations or emotions that seem overwhelming or intense. When you feel the intensity, try to relax, turn your mind to the ground or your feet or your hands, and lean into the energy of care that is being radiated from your homecoming circle.

5. Imagine that the energy begins to sink into your body and finds its way to where you are holding this experience of trauma. Let that energy of care hold the trauma.

6. If the sensation or emotion isn't too intense, imagine that you begin to offer the material out of your body into your homecoming circle in the form of a dark cloud of mist. Using the tonglen practice, take deep in breaths through your nose, and imagine that on the out breath through your mouth you send the dark mist of trauma out of your body into the circle.

Pray into your circle for this trauma to be held and cared for by the circle. Imagine that the energy of care begins to penetrate the cloud of trauma. Just sit and experience whatever is happening, and rest.

7. At the end of the practice, imagine that the energy of care from your circle completely dissolves the remaining dark mists of trauma. Then dissolve the care circle into white light and return your attention to the earth and being held by the earth.

8. Move through the ending practice sequence.

## —— EARTH TOUCHING TRAUMA RELEASE ——

This meditation is a mindfulness-based practice using breath to connect to the energy of the earth to create a sense of stabilization.

### —————— THE PRACTICE ——————

1. Start by moving through the beginning practice sequence.

2. Now bring your attention to the sensation of your body on the seat. If you are standing, start with bringing your attention to the sensation of your feet on the floor; or if you are lying down, bring your attention to the sensation of your body on the floor. Just notice the sensations, including the weight of your body and the seat or floor under you.

If you are seated, shift your attention to the floor under your seat. If you are sitting in a chair, notice your feet making contact with the ground. If you are sitting on a cushion, notice the sensation of your cushion on top of the ground. The ground is earth. Let your attention touch the earth.

3. Notice the energy of earth. Name the energy. The energy of the earth can express itself as the energy of stability, firmness, solidity, steadiness, sustainability, or others. Try to connect to the energy you most resonate with.

4. Now turn your attention back to whatever you are noticing as trauma in the body. Imagine that the earth energy you connected to begins to pull that trauma down through your body, out the bottoms of your feet, and into the earth. As this is happening, allow yourself to continue to relax and let go of the discomfort into the earth.

5. When you feel complete with the practice, move through the ending practice sequence.

# 14

# SKILLFUL MOURNING

*In my healing I am also mourning. Sometimes I am in despair. Mourning and despair are very private matters. It is my acknowledgment that there is suffering. It is my honoring of my discomfort as well as the discomfort of everyone else in the world.*

—LAMA ROD OWENS, *Radical Dharma*

*The trauma said, "Don't write these poems.*
*Nobody wants to hear you cry about the grief inside your bones."*

—ANDREA GIBSON

MUCH OF MY FREEDOM and joy is bound up in my capacity to mourn. Mourning is my attempt to acknowledge heartbrokenness, accept it, and offer it space to be in my experience so it may do its work of teaching me and passing through. Whenever I feel this energy, I allow it; and it is something that I am encouraging others to do as well. When we are sitting with someone, it is an expression of compassion to offer them the space to move through their heartbrokenness.

In my practice, I'm trying to be in power with my heartbrokenness. This means that I meet my woundedness, my discomfort, with a kind of friendliness. This friendliness is an expression of love, and that love is the energy that opens up the space around the discomfort.

## ─────── WORKING WITH CRISIS ───────

When we get bad news about someone we love, initially we may feel a really intense tightness or mental contraction. It's like being shocked. After that, we have the opportunity to relax into the crisis, even though that feels really intense to do. That relaxing is not an expression of not caring. It's not an expression of apathy. It's actually an expression of trying to be in wisdom, or trying to experience wisdom or clarity, which will help us make the best choices to be in a relationship with that crisis, or to handle the crisis, really.

That's what we're going for, and it's quite uncomfortable. If we get thrown into something, it's as if we're sinking, and it's hard. It's a really interesting instruction to be told, "If you find yourself sinking within everything that comes up within a crisis, just relax. Sink some more." This relaxing helps us to float above, or around, the thing itself. Now, the thing itself doesn't go away. However, you are giving it space now, and that's where we will experience different potentialities.

Now the crisis itself isn't dictating everything. We become a resource for other people.

## ─────── BASIC MOURNING PRACTICE ───────

The basis of this practice is space, holding space, and allowing ourselves to experience grief. In experiencing grief within spaciousness, we are able to allow grief to move through our experience, and we can slowly experience liberation over time from this energy.

## Type of Practice

This practice uses the Seven Homecomings, earth touching, breath practice, and other visualization practices.

---

### THE PRACTICE

1. Start by moving through the beginning practice sequence, ending with a breath practice.

2. Continuing with the breath, breathe deeply in through the nose and out through the mouth. Try to make both the inhale and the exhale as deep as possible. After a few minutes, take a two-second pause after the inhale through the nose before releasing the exhale through the mouth. Gradually make that pause longer, up to five to ten seconds, or however long is comfortable for you. In the pause between the breaths, notice the space and stillness that that opens up. If you can, try to rest in between those breaths. As you continue resting in the pauses, try to start experiencing the breaths as well as the pauses. Let the breath breathe you, and while doing so allow it to move you into a deeper sense of spaciousness and calm. Practice with the breaths as long as you want to.

3. Now move into evoking the Seven Homecomings and your circle of care.

4. Imagine that your circle begins to generate the energy of care for you, and feel that energy filling the space around you as warmth. Feel that warmth gently hold you and wrap you; and slowly begin to feel that energy of kindness, this warmth from your benefactors, slowly begin to sink into the body beneath the layer of skin into the muscles, the bones, and the organs as if you're being marinated in this energy of kindness. As you're breathing, imagine that you're breathing this kindness into your body and lungs; and when that kindness gets into your lungs, imagine this energy begins to circulate throughout the whole body in the same way oxygen is taken in by the lungs and distributed throughout all the cells in the body. Imagine the same thing is happening with this energy of kindness, that every cell gets fed by this energy. In the same way that you are being held by the energy of the earth, allow yourself to be held by the energy of kindness from your benefactors. Relax, open, and continue breathing.

5. In your experience right now there is comfort, as well as discomfort, but looking at the discomfort, what are you calling discomfort right now? Is it physical pain? Is it emotional discomfort? Is it sadness? Is it frustration? Is it anger? Is it despair? Is it a broken heart? Notice the discomfort, and just imagine directing the energy of the kindness from your benefactors into the experience of that discomfort. You can imagine that this energy is holding the discomfort.

Maybe you can imagine that this energy is trying to dissolve this discomfort, or you can imagine that you're directing this energy into the very heart of the discomfort, attempting to fill it up with kindness from your benefactors, and filling up this discomfort in the same way this energy of kindness is filling up your body.

6. Within the context of this kindness that you're experiencing from your benefactors, can you move a little bit further and allow this discomfort space to be in your experience? Can you accept it? Can you let it be there? Can you continue to take care of it with this energy of kindness? Can you let yourself experience this discomfort, and can you let yourself be held by the energy of kindness as you are experiencing it? Or can you let yourself fall into being held by this kindness as you fall apart?

7. Do you see your experience as an experience, not as who you inherently are? Keep breathing. You can even begin to send this energy of kindness back to a moment, to a time when you were hurt and didn't know how to deal with the hurt.

8. Now think about the younger version of yourself, that age you were when you were deeply hurt somehow, and when that part of yourself stopped growing. Returning back to that younger version of yourself, send this energy of kindness to them, helping them to hold space, to experience, and even to release the old hurts, all while falling back into being held by your benefactors within this energy of kindness, and falling back to the earth and being held by the earth.

9. Allow yourself to return back to the present if you're in the past, and turn your attention away from the discomfort back into your circle of benefactors around you. Imagine that your circle of benefactors begin to dissolve into this energy of kindness, compassion, and love that's been around you. Imagine that you absorb all this remaining energy into your heart's center. Return back to being held by the earth, and as you keep some intention anchored into the earth, turn the remaining attention back to your breath, and breathe any way that's comfortable for you right now.

10. Move through the ending practice sequence.

## THE LOSS OF MAGIC

Much of my mourning comes from feeling as if I have lost much of my magic. I mean the magic of rituals and relationships my ancestors relied on to keep them attuned to both the material and the unseen worlds, as well as the magic of creativity, passion, joy, and resilience.

I am bothered by folks who are terrified to remember that there are different ways to imagine God or the divine. That would mean exploring our unmetabolized trauma and our addiction to systems of power, including white supremacy, patriarchy, queerphobia, and capitalism.

I want to remember my magic. I want to remember how to divine the future, resurrect the past, and dance in the present. I need a return to reading the cards, bones, tea leaves, wind. I want to talk to the weather and the trees. I want to cast spells and write new rituals. I want to return back to the earth and ask it to teach me how to heal myself and others around me. I want to remember the secret names of ancient creatures who have learned to hide from modernity. I want to remember the gods and the goddesses, the rites of blood and coming of age. I want to remember the ceremonies for sun, moon, and water. I want to evoke the vulture and the horse. I want to have agency over demons. I need to remember that there is no such thing as death. I want to remember that I have a right to be free.

My magic was taken away from me, and everything I have done to understand my mind in contemplative and tantric practices has been an attempt to reclaim a magic that systems of oppression have conditioned me to be terrified of. But systematic oppression wields another magic, one that is darker and more sinister. Patriarchy has cast spells teaching me to hate women, queerness, and anyone or anything that is not rigid, brutal, silent, and violent. White supremacy took my ancestors' prayers, deities, and rituals away and gave us a theology that was used to enslave us. Capitalism has cast a spell on me, forcing me to believe that anything can be bought or sold, that our bodies have prices, and that I have to work and "do" something to be valued.

I want to teach others to remember their magic as well. I want to teach others to create and cast spells that return them to the way their spirits used to be before systematic reality began to reorganize and redefine us, which was essentially the violence of dismembering us into small bits and pieces so we could forget our wholeness as well as our holiness.

Remembering is a revolutionary act. It is defiance against forgetting. Authentic remembering is the evoking of our true self—not our racialized self or our traumatized self, but the remembrance of who we are that is the essential expression of freedom. This kind of remembrance is perhaps the most powerful spell we could cast for ourselves. And helping others cast this spell is the most important service we can offer to others.

## DIALOGUE ON HEALING AND RESILIENCY WITH SARAH BEASLEY

Adopted from "Lama Rod Owens on Social Justice, Rest, and Resilience" by Sarah Beasley appearing in *Buddhistdoor Global*

**Lama Rod Owens:** *The work of resiliency is something that's really important to me. It's something that I grew up with. I grew up in the Southern Black community, which was in the heart of a lot of segregation, prejudice, and violence, and so my family for generations had survived that by getting knocked down and getting back up again. It was like, you just keep going no matter what happens. For my community, that inspiration came from Christianity, which taught us that to be good and virtuous in the world meant that you would have to experience suffering just as Jesus did. Suffering is to be expected, and that if we deeply practice virtue and resilience in this life, then we're rewarded with heaven after we die. Of course for me, I was like, "No, I don't want to just suffer and then get rewarded for suffering." I just didn't believe in suffering.*

**Sarah Beasley:** *Then you became Buddhist?*

**LRO:** *Right. I guess the specific point was that I felt like there had to be a solution to suffering. I just didn't find it fair that just because I was born Black, I have to suffer. As I got older, I was just like, "I don't believe because you were born with certain characteristics, that you have to inherently be marginalized and to experience pain." I just didn't get that. And,* *that actually became a source of my interest in social justice. In my teens, I was very fortunate to have a mom who encouraged me to be community minded. My mother is always organizing. She was doing health fairs and mentoring groups for young women. She helped me understand that we have an obligation to be in service to other people.*

**SB:** *When you're talking about the Black Christian community, it can't be just "Keep going for yourself." It's "Keep going for all of* us*." Right? On behalf of everyone else.*

**LRO:** *Yeah. We help each other. If someone is experiencing a crisis in housing, we take them in. If someone needs money, we raise money. If they need food, we get food to them. It was just the ethic of my community. I didn't know I was taking it seriously, but I did.*

*But as I grew older, I started getting more intentional about how I sustained myself. So, that intention led into areas of self-care. I was inspired by Audre Lorde's understanding of self-care, where she expressed that self-care is self-preservation, and self-preservation is an act of political warfare. And, that's one of my favorite ideas, because it has helped me to understand that when I preserve myself, then I'm actually disrupting systems that want to get rid of me.*

*I wanted to do more than survive—I wanted to thrive within these systems of abuse. And so that elevated the work around resiliency. I've survived because I've been taught how to survive, and so much of that survival has come from being able to cultivate a sense of connectedness and stability within surviving. And then, self-care as self-preservation actually became a little more real for me. So, I think about James Baldwin, when he wrote that if you don't rest, then you won't survive the war. And so, rest became actually a part of my self-care and my resiliency.*

**SB:** *Literally, alone time to sleep or meditate?*

**LRO:** *Yup. And three-year retreat was really like the pinnacle of that for me. That actually was the deep grounding that I needed to cultivate a lifelong allegiance to rest. It was silence and practice and letting go of things that were unhealthy and toxic. My teacher said that if we could survive retreat, we could survive anything.*

**SB:** *It's like it can kill you or make you stronger.*

**LRO:** *That's exactly what he was saying. Every time I go through a really hard situation, I think about retreat and I tell myself, "But, I survived that. I survived that breakdown. I survived that illusion in my mind, and I can survive this."*

**SB:** *And are there tools in there? How did that inform the tools or methods you now use with students or the public or in your work?*

**LRO:** *I learned how to not take myself so seriously, because of the recognition of the illusionary nature of self. If someone calls me a name, I naturally think, "Oh, they don't know who I am though." And, they don't know who I am because they don't know who they are. They don't get their own innate wisdom. They don't understand their Buddha nature, whatever we want to call it, but they don't understand that they are expressions of goodness and virtue, and how that's just been clouded over by ignorance.*

*And so when you're trying to enact that kind of violence on me, then you're actually just responding to your own suffering in the moment. So, it has nothing to do with me. I may have triggered something, definitely, because we are interrelated and interdependent. Of course that's going to happen. But, if we actually could relate to and rest back into our own nature, then we could actually cut through the ways in which we're trying to make other people hurt as much as we're hurting. And, that's something that I talk to my students often about. It's this sense of knowing who you are, which was like growing up in church, and how we were raised to believe that we were children of God.*

*If you realize that, if you actually knew that to be certain, then you would have a very different experience in life. And it's the same for Buddhist communities. I think if we just believe or have some faith that we're more than the suffering, then I think that we could show up in a much more open and vulnerable way.*

*I also teach people to refrain. I think we're overengaged in things that are not meaningful. You need to actually rest and take a break. And that's such a cornerstone of my practice. Just to take breaks, to refrain from emails and social media, and just to be alone, to be silent, to limit all of these distractions around me, so I could actually have time to restore. And just this basic resting and really just letting go, relaxing. Definitely do what invites joy in. Joy is such a tool for renewal and resilience, to always retreat back into the things that make us feel good. And that's different for everyone.*

**SB:** *And I have this sense that you use humor as a tool.*

**LRO:** *For me, humor is an expression of what's happening for me in the moment. So, it's not this attempt to hide, or to perform, or to make people feel comfortable. It's more about "Oh, this is what I'm experiencing in the moment, and I'm going to articulate it. This is what I'm thinking about, so I'm going to share it," and it's disarming. And there's a transmission that comes right under that. For instance, good comedians can be the best social commentators. I think the same can be said with dharma teaching. I think that humor helps to invite joy, and it helps to release people into being themselves.*

**SB:** Do you find that having the label of *"Lama"* is both maybe a help and a hindrance in your work?

**LRO:** *I think initially it was a hindrance. I think when I first got out of the retreat and I was fortunate to teach at a Dharma Center, I definitely went through an identity crisis, where I just felt that I had this title, but people were trying to project their own meaning onto the title. And so, I was so grateful to have support from other senior lamas who had gone through this before. Well, it's like, "Okay, who do I want to be?" And so, I went through that process and just came out the other end, having a clearer sense of how I choose to show up in the world. And since then, it's not been a problem.*

**SB:** *Part of the reason I ask is that I think it's tricky enough for any Westerners to be lamas, right? And then, I'm just imagining it's probably as a person of color more challenging, people's perceptions and projections. And yet, it's so critical that we have more Western lamas and women, people of color, and people who identify in all kinds of ways. So it's: how to have it happen and make it authentic for everyone.*

**LRO:** *And that's the key, the authenticity. I had to figure out what it meant. I had to figure out what the title meant for me, not what I was being told by the lineage. I had to draw the line and say, "This is who I am." I wrote this article for* Buddhadharma *called "Do You Know Your True Face?" That was so important for me. I thought it was a basic exploration of intersectionality, but it was so radical and challenging for so many people because of how many identity locations I could occupy and still be a lama.*

*I think the work that a lot of Westerners are doing, particularly Western lamas, is asking how to best and more authentically represent who we are as well as this tradition. I believe*

*I can't really transmit dharma unless I am being completely authentic to myself, to my culture, to my race, to my class and my sexuality, to everything across the board. Dharma has to come through those identities for it to be authentic. As a junior teacher, I was trying to replace who I was with this understanding of what a lama was, and it just wasn't working. I think when Western lamas do that, they get into a lot of trouble. I think that creates a really intense shadow effect.*

SB: *It's funny, as we're talking, I'm thinking of my lama. He wore a robe for puja, but most of the time he wore jeans and a nice shirt and a Western hat. He was just very authentic.*

LRO: *I was going to do a second three-year retreat after my first one, and my teacher told me it would be better for me just to go into the world and to figure things out. My teacher gave me a lot of agency. That turned into confidence to embody this position in a way that I feel like is the most nonviolent way I can be right now.*

SB: *Well, that says a lot about you, because this world is so bananas. If you can rest and transmit the dharma and feel nonviolent in this insanity, then it says a lot about the retreat you had and about your own character and your upbringing because, man . . .*

LRO: *The more intense the world gets, the happier I get. It's a weird thing, but I think that, for me, part of it is like, "Oh, this is what I'm supposed to be doing now. This is the time." And I think that what advanced practitioners are being called to do now is to hold space. Everything is this illusion. It's also real at the same time. So if we can just straddle those two extremes, I think that creates this profound and fierce way of being in the world, where I can care, I can get involved, I can fight for people, but at the same time I can be reminded that this too will pass, that I will die like every other being will die, and then there will be another reality that I'll have to encounter, and it'll be that over and over again till I get the point, and then transcend the whole cycle.*

## LOVE AND RESILIENCY: A DHARMA SERMON

I am scared. Not only that, I feel ashamed for being scared. I have to interrogate all the ways in which I am told not to show up in a way that's vulnerable and open, as well as interrogate the ways in which I'm being told that it's not okay to mourn publicly. Resisting the ways in which I'm being told that I should just get over it and keep going. I can't get over it; I can't keep going. The best way to take care of myself is to acknowledge that my heart has broken and I don't trust a lot of people. I am suspicious of every person I see walking down the sidewalk, or on the subway, especially if they are not of color.

I don't know if this makes me a bad Buddhist, but I think it makes me more honest. But I know that I don't want to remain scared either. I'm not happy being suspicious. I do want to come from a place of love. However, as RuPaul has said, "My goal is to always come from a place of love . . . but sometimes you just have to break it down for a motherfucker." Sometimes I need to break it down for a motherfucker. I struggle with wanting to break it down too much. Sometimes I am the motherfucker that's breaking down.

These days I have had to keep it simple and work from the beginning of the Buddha's teachings. The Four Noble Truths are the first teachings that the Buddha gave after his enlightenment. He was in a position where initially he didn't want to break it down. He was like, "Listen, no one's going to get this, so I need to go about my way and hit Nirvana and be like, peace." In the mythology, he was convinced by spirits and deities. These beings approached him and pleaded with him and said, "You can do something. You can break a little bit of it down." He did, and the Four Noble Truths were the first teachings that he gave. Revolutionary teachings. The first noble truth is that there is suffering in life. Not that life is suffering, but there is suffering in our existence of living.

In Pali, one of the ancient Southeast Asian languages we study early Buddhism in, the word for suffering is *dukkha*. The sense of dukkha is not being okay, not being right. Even more precisely, it's feeling that things don't fit together, but we're going to force them and then trick ourselves into thinking that this is okay until it falls apart. It's like you're trying to find the top for the Tupperware, and you just find something that kind of fits and you jam it on. You're like, Okay, this works, everything's cool. Then it falls off. The second noble truth was: okay, so there's suffering; what's the root of that suffering? He said the root was desire, attachments. We're creating something that we don't actually need to experience, but we've lost our way from our true selves. The third noble truth was that actually there's a way out of this. The fourth noble truth was essentially the introduction of the path of dharma: the Eightfold Noble Path. The path of right understanding, right thoughts, right speech, right action, right effort, right livelihood, right concentration, and right mindfulness. These eight actions that we can engage in actually help to dissolve our fixations, to dissolve our desires and our attachments, and bring us into a balance that eventually dissolves the sense of ego that we think exists.

It's within this fourth noble truth that I've been trying to establish my life. What's right to do? What have I been believing in that I shouldn't actually be believing in? What am I trusting that's actually hurt me over and over again? What am I trying to understand that isn't understandable? What am I trying to think that's actually not of any benefit to me? Essentially, how am I letting go of this person that I used to be? Because the situation has flipped, and the person or the Rod that I used to be is no longer able to meet the coming occupation or the continued occupation. The one thing that I always come back to when I'm practicing and thinking about liberation is love. Always coming back to love. And I talk about love with the understanding and acknowledging that I have been someone who traditionally thought not to trust and believe in love.

My work and integrating into love were actually about coming into this space where I was able to hold space for the sum of all these mistakes that I kept making over and over again. The sum of all the violence that's been done to me. Also the sum of the violence that I had done to others. I had to come back and look at the ways in which I felt that I was fundamentally not good enough to receive love. Realizing that the world was trying to love me, that my family was trying to love me, friends were trying to love me, strangers on the street were trying to love me, but I fundamentally shut that down and sabotaged receiving love. I didn't think I was good enough to receive it, nor did I trust it.

Then slowly teachers created spaces where I could actually open up and be vulnerable and look at the pain, and allow the pain to be there. That's where loving started for me. Once I began to love these parts of myself that I felt unlovable, I began to love others. I began to become very sensitive to the way the world was loving me. It didn't matter how bad I felt for the world; all the spaces around me, they were seeds, they were shreds of light, they were channeling love. I became addicted to that. If you want to become addicted to anything, become addicted to love. That's a habit that will actually liberate you.

My experience wasn't about how pitiful I was, but rather that I had this potential to be something else. To identify in a different way. To let go of the things, to ask forgiveness of myself, to ask forgiveness of others. That holding space and loving actually helped me to move into the work of compassion, which is for me a little different than loving. Compassion is the wish for others to be free from suffering. All these practices make us sensitive, deeply sensitive, not only to our experience but to the experience of others around us. I've moved through the world, not just thinking, "Oh, I am heartbroken." I move also through the world thinking that "So is everyone else." The strategy moving forward isn't about arming ourselves—it's about de-arming. This is a different kind of battle that we have to fight now. I think so many people are alone and isolated, and I want to see more communities of healing taking place. Some of us aren't agents of feeling, and we have to be real about that. Some of us create division, and how can we even heal that in our experience? Sometimes it's just our distrust—it's our unwillingness to be vulnerable. It's our coming from histories where we've been hurt in groups, and we don't want to deal with that anymore. How can we go to that forefront and work with that trauma?

When I think about the ancestors, I think about the ones who allowed themselves to be annihilated through love and how they created change for me to show up now. We have to become people willing to allow ourselves to die in love. I think what needs to die is something that we don't even need to begin with. We think we need it. I'm right there with you. I don't want to do this; I was looking forward to vacation next year. I don't want to organize and act up, but you know what? We're made for these times. I really believe that we are intentionally born into this very moment, this very time, because we were ready for this. We just have to trust ourselves; we need to trust the love, we need to trust the ancestors. As long as you keep one foot out, suffering is going to compound and compound.

You have to let go of that. It scares the shit out of me as well. People are depending on you. Of course I think, "Oh, this isn't fair for brown people to have to do this again. I'm tired of this— why does it always have to be us? Why is it always us having to call people out?" It's because we can. We've been put in this unique position to understand what suffering is, and we're connected to this strength that's love that derives from a lineage of people who have survived over and over again and who have actually thrived.

Now is the time to actually build a movement. We talk about unity and different ethnic groups and our different identity locations. Now is actually the time to do that. It's also time to not just talk about Black love, but to do it.

When I was growing up in church, we'd always say, "The storm comes in the night, but joy comes in the morning." That's how my ancestors survived. What is that T-shirt that I'm seeing around? "I am my ancestor's wildest dreams." We are. No matter who and what our ancestry is, we have survived, and we carry their lineage, their blood, their blessings, their spirit. If we don't honor that, then it's like we're throwing that back in their faces and we're not grateful. My ancestors literally died so I could have this life; if I don't maintain that freedom, then why did they do it? We have a responsibility to the ancestors to continue to work for liberation.

I just want to go to Target and buy something, but I have to go to this rally. I just want to stay in bed, but I have to go organize something. But this is why I feel like I was born. Then when I die, I'll be able to look back over my life and to say, "This is what I did to help."

# 15

# SELF-CARE

*Caring for myself is not self-indulgence, it is self-preservation, and that is an act of political warfare.*

—AUDRE LORDE

*Are you sure, sweetheart, that you want to be well?... Just so's you're sure, sweetheart, and ready to be healed, cause wholeness is no trifling matter. A lot of weight when you're well.*

—TONI CADE BAMBARA, *The Salt Eaters*

*We must drink as we pour.*

—MA JAYA SATI BHAGAVATI

*In America, I was free only in battle, never free to rest—and he who finds no way to rest cannot long survive the battle.*

—JAMES BALDWIN

SELF-CARE IS A new frontier for me. I have grown up in a culture that on one hand has sought to annihilate me through systematic violence, while at the same time telling me that self-care is important only as an expression of self-indulgence.

272 Love and Rage

Self-indulgence is about isolation and placing our needs above others' needs. It is an act of compromising what other people need. Authentic self-care may look like self-indulgence in practice, but the intention of authentic self-care is about doing the things we need to do to care for ourselves. Authentic self-care is about asking ourselves what we need in order to do the work of benefiting others, especially the communities we identify with.

Mother Audre's teaching of how authentic self-care is self-preservation is so uncomfortably truthful because the goal of systems of violence is to annihilate us. If we are practicing self-preservation, then we disrupt the work of these systems, which is an expression of warfare. The following section is an informal exploration of how I have waged, and continue to wage, warfare against systematic violence through self-care as self-preservation.

## RITUALS

*The LGBTQ+ community has been excluded from many modern rituals. We were denied dating rituals in our teen years. We did not go to the prom. And so we developed our own rituals out of necessity.*

—RUPAUL

The first point of self-care for me is the development of rituals. Because I spend my life as this traveling evangelist, I have figured out what I need to make travel restorative. I know what I need in order to be well enough to continue moving from place to place.

I often say that the violence we experience is highly ritualized. If that is the case, then our self-care has to be even more ritualized and methodical to meet this violence.

## RESTING

*There is rest for the weary.*

         —AS SUNG BY SWEET HONEY IN THE ROCK

The practice that keeps me restored is rest. I know how to rest. Sitting in a chair at the airport waiting for a plane, I can rest even if it's only thirty minutes. I can rest on any mode of public transportation.

When I say rest, I don't mean sleep. Sleeping and resting are not the same thing. Resting means there's a sense of letting go, letting be, dropping things, and just resting the mind, just being with things as they rise. That's my sense of rest.

I can go to sleep for hours and hours. It doesn't mean I let go of anything in that rest, in that sleeping. That comes directly from meditation practice.

Something that looks self-indulgent actually becomes something that's about self-preservation, because it is giving me a way and a release to come back into the work that I'm called to do.

## LOVE

*Searching all directions*
*with one's awareness,*
*one finds no one dearer*
*than oneself.*
*In the same way, others*
*are dear to themselves.*
*So one should not hurt others*
*if one loves oneself.*

         —BUDDHA

In my teens and early twenties, love was nothing I really ever thought about; I thought it was pointless. Everything that I knew about love was informed by romantic comedies or R&B and pop love songs.

All of that seemed like a lot of suffering. (It still does!) For me, the message in these songs seemed to be: If you leave, I'll die. Why fall in love then? It just never made any sense to me. I felt as if love was nothing but suffering, a sentiment I may or may not still be working out. I've never really been in a serious relationship before and I'm forty.

This is something I would never talk about either. It's definitely not as if I'm a forty-year-old virgin. If we're talking about sex, let's just say I've been around that block so much, it's named after me. I have been in many relationships, but never anything I could commit to long term.

I learned to understand love as the wish for others to be happy and free, and I want to bring that to my romantic loving.

Loving as self-care is imperative. The care I have for myself is the same care I want to offer to others around me. Love puts me into a beautiful but difficult acceptance of things as they are, including myself, including others around me.

Love makes me do the things that reduce violence in the world. I must always return to being loved and loving if I am to experience the liberation of authentic connection to others.

## COMPASSION

*You think your pain and your heartbreak are unprecedented in the history of the world, but then you read. It was books that taught me that the things that tormented me most were the very things that connected me with all the people who were alive, who had ever been alive.*

—JAMES BALDWIN

Compassion is important as a part of my self-care for myself and for others. First and foremost, it's touching into relating to my discomfort and wanting myself to be free from this discomfort.

Then turning my attention outward into the world, wanting the same liberation for other people and other beings. That's how I remain tenderhearted, and this tender heart is a heart that is kept open and pliable and less likely to shut down.

The tender heart thrives in the space we cultivate, and that space helps us to also hold the woundedness we experience from others.

## — SILENCE —

*Listen! Clam up your mouth and be silent like an oyster shell, for that tongue of yours is the enemy of the soul, my friend. When the lips are silent, the heart has a hundred tongues.*

—RUMI

Silence is so crucial for me. I have to wake up in silence. I don't like to get up and just start talking. This is why not being in a relationship is wonderful!

I am a child of silence. There's enough going on in my head and my heart. I need the space silence offers me to be with all that material, to figure out how to translate it into wisdom and eventually share this wisdom with other people.

This is where all my teaching comes from. It comes from the silence that I experience; and if I had no silence, there would be no dharma for me.

Silence is also how I figure out how to be in the world. Silence takes care of me, and I can move through the world not needing everyone and everything to do that caretaking.

## SOURCES OF REFUGE

*The ache for home lives in all of us. The safe place where we can go as we are and not be questioned.*

—MAYA ANGELOU

I need places to go to feel loved and to be held. This is why the earth and our homecoming circle are powerful things to take refuge in.

We can only be vulnerable with a very few, if any. I'm talking about people you can just call up and say, "Oh my God, can you believe this thing that just happened to me?" And they say, "Yeah, I get it." They're not like, "Oh, you're horrible."

When we are practicing vulnerability, we are taking refuge first in ourselves and then getting refuge by being seen and held kindly. It is hard to experience care if we can't trust someone with our vulnerability.

## BELOVED COMMUNITY

*Beloved community is formed not by the eradication of differ-ence but by its affirmation, by each of us claiming the identi-ties and cultural legacies that shape who we are and how we live in the world.*

—BELL HOOKS

Beloved community is a community where we can be different, but we can also do the work of understanding how certain dif-ferences carry different kinds of power within the community. We want to be in power with each other, not having power over or not having power under, but be in power with.

My personal ethic is to try to understand what it means to be in power with myself, to be in power with others. Again, when I'm in power with, there's not this domination happening; there's not this power struggle.

## THE POWER OF NO

*If I can't dance, I don't want to be a part of your revolution.*

—EMMA GOLDMAN

"No" is a complete sentence. I actually don't say no—I say nope.

I say, "Nope, and I don't want to talk about it." Because it's a complete sentence, right?

If I can't be myself, then please don't invite me to your party, to your revolution.

No is the mother of boundaries. Without no, there is no protection of our energy. It is hard for us to say no because we are so invested in other people's needs and not disappointing them.

No is also how I learned to stop going places that didn't love me. If I am not being loved or not being encouraged to love, it's not my community, and I must refrain by saying no.

## SPEAKING

*If you are silent about your pain, they'll kill you and say you enjoyed it.*

—ZORA NEALE HURSTON

I come from a history of being silent, because I didn't ever feel like I was being heard, validated, or seen. I've had to work hard to be noticed.

First and foremost, I want to be heard, and I want to be understood. I don't need to be agreed with. That's not really the point. I just want to be heard. I want it to be understood that I have an opinion, that this is what I believe, this is what I need to happen.

Speaking is how I shape my reality and become what I need to be, to be able to experience the deepest kind of liberation.

## CRYING

*Cry. Dry your tears. Then continue. Repeat if necessary.*
—LAMA ROD

Some of us grew up in situations where we weren't allowed to show emotion, especially sadness and tears. I had to reverse that conditioning.

I had to learn how to cry, and to cry publicly. Letting that energy pass through to mourn and to allow those tears to come and just be like, "Yeah, this is fine to cry."

Crying is release. It is cleansing. It helps us to reset. It also renders us utterly vulnerable.

## RITUALS OF RESISTANCE, RESILIENCE, AND SUSTAINABILITY

Rise early in the morning. Hear in the stillness of morning what you can't hear anytime else.

If you cannot or choose not to speak, go in silence. Think of those who have always loved you. Reflect on their love. Imagine that your silence is saturated with their love.

Remember those who have cared for you or who have worked for your happiness. Give rise to gratitude for them.

Remember those who came before you and helped you to be alive now. Ask them to abide with you. Call them ancestors. Believe that you are never alone.

Cry. Dry your tears. Then continue. Repeat if necessary.

When you are tired, rest. When hungry, eat. When thirsty, drink. If possible, do this and think that you are taking rest, food, and drink not just for yourself, but for others who cannot.

If you choose to make love, surrender to lovers who can also make love to your pain.

Create energetic barriers by imagining a wall of light around you that keeps the darkness of negativity from touching you.

Avoid people who do not want to do the work of sustainability.

Avoid people who intentionally keep you from practicing sustainability.

If you are the person who keeps you from being sustainable, seek out individuals and communities that teach you to sustain.

Swim in natural water like lakes or ponds. Let the water cleanse your spirit.

Baptize yourself in the name of whatever helps you to survive, and imagine that you are being reborn.

Keep being reborn.

Go and lie on the earth. Let the earth hold you. As it holds you, let it love you. Offer to the earth what you cannot hold.

Wear white, and imagine that your body is releasing old or toxic energy it cannot use or transform.

Fast, and ask to be guided.

Read sacred scriptures and writings.

Go and sit with the elders. Ask them to tell you stories.

Spend time with people who do not want anything from you.

Cook a meal. Before eating it, set aside a small portion of it for the spirits of those who have passed.

Meditate under the light of the moon. Imagine that the light is cleansing you.

Write down everything you struggle with on a piece of paper. Burn it outside. Imagine that you are burning away the obstacles that keep you struggling.

Burn sage and lavender, and cleanse your body and your personal space.

Dwell in spaces that love you.

Burn incense.

Pray.

*Refrain.*

# —ABOUT THE AUTHOR—

LAMA ROD OWENS is an author, activist, and authorized lama (Buddhist teacher) in the Kagyu School of Tibetan Buddhism and is considered one of the leaders of his generation of Buddhist teachers. He holds a Master of Divinity degree in Buddhist Studies from Harvard Divinity School and is a coauthor of *Radical Dharma: Talking Race, Love, and Liberation.* Owens is the co-founder of Bhumisparsha, a Buddhist tantric practice and study community; has been published and featured in several publications, including *Buddhadharma, Lion's Roar, Tricycle,* and the *Harvard Divinity Bulletin;* and has offered talks, retreats, and workshops in more than seven countries.

## ALSO BY LAMA ROD OWENS
*available from North Atlantic Books*

*Radical Dharma*
978-1-62317-098-1

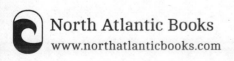

North Atlantic Books
www.northatlanticbooks.com

North Atlantic Books is an independent, nonprofit publisher committed to a bold exploration of the relationships between mind, body, spirit, and nature.

# About North Atlantic Books

North Atlantic Books (NAB) is an independent, nonprofit publisher committed to a bold exploration of the relationships between mind, body, spirit, and nature. Founded in 1974, NAB aims to nurture a holistic view of the arts, sciences, humanities, and healing. To make a donation or to learn more about our books, authors, events, and newsletter, please visit www.northatlanticbooks.com.

North Atlantic Books is the publishing arm of the Society for the Study of Native Arts and Sciences, a 501(c)(3) nonprofit educational organization that promotes cross-cultural perspectives linking scientific, social, and artistic fields. To learn how you can support us, please visit our website.